Exorcism
AND THE CHURCH MILITANT

Exorcism
AND THE CHURCH MILITANT

By Rev. Thomas J. Euteneuer

With a Foreword by

Rev. John A. Corapi, SOLT, STD

Human Life International

© 2010 Human Life International®

Human Life International
4 Family Life Lane
Front Royal, Virginia 22630 USA
www.hli.org

All rights reserved.
Portions of this book may be reproduced for educational
purposes provided full credit is given.

Cover illustration: "Descent into Hell," from Altarpiece of the
Holy Sepulchre, 1381-82 (detail)
Artist: SERRA, Jaime : 1358-89 : Spanish
Credit: The Art Archive / Museo de Zaragoza (Saragossa) /
Gianni Dagli Orti

Printed in the United States of America.

ISBN: 978-1-55922-060-6

We do indeed live in the body but we do not wage war with human resources. The weapons of our warfare are not human. They possess God's power for the destruction of strongholds. We demolish sophistries and every proud pretension that raises itself against the knowledge of God; we likewise bring every thought into captivity to make it obedient to Christ. (2 Cor 10:3-5)

Dedication

To the Immaculate Virgin Mary, Comforter of the Afflicted
and
St. Joseph, Terror of Demons

To my parents, Joseph and Mariann, in gratitude for handing on to me
the Faith of our Fathers

To Fr. Jerome Herman, my dear friend in the priesthood who taught me the most about spiritual warfare and who now belongs to the Church Triumphant.

The people who walked in darkness have seen a great light; upon those who dwelt in the land of gloom a light has shone. You have brought them abundant joy and great rejoicing, as they rejoice before you as at the harvest, as men make merry when dividing the spoils. For the yoke that burdened them, the pole on their shoulder, and the rod of their taskmaster you have smashed, as on the day of Midian. For every boot that tramped in battle, every cloak rolled in blood, will be burned as fuel for flames. For a child is born to us, a son is given us: upon his shoulder dominion rests. They name him Wonder-Counselor, God-Hero, Father-Forever, Prince of Peace. His dominion is vast and ever peaceful, from David's throne, and over His Kingdom which he confirms and sustains by judgment and justice, both now and forever. The zeal of the Lord of hosts will do this![1]

---

[1] Isaiah 9:1-6; all Scripture quotes taken from *The New American Bible*, Catholic Book Publishing Co., Inc., 1970 unless otherwise noted.

Acknowledgements

I would like to thank, from the bottom of my heart, all those generous souls who assisted in the preparation of this work on exorcism. In addition to people who attended and offered feedback at the numerous talks I have given on this subject, I owe a great debt of gratitude to the priests who gave their valuable time to reviewing this work, primarily Fr. Jeffrey Grob, and Fr. Ken Yossa. Most helpful of all was Fr. Clement Machado who spent many hours with me refining my understanding and precision of concepts that are critical to the ministry of exorcism. Their professional advice rooted out many errors and inconsistencies in the work and held me accountable to my own theological training.

I also wish to acknowledge my many generous "editors" who provided a wealth of insight to my work: above all, Anne Lotierzo, who also regularly edits my *Spirit and Life* e-newsletter; Patricia Bainbridge, HLI's Board Chairman; Mike Mueller, Executive Vice President of HLI; Don Kazimir, Respect Life Director of the Diocese of Palm Beach; Neal Lozano, Helani Scurfield and several others who through comments and encouragement have helped to bring this work to completion. Finally, thanks to Anthony Mioni, my publicist, who has worked his technical marvels to put this work into book form.

I could never have accomplished this task without so many angels of light and life to assist me!

Contents

Dedication vii
Acknowledgements ix
Foreword xxi
Introduction: *Ecclesia Militans* xxv
    The Real Power of Satan xxvi
    The Authority of the Church Militant xxix
    Goals of this work. xxx
    A Note on Terminology xxxiv
    St. Michael, Patron of Exorcists xxxv
Chapter 1: Jesus, Chief Exorcist 1
    1. Was Satan's expulsion from heaven an exorcism? 2
    2. What did Jesus say about exorcism in the Gospels? 3
    3. What evidence is there that Jesus performed exorcisms? 4
    4. Why did Jesus need to exorcise the world? 5
    5. What other Old Testament images did Jesus likely have in mind when He performed exorcisms? 6
    6. What is the main paradigm of spiritual liberation for the Jewish people? 7
    7. Why is exorcism important to Jesus' Kingdom? 8
    8. What reactions did people have to Jesus' exorcism ministry? 9
    9. How does Jesus carry on the ministry of exorcism in His Church? 10
    10. Why do exorcists or those who perform deliverances use the Name of Jesus? 11
    11. Can other religions perform successful exorcisms? 11

12. Will there be a final exorcism of evil by Christ?.........13

Afterword to Chapter 1: Priestly Assistance from Heaven 14

Chapter 2: The Devil, His Minions and His Activities. 17
   1. How do we know that evil really exists?................18
   2. What do we call the devil and why? 19
   3. What does the *Rite of Exorcism* call him?...............20
   4. Who is Beelzebul then?............................22
   5. Which are the wickedest demons that may afflict humanity?......................................24
   6. Was Jesus concerned about the devil? 24
   7. What is the difference between angels and archangels? 25
   8. What is the difference between demons and devils?.......26
   9. How are demons different from the devil?..............26
   10. Are demons supernatural beings?.....................27
   11. Are demons male or female? 28
   12. What do demons look like?.........................29
   13. Is it possible for the devil or a demon to look beautiful? ..30
   14. What is a demon's "personality" like?..................30
   15. When the apostate angels rebelled, what happened to their hierarchy?......................................31
   16. Can demons repent after they sinned?.................33
   17. What are the levels of the devil's activity against God's children?...33
   18. Are good angels always stronger than demons? 34
   19. If a demon is not a material being, how can a demon be "in" a body?......................................35
   20. If the body is God's temple, how can a demon and the Holy Spirit co-exist in the same body? 36
   21. How much power does the devil have over us in normal circumstances?....................................36

22. Can a demon kill someone or make him commit suicide? 37
23. Why does the devil possess people? 38
24. Why does the devil possess some people and not others? . . 39
25. What is a state of "perfect possession"? 40
26. What does a demon actually "possess," the body or the soul? 41
27. Can a person become possessed inadvertently? 42
28. Can a demon possess a house or building? How about an animal? 43
29. Can one demon control another? 44
30. Will a person go to hell if he is possessed? What if he dies possessed? 45
31. How much power does the Church actually have over demons? 45
32. Do sacraments protect a person against evil? 46
33. What is a state of grace? 46
34. How powerful is St. Michael the Archangel against the devil's action? 47
35. Can an exorcist permit a demon to leave one body and go to another? 47
36. How does God use the devil and demons in His Providence? 48
37. Is there really a Church of Satan? 49

Afterword to Chapter 2: The Psychology of Demons **50**
   Description 50
   Analysis 51
   The antidote to demonic possession: family 54

Chapter 3: Exorcism and Church Authority **56**
   1. How do we define exorcism? Is it a sacrament? 57
   2. What other ways does the Church understand exorcism? . . 57
   3. What is exorcism *not*? 59

4. Why do we need exorcism? 59
5. Where does the word "exorcism" come from? 60
6. Who may authorize an exorcism? 60
7. Who has the authority to perform an exorcism? 62
8. May a lay person ever perform a solemn exorcism? 62
9. How many exorcists are there? 64
10. Why aren't there more exorcists? 64
11. How may a priest become a qualified exorcist? 66
12. Isn't the identity of an exorcist supposed to be kept secret? 67
13. Does an exorcist ever charge for his services? 67
14. How common is exorcism? 68
15. What is the difference between a "minor" and a "major" exorcism? 68
16. Was there a change in the regulations concerning exorcism in the new 1983 *Code of Canon Law*? 69
17. Other than the *Code of Canon Law*, what else has the Holy See said about exorcism in recent times?. 70
18. Wasn't there an "order of exorcist" prior to Vatican II? What was that? 73
19. Must each diocese have an appointed exorcist? 75
20. What if a bishop denies a priest the authority to exorcise when there is a real need? 75
21. Does the Church keep records or recordings of exorcisms? 76
22. Does the Church allow exorcisms for non-Catholics? 77
23. Does a person have to officially consent to an exorcism? . . 78
24. Can Protestants do exorcisms? 78
25. Who wrote the exorcism ritual? 79
26. How is the *Rite of Exorcism* organized? 80
27. Must the priest always use the words of the ritual in an exorcism? 81

28. Must a priest conduct the exorcism in Latin or may he use another language? 82
29. Can a priest ever do an exorcism in secret? 83
30. What are some of the deceptions that a demon may employ in an exorcism? 83
31. How do you define success in an exorcism? 85
32. How do you define failure in an exorcism? 86
33. Does the devil attack exorcists? 88
34. Can an exorcist be deceived by the devil and end up in spiritual trouble? 89
35. What did Pope John Paul II say about the devil? Did he really do an exorcism as Pope? 90
36. Is Freemasonry still forbidden by the Catholic Church? ..91

Afterword to Chapter 3: Practical Advice for Petitioning an Exorcism 92

Chapter 4: Discernment Issues 97
1. Why should an exorcist be concerned about discernment? .98
2. What forms of discernment may a team employ to understand more about demonic presence and actions? ...98
3. In discerning demonic presences what "types" of demons are there? 101
4. What is the difference between demons and ghosts? 103
5. Can damned human souls possess or torment people? 105
6. How does a person know he needs an exorcism? 106
7. What if a person needs it but refuses to get an exorcism? ..107
8. How can a Christian have a demon? 108
9. How does the Church determine that a person is possessed? 109
10. Can the exorcism prayers be used "diagnostically" even if a priest is not sure a person is possessed? 110

11. What other "symptoms" might the Church
    acknowledge as signs of possession?................110
12. How does the Church determine that a person has a
    demon but is not fully possessed?..................112
13. What types of demonic manifestations do we see in
    people who are obsessed and need only deliverance?....113
14. What is the "line of demarcation" between deliverance
    and exorcism?.....................................114
15. In general how does the Church distinguish between
    demonic influences and mental/psychological disorders? 115
16. What is a person to do if he suspects that he or a loved
    one suffers from demonic problems?................116
17. If demons can infest both persons or localities, how
    can you tell, in any given situation, whether a demonic
    problem is related to the person or the place?.........117

**Afterword to Chapter 4: Eight Degrees of Difficulty in
Expelling Demons............................... 117**
   A Final Word about "Perfect Possession".................124

Chapter 5: Healing and Deliverance.................... 126
1. What is the Church's concept of healing?.............127
2. What is the Church's concept of deliverance?..........127
3. Why does the Church have two forms of dealing with
   demonic entities, exorcism and deliverance?..........128
4. Which is more common: deliverance or exorcism?......129
5. What priority did healing have in the Public Ministry of
   Jesus?...129
6. How do we know that He handed on the healing
   ministry to His Church?..........................130
7. What are the four types of prayer needed to heal body,
   soul and spirit?...................................132
8. What are healing services?.........................133

9. Does the Church have any regulations regarding healing services? 134
10. How are deliverance prayers prayed? 134
11. What is the "pastoral approach" to deliverance ministry? 135
12. Does the Church forbid lay people from commanding demons directly? 136
13. What specific restrictions does the Church put on the laity, then? 138
14. What are examples of deliverance prayers and commands? 139
15. When and where are deliverances to be performed? 145
16. How can a deliverance go wrong? 146
17. What is the most necessary quality for a person who wants to do deliverance ministry? 148

Afterword to Chapter 5: Case Study of a Successful Deliverance 148

Chapter 6: The Conduct of an Exorcism 154
1. What analogy best describes what happens in an exorcism? 155
2. What other analogy describes exorcism well? 156
3. What must a priest do to prepare the exorcee for an exorcism? 156
4. What is the role of prayer support in an exorcism? Must those who pray be present at the exorcism? 157
5. What must a priest do to prepare his team of helpers for the exorcism? 158
6. What personal preparations must the priest undertake for an exorcism? 159
7. What if the person resists going to an exorcism? 161
8. How many exorcisms does it take to release a person from a demon? 161

9. What religious objects does a priest use during the course of the exorcism? 163
10. Can a priest use the Eucharist to expel a demon? 164
11. What happens if the person does not get help from one exorcist or wants to change for another? 164
12. How long does an exorcism session last? 165
13. Are there ever any breaks in an exorcism? 165
14. Can't the demon re-gain his strength if the exorcisms are not all done at once? 166
15. How should a chapel or a room be arranged for an exorcism? 167
16. What is the position of the victim in an exorcism? 168
17. Are exorcisms always violent? 169
18. Is a person always unconscious during an exorcism? 170
19. Does the devil speak in a guttural voice in a possession? .170
20. Does an exorcee feel pain during an exorcism or does he feel the pain of the demon? 171
21. Can a demon jump from one person to another in an exorcism? 172
22. Does a demon act on his own or in concert with others? 173
23. Can a demon hide from the exorcist to avoid being expelled? 173
24. Do demons always talk in an exorcism? 174
25. What language does the demon speak in an exorcism? ..175
26. Do the demons really yell out your sins to you in an exorcism? 176
27. Can demons read a person's thoughts? 177
28. Should an exorcist ever mock or taunt a demon in an exorcism? 178
29. Does a victim "see" the demon at any time? 179

30. Can a person experience a holy vision in the course of an exorcism? 179
31. What is the role of angels in an exorcism? 180
32. What are the "signs" by which an exorcist or a victim knows an evil spirit has departed? 181
33. Do all demons give signs when they depart? 182
34. If the exorcism is performed correctly, why would a demon not leave? 182
35. How does an exorcist know when all the demons are gone? 183
36. What does it actually mean to "cast out" a demon? 183
37. Where do demons go when they are cast out? 183
38. Does the "Foot of the Cross" actually exist? 184
39. What does the victim feel after a demon has left? 184
40. Is the exorcee persecuted before, during or after an exorcism? 185
41. Can a person be re-possessed? 186
42. Does the devil retaliate against the priest if he does exorcisms? How about those who help him? 187

Afterword to Chapter 6: Outline of an Exorcism 188

Chapter 7: Pastoral Considerations 198
   Cura animarum 199
   The priestly role in helping people to discern the power of evil 203
   Basic principles for giving spiritual help 205
   The state of grace and the Toehold-Foothold-Stronghold analogy 209
   Teach them to close the doorways to the occult 211
   Parish-based initiatives and preaching 216
   Spiritual resources for busy people 218
   Best resources on spiritual warfare 219

Best websites for spiritual warfare and healing resources 219
Best overall teachers on spiritual warfare and deliverance from a Catholic perspective. 219
Best resources for deliverance and healing 220
Best resources for healing the family tree 220
Best resources on the angels. 221
Best resources on the art of discernment 221

Appendix A: General Rules Concerning Exorcism (Part I of the 1614 *Rite of Exorcism*) 223

Appendix B: *Ritus Exorcizandi Obsessos A Daemonio* (Part II of the 1614 *Rite of Exorcism*) 228

Appendix C: Exorcism Against Satan and the Fallen Angels (Part III of the 1614 *Rite of Exorcism*, also known as the Exorcism of Pope Leo XIII) 250

Appendix D: "The New *Rite of Exorcism:* A Potent Weapon Is Weakened" 255

Appendix E: Commentary on the 1985 Letter of the Congregation for the Doctrine of the Faith: *On the Current Norms Governing Exorcism* *260*

Appendix F: *Instruction on Prayers for Healing*, September 14, 2000 267

Appendix G: Pope John Paul II's Catechesis on the Fallen Angels 271

Appendix H: The Redemptive Suffering of Anneliese Michel 277

Appendix I: Other Scripture Passages Related to Deliverance 281

Bibliography 283

About the Author. 304

Foreword

by Rev. John A. Corapi, SOLT, STD

Looking back on the previous twenty five years of my life in the Catholic Church, I can tell you that one of the most commonly misunderstood and neglected areas concerns that extraordinary form of combat against the forces of darkness we see in exorcism and deliverance. Perhaps it's the excesses of Hollywood, or the numbing effect of a rampant secularism that makes some who should know better ashamed of some facets of the doctrine of the faith: mainly sin, grace, angels and demons, heaven, hell and purgatory. The existence of all of which are required tenets of Catholic faith.

As the *Catechism of the Catholic Church* reminds us in #409:

"This dramatic situation of 'the whole world [which] is in the power of the evil one' (1 Jn 5:19; cf. 1 Pet 5:8) makes man's life a battle:"

> The whole of man's history has been the story of dour combat with the powers of evil, stretching, so our Lord tells us, from the very dawn of history until the last day. Finding himself in the midst of the battlefield man has to struggle to do what is right, and it is at great cost to himself, and aided by God's grace, that he succeeds in achieving his own inner integrity (Vatican II, *Gaudium et Spes*, 37:2).

A defined element of Catholic faith concerns the existence and activity of the angels and the fallen angels commonly called demons. As #328 of the *Catechism of the Catholic Church* asserts, "The existence of the spiritual, non-corporeal beings that Sacred Scripture usually calls 'angels' is a truth of faith. The witness of Scripture is as clear as the unanimity of Tradition."

There is no doubt whatever that angels and demons are real, creatures originally created by God as good, very good. Behind the fall of the angels (demons) is pride, the genesis of all sin. The *Catechism* sheds further light on this by teaching, "Behind the disobedient choice of our first parents lurks a seductive voice, opposed to God, which makes them fall into death out of envy (cf. Gen 3:1-5; Wis 2:24). Scripture and the Church's Tradition see in this being a fallen angel, called 'Satan' or the 'devil'" (CCC 391; cf. Jn. 8:44; Rev. 12:9).

One might say that this is clear and always has been, so why mention it? From time to time throughout history, errors and deceptions weave their way even inside the Church. In recent years it has become almost fashionable, even commonplace for priests and theologians—the pseudo-educated, pseudo-sophisticated variety—to call into doubt defined elements of the Church's teaching. I have encountered this many times personally. The results of such errors confuse the faithful and call doctrine into question when there is no question. Angels and fallen angels exist. A poor derelict man who ended up in prison, long previously enslaved to drugs and alcohol perhaps said it best: "I know there has to be a God because I've lived with the Devil for years and he is very real. I know evil and its end is death. There has to be a God Who is goodness and life."

In 1975 the Sacred Congregation for the Doctrine of the Faith commissioned an expert to prepare a study on *Christian Faith and Demonology*. That Congregation of the Roman Curia strongly recommended it as a sure foundation for the reaffirmation of the teaching of the Magisterium on the theme of *Christian Faith and Demonology*. At the outset, this document felt the need to condemn and discredit those teachers or teachings that either eliminate or question the reality of angels and demons and the spiritual warfare that is so much a part of everyday reality.

Obviously, if there is no Devil, no demons, and no battle between the concrete personal realities that represent good and evil, truth and lies, then the whole idea of exorcism or deliverance from the forces of darkness becomes a non-question. I can assure you it is a very serious, relevant, and constant battle. My own personal ministry and experience of twenty-five years bears this out. Fact is often wilder than the wildest of fiction. This combat with the Devil, who is a real, personal, and living being—a fallen angel, at once perverse and perverting—is absolutely real.

Denying or doubting reality is not helpful; especially when it is a life-or-death matter, and this is surely a matter of eternal life and eternal death. That being said, it is good to always remember that we know the ultimate outcome of this fierce combat: we win. Jesus nailed sin, Satan, and eternal death to the Cross. Dying He destroyed our death and rising He restored our life. Therefore, we can fight this good fight with absolute confidence, having no fear of the forces of darkness. God is stronger, and, indeed, "If God is for you, who can be against you."

Father Thomas Euteneuer has performed a valuable service in giving us his book *Exorcism and the Church Militant*. Everyone seeking a more complete knowledge of the Catholic-Christian faith, indeed, reality itself, can profit from a careful and prayerful reading of this book. Priests especially should profit from this material, for it is my personal experience that the need for it has increased exponentially in recent years. Preparation for this dimension of spiritual warfare is singularly lacking in almost all seminaries, novitiates, or other Catholic institutions of learning. One of the reasons for this is that many such institutions have faculty that from all indications don't necessarily believe what the Church believes. This leaves a terrible void, so much so that it is often extremely difficult to find a priest with even the most rudimentary knowledge of this essential facet of priestly ministry. The effect on souls can be devastating. Hopefully this fine book will inspire many priests to equip themselves with the necessary weapons to fight for souls in this arena, remembering that:

> We are warriors now, fighting on the battlefield of faith, and God sees all we do; the angels watch and so does Christ. What honor and glory and joy, to do battle in the presence of God, and have Christ approve our victory. Let us arm ourselves in full strength and prepare ourselves for the ultimate struggle with blameless hearts, true faith and unyielding courage. (Office of Readings, Common of Several Martyrs)

Introduction
Ecclesia Militans

Draw your strength from the Lord and his mighty power. Put on the armor of God so that you may be able to stand firm against the tactics of the devil. Our battle is not against human forces but against the principalities and powers, the rulers of this world of darkness, the evil spirits in regions above. You must put on the armor of God if you are to resist on the evil day; do all that your duty requires, and hold your ground. (Eph 6:10-13)

Ergo, draco maledicte et omnis legio diabolica, adjuramus te per Deum + vivum, per Deum + verum, per Deum + sanctum… Vade, satana, inventor et magister omnis fallaciæ, hostis humanæ salutis. Da locum Christo, in quo nihil invenisti de operibus tuis; da locum Ecclesiæ uni, sanctæ, catholicæ, et apostolicæ, quam Christus ipse acquisivit sanguine suo.[1]

---

1 "Therefore, accursed dragon and every diabolic legion, we adjure thee by the living + God, by the true + God, by the holy + God… Get thee gone, Satan, founder and master of all falsity, enemy of mankind! Give place to Christ in Whom thou didst find none of thy works; give place to the One, Holy, Catholic, and Apostolic Church which Christ Himself bought with His blood!" Cf. Rev. Philip T. Weller, STD, Trans. *The Roman Ritual, Vol. II, Christian Burial, Exorcisms, Reserved Blessings, Etc.*, The Bruce Publishing Co., Milwaukee, WI, 1964, pp. 227 and 229. All quotes from the exorcism ritual hereafter cited as Weller, *Rituale*, page number, and are taken from Volume II of the series. Note that Weller's is not an "official" English translation of the Latin ritual. There has never been one for liturgical use. However, as a "study edition" it is useful.

✣

The One, Holy, Catholic and Apostolic Church has been commissioned by the Lord Jesus Christ to fulfill a most dramatic mission; it is perhaps the most dangerous and exhilarating of missions ever entrusted to men. It is the mission of saving souls.

This mission cannot be accomplished without entering into conflict with "the world, the flesh and the devil." It is not a mission for the fainthearted or for those who wish to take the wide road to heaven. It is the path of warfare, of spiritual battle. And although we know that Our Lord has fought that battle before us, and won, every age of the Church must take up arms anew and fight it until the end of time. Let it be said with certainty that those who embrace wholeheartedly the Church's mission to save souls will live a difficult life, one full of challenges and at times real sorrows, but, at the same time, a life imbued with immense blessings that accrue only to those who risk everything for Christ. It is for those who "fight the good fight" for souls in hand-to-hand combat with the devil that this book is written, to support, encourage and strengthen them in their conflict with the forces of evil arrayed against man's salvation. Theirs is the work of the Church Militant.

The Real Power of Satan

In today's day and age, Satan is growing exponentially more powerful due to the enormity of human sinfulness, and the Church must confront his power either willingly or unwillingly. Satan is normally "hidden in the dark sea of human sin and error,"[2] like Leviathan of the Old Testament, but nowadays he is walking tall in powerful *structures of sin* like abortion, pornography, sex slavery, rapacious greed and terrorism. He flexes his muscles

---

[2] Rev. Jeremy Davies, *Exorcism: Understanding Exorcism in Scripture and Practice*, The Incorporated Catholic Truth Society, London: England, 2008, p. 5.

in the *massive diffusion of errors and sinful practices* like the doctrines of myriad false religions, pernicious ideologies like radical feminism and "pro-choice" extremism, the militant homosexual movement and the aggressive mass media which is the ministry of propaganda for Satan and all his works and all his empty promises.

Never in all of history have we seen evil promoted so effectively and the true good so roundly mocked and rejected as in this age of extreme technological prowess. Although evil has existed since the dawn of time and manifested itself to the world, the difference between the modern world and past generations is that Satan has a greater ability to use groups and institutions for increasing his wicked reach into human life and society.[3] No longer is evil just practiced in the haunts of cemeteries, seedy parlors and hidden covens. Nowadays, objective evil is displayed out in the open air with impunity, celebrated in the public forum and strategized in plush board rooms. Whole industries and power groups are dedicated to its promotion and dissemination, and sometimes the sheer power of these industries of immorality defies imagination. They target the younger generations with an immense seductive force, and the young are almost entirely unequipped to deal with this tyranny of sin due to unparalleled attacks on faith, marriage, family and innocent human life in modern times. Not only do young people not know the truth about their salvation; they don't even know that they don't know it.

The 21st century is a moral and spiritual battlefield of such immense proportions that no era of human history will have ever seen a war like it.[4] Satan is using the cumulative force of this world's sinfulness to re-define life as we know it. Now, this war is

---
3 Malachi Martin: Audio Cassette Series, *The Eternal War*, "The Kingdom of Darkness," Tape 1.
4 Pope John Paul II, *Evangelium Vitae*, n. 17.

not just against trained combatants. It is total war against all that is sacred and natural. It is a war against humanity itself, something unseen before in all of history with the possible exception of atheistic Communism.

The devil now arrogates to himself the right to control the totality of human existence even in so-called free societies: from manipulating the very act of creation (*in vitro* fertilization, cloning, Human Genome); to the authority over life and death (abortion, embryonic stem cell research, euthanasia); to the definition of human sexuality and marriage (birth control, divorce, homosexual unions); to the very prospect of human annihilation (nuclear war, genocide and the impending New World Order). Nothing escapes the rebellious forces of hedonism and secularism in their violent march through our world. They creep into the fabric of our lives and families like a vapor until they have poisoned the entire environment and make everyone believe that their toxicity is "normal." If the measure of a war's ferociousness is the number of casualties, the modern war to exterminate souls is unprecedented in the history of humanity; it is nothing short of history's worst nuclear holocaust in spiritual terms.

Malachi Martin, in the 1992 preface to his book, *Hostage to the Devil*, said that "ritualistic Satanism and its inevitable consequence, demonic Possession, are now part and parcel of the atmosphere of life in America….such pervasive cultural desolation is the most fertile ground one could possibly imagine for the causes of Possession to take root and flourish in almost unimpeded freedom."[5] It must be kept in mind that such a frightening observation was made at a time before the advent of the Internet, the massive diffusion of New Age beliefs and the Harry Potter books and movies. Martin's observations suggest that this evil is so all-encompassing that only the

---

5 Malachi Martin, *Hostage to the Devil: The Possession and Exorcism of Five Americans*, HarperSanFrancisco, ed.: San Francisco, 1992, pp. xiii-xiv.

authority of God Himself, borne and administered by the Church, is adequate to meet this challenge.

The Authority of the Church Militant[6]

We know from our catechism that the whole Church of Christ is not confined just to this earthly realm.[7] The battle against Satan has already been won in heaven and purgatory, and only in this earthly realm is the devil allowed to work. God, in His Mercy, certainly has not abandoned us to the forces of evil, though. There is one spiritual force on earth that can counter the hubris of Satan and his apostate angels and conquer them. That force is the "One, Holy, Catholic and Apostolic Church," which, in my opinion, has been singularly unprepared for and *unengaged in* the hard work of spiritual warfare since the Second Vatican Council. By this I mean that if the institutional Church on earth were ever to train its members to be spiritual combatants and aggressively apply its great authority against the power of evil in this world, the evils mentioned above would simply not be able to exist in their potency or scope. As it is, the Church has yet to seriously enter the battle and become what it is called to be, namely, the Church Militant.

The hour is late, Satan's forces are already assembled, and the Church's army and its officers must stir for battle. The trumpet call of Christ our Commander beckons. Souls are at stake, and the devil's only real hope for victory is that the Church will sit

---

6 The terminology describing the Church as "Militant" is consistent with imagery in St. Paul's letters which express this reality better than I. He variously uses terms such as "soldier of Christ,"(2 Tim 2:3) "armor of God" (Eph 6:11) "weapons of our warfare"(2 Cor 10:4) and "fight[ing] the good fight"(1Tim 1:18) in outlining the work of the Church and its leaders.

7 Traditional theology tells us that the full Body of Christ consists of the Church Triumphant (Heaven), the Church Suffering (Purgatory), and the Church Militant (Earth).

this one out. The devil certainly "knows that his time is short"[8] and would be much shorter should the Church of Christ ever take the call to spiritual warfare seriously. When our Lord healed a paralytic by forgiving his sins and restoring him to health, the Gospel said that "a feeling of awe came over the crowd, and they praised God for giving such authority to men."[9] Indeed, that spiritual authority *has* been given to the men of the Church for the protection, sanctification and saving of souls—it only has to be used.

Goals of this work

First goal: to communicate a proper understanding of exorcism

The transformation of exorcism into a popular cultural phenomenon in recent decades has led to a major distortion of both the Church's mission to expel demons and the power of the devil. A main concern of this present work is the taking back of this important pastoral ministry of the Church from the realm of the internet, movies and tabloids and placing it back in the hands of priests where it belongs—the true officers of the Church Militant.

Exaggerated pop images of exorcism falsely define people's understanding of the Church's ancient ritual that is meant to liberate victims of the devil from these very deceptions. Popular movies like *The Exorcist* (1973) and *The Exorcism of Emily Rose* (2005), while containing some truthful elements, have done very little to present a correct picture of exorcism itself. These movies and others, for the sake of sensationalizing the power of the devil, present the Church and her priests as being the underdogs in a fight against the devil and oftentimes as weak or reluctant combatants. While there are certainly moments of heroism de-

---
[8] Rev 12:12
[9] Mt 9:8

picted in these movies, the devil is shown as powerful and tantalizing, sort of like one who always seems to have the upper hand against the Church. Nothing could be farther from the truth! Exorcists are never in a position of subjugation to the evil one during the course of an exorcism, nor is the devil ever entertaining and enthralling like he is portrayed in the movies. He is pure evil, and that is never lost on the one who has to face him down in a possession.

A correct understanding of exorcism can also divest many people of a dangerous fascination with the occult. No sane person who truly understands the nature of demons would be fascinated with them or their works. Due to its mysterious nature, exorcism will never be totally removed from popular distortions or fear, but priests can assure that the Church's rightful patrimony is understood by the faithful and people who need sacramental assistance against demons. The priest's work is to fortify Christians to "reject Satan and all his works and all his empty promises."[10]

The organization of the chapters in this book is meant to introduce people to the diverse dimensions of exorcism. Through a discussion of the nature of Christ's high-priestly ministry of exorcism,[11] the nature of the demonic forces that afflict men[12] and the rightful authority of the Church over evil,[13] readers will understand better the theological and pastoral dimensions of exorcism. Furthermore, I have made every attempt to rely on only the most reputable sources on exorcism from the tradition and modern writings that are tested and orthodox. I pray that this

---

10 From the traditional baptismal promises.
11 Chapter 1
12 Chapter 4
13 Chapter 2

work will become a resource for many in their fight against the forces of evil.

Second goal: to motivate priests

Exorcism is best understood in the context of evangelization and the care of souls, and, as such, is the proper office of ordained Catholic priests.[14] As such, the second purpose of this work is precisely to help Catholic priests recognize that exorcism is a normal and very important form of pastoral ministry in the care of souls. In times to come, priests will be increasingly called upon to expel real demons from truly demonically-afflicted individuals who have, in one way or another, fallen into the seductions and empty promises of the master deceiver.

Occult influences have been unleashed into our modern world like the emptying of a demonic Pandora's Box of unclean spirits. The popularity of the New Age movement, the rise of Satanism as an organized and institutionalized force, the flood of satanic video games and Heavy Metal music, the massive diffusion of occult terminology and images through the immensely-popular Harry Potter series and other youth-targeted entertainments, like the rash of modern vampire movies, assure that Catholic priests will be very busy in the next decade.

To aid priests in a proper understanding of the nature of exorcism, one chapter explains how exorcisms are actually conducted,[15] which may help to take away some of the mysticism or fear related to a ritual that *any* priest can perform (with the proper authorization). I also attempt to provide some clarity in the nebulous area of differences between the ministries of

---

14 English exorcist, Fr. Jeremy Davies, says that exorcism "is an intrinsic part of the Sacrament of the Priesthood," *op. cit.*, p. 41.
15 Chapter 5

exorcism, deliverance and healing and some practical rules for discernment of ambiguous cases.[16] Chapter 7 will show priests that exorcism is a truly pastoral ministry, worthy of their engagement, and will give them principles and best practices for helping their parishioners discern the presence and power of evil in their lives. It concludes with some of my personal recommendations for resources on spiritual warfare and discernment which will be helpful to any priest wishing to give people guidance and direction in these matters. The bibliography included at the end of this book will be a resource for information on exorcism and deliverance.

This book is essentially for priests, but it may be read with benefit by any lay person who is interested in spiritual warfare. It offers only one priest's point of view but has been written after fairly extensive consultation with other priests in the ministry and attempts to be as comprehensive as possible on the subject while keeping the text relatively short and readable. I have organized six of the seven chapters in a short question and answer format to facilitate the book's use as an ongoing reference source, and not just something that is read from cover-to-cover. The detailed Index and Table of Contents are given for this same purpose.

As in all things related to faith and morals, I submit my views on these matters to the final judgment of the Church's Magisterium and welcome any feedback and correction from priests, more capable than I, who are involved in this ministry. We can all benefit from further fraternal dialogue on these matters. It is my thesis that the devil's spiritual warfare on our flocks will intensify as the years proceed and that all Christians, but especially priests, will have no choice but to engage more deeply

---

[16] Chapters 4 and 5

in the spiritual battle for souls. There is no time like the present to begin the training.

A Note on Terminology

A final note on terminology: in this work I use the word "exorcism" to speak about something very particular, albeit complex. Exorcism is often confused in religious and secular parlance with "deliverance" (which is defined more distinctly in Chapter 5), but in this book, the term "exorcism" will always mean what the Church means by it: namely, a rite for expelling demons from persons who are possessed, authorized by a bishop and limited by canon law to the ministry of priests. Solemn exorcism has a long historical development and practice and a theological grounding in the Tradition of the Church. It should also be understood that this work only deals with "exorcism" as it applies to the Roman Catholic Church. There are other expressions and understandings of exorcism in the Eastern Church and Protestant churches which I do not attempt to illuminate in any systematic way in this work.

In this work, I am also very careful about the term *possession* which often gets used to describe demonic infestations of a lesser severity. Too-liberally labeling demonic activity as "possession" creates the unfortunate impression that the devil has more power over us than he actually has. The term "possession" will apply to those individuals whose bodies and faculties are judged by the Church to be fully or near-fully taken over by demonic forces and who lose most or all of their freedom to fight the evil one on their own. They need the help of the Church, and it is these afflicted individuals who are the proper subjects of the Church's ministry of solemn exorcism.

Finally, according to custom and general usage, I usually refer to the devil and his minions with masculine pronouns rather than to try to encumber the text with neutral pronouns which attempt to describe spiritual beings as genderless. Since Scripture and Tradition generally refer to demons with masculine pronouns, that will be sufficient enough reason to do the same in this work.

St. Michael, Patron of Exorcists

May St. Michael the Archangel, heaven's exorcist angel, defend us in our battles against "the principalities and powers, the rulers of this world of darkness,"[17] help us minister to the many souls who are immersed in the devil's darkness, and draw us into the reign of Light of the true Shepherd of our souls, Jesus Christ.

Rev. Thomas J. Euteneuer
Human Life International
March 3, 2010

---

17 Eph 6:12

Exorcism
AND THE CHURCH MILITANT

Chapter 1
Jesus, Chief Exorcist

Peter said to Cornelius, "I take it you know what has been reported all over Judea about Jesus of Nazareth, beginning in Galilee with the baptism John preaches; of the way God anointed him with the Holy Spirit and power. He went about doing good works and healing all who were in the grip of the devil, and God was with him." (Acts 10:37-38)

I cast thee out, thou unclean spirit, along with the least encroachment of the wicked enemy, and every phantom and diabolical legion. In the name of our Lord Jesus + Christ, depart and vanish from this creature of God. + For it is He Who commands thee, He who ordered thee cast down from the heights of heaven into the nethermost pit of the earth. He it is Who commands thee, Who once ordered the sea and the wind and the storm to obey.... Him thou shalt fear! (Roman Ritual, *Rite of Exorcism*, n. 4)[1]

---

[1] Weller, *Rituale*, p. 185. "The *Roman Ritual* (Latin: *Rituale Romanum*) is one of the official ritual works of the Roman Catholic rite. It contains all of the services which may be performed by a priest or deacon which are not contained within either the *Missale Romanum* or the *Brevarium Romanum*." (Cf. Wikipedia.) The edition of the *Rituale Romanum* to which I will refer in this book is the second of the three volume work translated by Rev. Philip T. Weller, STD. The three volumes are the following: *Vol. I: The Sacraments and Processions,* Copyright 1950; *Vol. II, Christian Burial, Exorcisms, Reserved Blessings, Etc.*, Copyright 1964; *Vol. III: The Blessings,* The Bruce Publishing Co., Milwaukee, WI, 1946.

✜

1. Was Satan's expulsion from heaven an exorcism?

The story of Satan's expulsion from heaven is found in Chapter 12 of the Book of Revelation. When the devil is cast down to the earth, the passage notes that the heavenly choirs and all of the redeemed sing for joy that "the accuser of our brothers is cast out."[2] Even some of the free angelic creatures whom God created to love, honor and serve Him rebelled and had to be expelled from heaven because "nothing unclean will enter there."[3]

If exorcism is defined in general terms as the expulsion of demons from some place, then this passage from Revelation does reveal a sort of exorcism. It was not, however, an exorcism in the technical sense that the Church understands it; namely, as an adjuration of an unholy spirit and its separation from a human body.

The passage says that St. Michael (an Archangel) and his angels performed the expulsion of Satan from heaven. Being of a lower order of angels than Lucifer (a Seraphim angel), St. Michael had less *natural* angelic power to expel a powerful Seraphim. He could only act under some authority and power greater than that of a Seraphim angel to perform this work.[4] The authority was that of Jesus Himself, the Son of God, who is featured in the same passage as the male child "destined to shepherd all the nations with an iron rod."[5] This battle was thus a celestial David versus Goliath battle and, here too, the smaller party won "in the name of the Lord of Hosts."[6] Analogously,

---

2 Rev 12:10
3 Rev 22:3
4 St. Thomas Aquinas, *Summa Theologica*, I.109.4.ad3.
5 Rev 12:5
6 1 Sam 17:45

the flesh-and-blood exorcist has no power of himself to expel demons that are much stronger than he, spiritually. He has only the power of the Name of Jesus and the authority of the Church which makes the work of exorcism possible.

2. What did Jesus say about exorcism in the Gospels?

Perhaps wary of the human fascination with occult things, Jesus did not give many teachings about the devil or exorcism. However, His few teachings almost always relate to the devil's defeat and expulsion. For example, when His disciples returned from their first missionary excursion into Palestine, He told them that He saw "the devil fall like lightning from heaven."[7] The night before He died, He told them that "the prince of this world is cast out."[8] He told them that "the gates of hell shall not prevail,"[9] meaning that the gates of evil will not withstand the onslaught of the Church's attack. And He even told them that various evil things they would encounter in their ministry: poison, snakes, sickness, etc., would be powerless to harm them if they carried out His mission with fidelity.[10] The Lord's few references to the devil emboldened His disciples to use the spiritual authority of Christ against evil with confidence that they would always prevail.

The Lord did give His disciples explicit instructions about exorcism in several places though: first, when He sent them out on their inaugural public mission for the Kingdom, He explicitly instructed them to cast out demons.[11] The disciples were so noticeably affected by their "success" against demons that Jesus had to remind them that it was not their power but their election in

---

7 Lk 10:18
8 Jn 12:31
9 Mt 16:18
10 Cf. Mk 16:17-18
11 Cf. Mt 10:8

heaven that mattered most.[12] Secondly, He also gave Peter and the Church the power to "bind and loose,"[13] which is interpreted as a spiritual/moral power to hold humans and demons accountable to God through His Church. Finally, at His Ascension into heaven, the Lord told His disciples that a sign of His Kingdom on earth would be that they would "expel demons in my Name."[14]

3. What evidence is there that Jesus performed exorcisms?

There is so much biblical evidence of Jesus casting out demons that it is impossible to deny this aspect of His Public Ministry. These instances are not, as some have said, psychological problems of neurotic people that Jesus enlightened and freed. They are revealed to us as actual *demons* inside of people's bodies, individual alien personalities, some committing great violence and some with specific names. In Matthew's gospel, he freed two men in the Gadarene territory from thousands of possessing demons.[15] The parallel story of a possessed man in Luke shows that the thousands of demons had the collective name of "Legion."[16] He freed a boy from a demon of epilepsy (literally "seizure") which the father described as an unclean spirit that "throws him into the fire and water...."[17] He also commanded demons who revealed Him as the "Son of God" before His time to come out of the possessed.[18] Indeed, in Mark, Chapter 1, there are three references to Jesus' casting out demons on the first day of His Public Ministry.[19] The purpose of Jesus' work was to "destroy the works of the devil."[20]

---

12 Cf. Lk 10:20
13 Cf. Mt 16:19
14 Mk 16:17
15 Mt 8:28-32
16 Lk 8:25-37
17 Mk 9:18 and Mt 17:15
18 Cf. Lk 4:41 and Mk 1:34
19 *Ibid.*
20 1 Jn 3:8

Jesus' most significant demonic expulsion, however, was accomplished from the Cross.[21] Just as Jesus commanded the expulsion of the devil[22] *from heaven* at the dawn of time by St. Michael, so it was His work to expel the devil *from the earth* and supplant the kingdom of darkness by His Death and Resurrection. One week before His death the Lord Himself solemnly proclaimed that He had authority over evil: "Now has judgment come upon this world; now will this world's prince be driven out, and I—once I am lifted up from the earth—will draw all men to myself."[23] In the Old Testament, Moses was commanded to make a bronze serpent, mount it on a pole and "lift it up" to heal all who were bitten by the seraph serpents in the desert because of their complaints against God.[24] Those who looked upon it had this evil (i.e., ailment) *driven out* of them.

The redeeming Death of Christ manifested His power over evil in a decisive fashion. Jesus was not conquered by death, which the Book of Wisdom tells us is the devil's instrument.[25] Rather, He submitted Himself humbly to death and was victorious over it by driving the prince of death from this world. While it is clear that the devil still exercises his works of death everywhere in the world, after the Death and Resurrection of Jesus, he no longer does so in a definitive way.

4. Why did Jesus need to exorcise the world?

If the Church is the "Mystical Body of Christ," then the world is the "mystical body of Satan."[26] As Christ's Mystical Body is a liv-

---

21 This is also a theme echoed in the recent publication by English exorcist, Fr. Jeremy Davies, *Exorcism: Understanding Exorcism in Scripture and Practice*, The Incorporated Catholic Truth Society: London, England, 2008, p. 8.
22 Rev 12:9
23 Jn 12:31-32
24 Cf. Nm 21:4-9
25 Cf. Wis 2:24
26 Nicolas Corte, *Who is the Devil?* Hawthorn Books: New York, 1958, p. 89.

ing community, intimately united to Christ the Head, the analogy of the world as the body of Satan is clear. The world and the flesh and all those who serve these things, whether consciously or not, are united to the "prince of this world" and become vehicles for all the actions of the devil. Explicit Satanism and devil-worship is the most evil expression of union with the devil, but there are many "worldly" people who serve the demonic agenda. It was this world that Christ came to redeem because it was created good in the beginning and was corrupted by the devil and all his malice.

5. What other Old Testament images did Jesus likely have in mind when He performed exorcisms?

Jesus understood His ministry of exorcism as an expression of His authority to judge organized evil in the world and destroy its power. A familiar biblical precedent of God's judgment on evil was the destruction of Sodom and Gomorrah,[27] which was so wicked that it could not be saved. The same was true of the destruction of the city of Jericho, which was considered an abomination to the Lord once the people entered into the Promised Land.[28] His words in the Gospel of John, "[N]ow has judgment come upon this world,"[29] are indicative of this attitude of righteous judgment upon unrepentant evil.

God's power over evil is manifest also in His purification of the promised land of the peoples who worshipped false gods. His action is described as a quasi-exorcism, a "driving out" of evil from their midst. We must be careful, however, not to interpret such passages literally. When the Old Testament speaks of "driving out" nations, it does so as a command to the Israelites to separate themselves from evil but is not to be interpreted in modern

---

27 Cf. Gn 19:1-29
28 Cf. The Book of Joshua, Chapter 6
29 Jn 12:31

times as commanding anyone to do violence. The Church applies exorcism and "driving out" only to demons, not humans. The following passage describes Yahweh's actions as a type of exorcism:

> *When you come into the land which the Lord your God is giving you, you shall not learn to imitate the abominations of the peoples there. Let there not be found among you anyone who immolates his son or daughter in the fire, nor a fortune-teller, soothsayer, charmer, diviner, or caster of spells, not one who consults ghosts and spirits or seeks oracles from the dead. Anyone who does such things is an abomination to the Lord, and because of such abominations, the Lord, your God, is driving these nations out of your way.*[30]

6. What is the main paradigm of spiritual liberation for the Jewish people?

The Exodus from Egypt[31] was undoubtedly the focal point of Israel's self-understanding of their liberation from the bondage of slavery. The elements are clearly those of a possession and deliverance by the mighty hand of God:

- A chosen people under severe oppression and in a state of cruel slavery (Israel);

- A totalitarian overlord (Pharaoh) who knows or cares nothing of the One True God and whose magicians imitate and mock His sanctity;

- An army of cruel task masters to do the overlord's bidding and cause the people to suffer (the slave drivers building the supply city of Raamses);

- A holy liberator (Moses) who is sent in to free the people of God from their bondage.

---
30 Dt 18:9-12
31 The Book of Exodus, Chapters 1-15

By extension, Jesus is the New Moses sent to liberate His people from bondage, only this time the deliverance was not the physical exodus from a land of slavery, but the definitive spiritual liberation of His people from the devil's power. His death and Blood freed the new People of God from the oppression of evil by driving the devil out of His Kingdom and bringing His people through the waters of Baptism to a new Promised Land, namely heaven.

In a fulfillment of all the Old Testament images, Jesus did for us what no other death or human act could accomplish. He became the *Paschal Lamb* that was slain for the sins of His people; He is the new *Passover sacrifice* celebrated as His people depart the land of slavery; His is the *Blood* on the *doorposts and lintels* of His people's hearts guarding them from the angel of death. He is that *destroying angel* putting an end to the reign of terror of the evil one. Finally, on the day of His Resurrection, He became the *New Moses* who, as he looks upon the vanquished forces of the enemy, sings the final song of victory over evil.[32]

For this reason in the Roman Catholic Good Friday liturgy, the Church "lifts up" the Cross of Christ for all men to see! There is no greater sign of our triumph over the devil and no sign that the devil loathes more than the Sign of the Cross.

7. Why is exorcism important to Jesus' Kingdom?

Jesus' manifestations of spiritual power in His Public Ministry were intended to give His followers *hope* in His power as Savior. His Kingdom aims at restoring man to the state of original innocence. Hence, He cured the sick, raised the dead, preached the good news, cast out demons and exercised power over natural forces, all of which were signs of His messianic authority over all

---

32 Cf. Ex 15:1-18

of creation. The power He showed over these realities would be a sign of the Kingdom of God breaking into human history. It was the spiritual power to "bind and loose" which He later delegated to His Church before His death.

Exorcism is one of the many spiritual powers that the Lord gave to His Church. The Church has power over sickness and sin through its Sacraments of Confession and Anointing of the Sick; it proclaims the power of life over death through its *Rite of Christian Burial*, etc. Saints and communities have even been known to pray for deliverance from natural disasters, plagues and chaos and have been heard by God because of their piety.

Indeed spiritual protection from the devil was important enough to the Lord that He included it as the last petition in the Lord's Prayer: "Deliver us from evil." If the Lord did not think that evil had power over human beings, He would not have asked us to pray for deliverance from evil as a regular petition in the Church's principle prayer. Praying for deliverance from evil is thus at the very center of our faith because, in praying this way, we recognize that only God can truly save us from the power of the devil. We recognize, more importantly, that we cannot save ourselves.

8. What reactions did people have to Jesus' exorcism ministry?

The reactions to His exorcism ministry were varied. Many marveled at His unparalleled authority over evil and "praised God that such power had been given to men."[33] They continued to bring demoniacs and oppressed people to Him and His disciples for deliverance. The spiritually proud elite leaders of Israel, however, remained resolutely opposed to the authority that was

---

33 Mt 9:8

made manifest for their belief, and they contradicted His work by saying that it was "by the power of Beelzebul that He casts out demons."[34]

Attributing His spiritual power to the devil caused the Lord to issue the most stringent warning about eternal damnation; He warned that such a blasphemy was a sin against the Holy Spirit, "the sin that will never be forgiven."[35] The sin is not "unforgivable" in the sense that the Lord is incapable of purging it; rather, it indicates that the *heart* from which that blasphemy issues is totally closed to the obvious manifestation of Christ's salvific power. Such was the sin of proud Lucifer in the beginning when he refused to submit to God and decided to set up his own atrocious kingdom.[36]

9. How does Jesus carry on the ministry of exorcism in His Church?

Jesus Himself acts whenever an exorcist uses His Name to drive out demons; namely, the exorcist acts *in persona Christi*. Ordination confers a spiritual power and mandate to bless, and some priests are given special permission from the bishop to perform in a direct way the ministry of exorcism, which is a unique type of blessing reserved for those most oppressed by the power of evil.

While the performance of an exorcism is limited to priests, the Church's power to combat evil is not. Anyone who is a baptized Christian has authority to fight evil in whatever way is appropriate to their state in life. Most Christians do not recognize that Christ bestowed this authority upon them and therefore don't use that authority to confront the evils they face in their

---

34 Lk 11:15
35 Mk 3:29
36 Cf. Is 14:12-15

daily lives. In most cases, Christians can fight evil by invoking the Name of Jesus against any manifestation of evil and by binding and rebuking it. If they encounter truly serious cases of demonic possession, they can refer these to the ordained ministers.

10. Why do exorcists or those who perform deliverances use the Name of Jesus?

Jesus Himself said that His disciples would use His Name to drive out demons. Mark 16:17 shows how Jesus made His Name our most potent weapon against demons and all other spiritual strongholds of evil. St. Peter says in Acts 4:12 that there is "no other name in heaven or on earth by which men are to be saved." When we use His Name, we act as ambassadors of Christ—in the same way that an actual ambassador acts in the name of his government, president or prime minister.

11. Can other religions perform successful exorcisms?

In a 2007 talk on exorcism at Mundelein Seminary near Chicago, Father José Antonio Fortea,[37] Spain's chief exorcist, provided a number of insights regarding the phenomena of demonic activity.[38] He described the action of exorcism as a battle in which people engage with spiritual weapons. Objectively speaking, Catholics and Orthodox Christians have essentially the full range of spiritual weapons provided to them by the Church, which they can use with great power against demons. This is because these two churches are heirs of the apostolic Tradition (which includes the ordained priesthood). Since it was to the

---

[37] Fr. José Antonio Fortea Cucurull, (Barbastro, Spain, b. 1968) is a priest of the diocese of Alcalá de Henares (Madrid) and a theologian specializing in demonology. He wrote his licentiate thesis on exorcism (1998) and is the pastor of the parish Our Lady of Zulema in his diocese.

[38] Conference on Healing, University of St. Mary of the Lake/Mundelein Seminary, Mundelein, IL, conducted from August 13-17, 2007. (Hereafter referred to as Mundelein Conference, 2007.)

Apostles that the power to "bind and loose" was given, the spiritual power of the apostolic churches is greatest. While this ministry and spiritual power is objectively held by the Church, the subjective application of spiritual warfare with these weapons will very much depend upon the individual exorcist's faith and holiness.

Other Christian churches have fewer weapons to fight spiritual evil, but they do have a certain spiritual power through using the Name of Jesus and through the intensity of their faith. I have seen situations where Protestant deliverance ministers could not handle cases of possession and actually referred them to the Catholic Church for expulsion. This is only to say that other Christians often lack the full range of spiritual weapons to combat potent evil. However, their potency of faith and pursuit of holiness in Christ is oftentimes extremely admirable and powerful against demons.

Fr. Fortea said that (modern) Jewish rabbis have no real tradition of exorcism and do not practice it as such. They certainly would not use the Name of Jesus to exorcise, or if they did, they would not use it with the faith in His divine power required for it to be effective. The Acts of the Apostles recounts the humorous story of the Jewish "sons of Sceva" who were beaten up by a demon when they attempted to cast it out using Jesus' Name, but without faith.[39]

Muslims have no priesthood and lack a coherent centralized spiritual authority to call upon in dealing with the demonic. They do have some inchoate practice of exorcism which is done by the recitation of parts of the Q'uran that give praise to God. This, Fr. Fortea says, causes the demons to suffer. They also use religious symbols like incense and water effectively. The devil understands

---

39 Cf. Acts 9:13-16

the symbolic value of these symbols of worship, and if there is sufficient prayer, an exorcism can be successful. Nevertheless, as Muslims have fewer weapons to fight evil, only relatively easy cases will be resolved, and these will take much longer.

Some Buddhist monks have even been known to perform successful exorcisms,[40] but their power over evil is related simply to the blessing that God bestows upon people of sincere faith, whatever their religious tradition. We can see how good God is to all people in that He provides some sort of spiritual remedy against evil when He finds authentic faith. There are many fonts of God's mercy flowing out of His Most Sacred Heart, but undoubtedly the Name of Jesus and the Apostolic Succession is the widest and deepest river from which to draw resources and weapons for battle.

12. Will there be a final exorcism of evil by Christ?

The Book of Revelation contains the story of both the first exorcism (see Question 1 above) and the last series of exorcisms of the world's possessing spirits (Rev 20:11-15), and we should pay close attention to these in order to bolster our faith and chasten our desire for sin. Although His patience is infinite and directed toward our salvation, in the end, God will not be mocked[41] or rejected. He does not deal lightly with the devil or his unrepentant companions, be they human or angelic.

The final exorcism of evil from the world is at the end of time when the old world passes away and when "new heavens and a new earth" are given to those whose names are written in the Book of the Lamb.[42] The devil has already been judged at

---

40 *Ibid.*
41 Cf. Gal 6:7
42 Rev 21:1

Calvary according to the Gospel of John.[43] In the final exorcism, the devil will join the false prophet and the beast that were cast down there before him into the pool of fire.[44] Then Jesus will judge all human beings who reject God and refuse to worship Him.[45] Following these, death itself will be judged and, together with the nether world, will be also thrown into the pool of fire, the second and definitive death.[46] There is no more evil to cast out then. All creation will thus be purified of its evil. In that final episode, Christ Himself will be the exorcist.

We have been forewarned.

Afterword to Chapter 1
Priestly Assistance from Heaven

One of the most fascinating deliverances I ever performed involved a middle-aged woman who had suffered for many years with unknown afflictions and pains, none of which could be cured by any medicine or therapy. The woman needed to be delivered from a host of lesser-strength demons which had literally infested her body over the course of many years for various reasons but which were now causing an escalating series of sorrowful events and persecutions. She was a very faithful Catholic, but her fidelity only seemed to enrage the unclean spirits that persecuted her every time she began to pray or get close to God. Chief among her devotions was her love for Padre Pio and Pope John Paul II (after his death).

---

43 Jn 12:31
44 Cf. Rev 20:10
45 Cf. Rev 20:12-13
46 Cf. Rev 20:14

When this lady asked for deliverance prayers, my assistant and I did not know that she had so many demons inside her body, but we prayed for her because of her expressed need. At the final count we estimated that there were several hundred distinct demons that exited her body through the four sessions of prayer and deliverance we conducted with her. Because these were not deeply-rooted demons, the process to expel them was very simple: silent prayer before the exposed Eucharist and then a command to each unclean spirit to leave her one after another. Each was commanded to tell its name as it came to the Light and say, "Hail Mary, full of grace," as its sign of departure. The list of names was unbelievable: Abortion, Anti-Christ, Belial, Betrayal, Birth Control, Black Cats (this one hissed and put up claws), Blasphemy, Fortune Telling, Horoscope, "Innocence" (this one spoke with a deceptively sweet, innocent voice), Illness, Pride (this one sat upright as if indignant and said, "I don't have to leave...."), Racism, Rape, Slave, Snake, Suicide and many, many others.

The most interesting insight into the demonic mind was the demons' resounding fear of this lady's favorite holy men: Padre Pio and Pope John Paul II. At one point the lady said that she could even sense the presence of these saintly men in the chapel. The demons *certainly* sensed it because each time a demon resisted the command to leave, it was very easy for me to say, "Well, I will just have to call on the Polish Pope to deal with you" or ask, "Should I call my priest friend with the stigmata to get you to leave?" Every mention of these holy men evoked a blood-curdling scream from the demons who sometimes yelled, "Get those $%^&* gloves off of me!" or "Keep that #@$% priest in white away from me—I'll go! I'll go!" We also used relics of the holy men which seemed to burn the demons like fire any time they were touched to the lady's person.

By the end of the fourth session, the woman was totally freed from hundreds of lesser-strength demons that left because of her personal faith in God and her deep devotion to two holy priests who assisted her from heaven.

Chapter 2
The Devil, His Minions and His Activities[1]

How you have fallen from the heavens, O morning star, son of the dawn! How are you cut down to the ground, you who mowed down the nations! You said in your heart: "I will scale the heavens; above the stars of God I will set up my throne; I will take my seat on the Mount of Assembly, in the recesses of the North. I will ascend above the tops of the clouds; I will be like the Most High!" Yet down to the nether world you go, to the recesses of the pit! (Is 14:12-15)

Evil is not merely a lack of something, but an effective agent, a living spiritual being, perverted and perverting. A terrible reality. Mysterious and frightening. It is contrary to the teaching of the Bible and the Church to refuse to recognize the existence of such a reality, or to regard it as a principle in itself which does not draw its origin from God like every other creature; or to explain it as a pseudo-reality, a conceptual and fanciful personification of the unknown cause of our misfortune. (Pope Paul VI)[2]

---

1 This chapter deals only with the theological and biblical dimensions of the power of evil and will not specifically address concrete occult situations or problems that may be rooted in culture. See Chapter 7 for references and resources concerning cultural aspects of occultism.
2 Pope Paul VI, General Audience, November 15, 1972.

1. How do we know that evil really exists?

St. Thomas Aquinas asked a similar question in his treatise *De Malo* (*On Evil*).[3] He asked "whether evil is something" and gave a very complex theological answer. I hope to provide here a much simpler answer to his complex theology! In talking about evil (and hence the devil and his demons) we must first talk about good. St. Thomas says that good is what all things naturally desire. That is, everyone and everything tends toward something good, whether it be a universal good or some particular good. Common sense tells us that "whatever is numbered among *the things that are* has an affinity with some good."[4] We can say that God is the universal Good to which all things aspire, and from Him there is a progression of lesser goods to which particular things aspire.

However, evil by definition is the opposite of good in that it wishes to *deprive* things of their true good, and for that reason it cannot be an actual *thing* (i.e., an object or goal). It is an anti-thing, that is, a deprivation of something good. St. Thomas says that, "if evil were a real thing, it would desire nothing, nor would it be desired by anything."[5] Evil is, rather, an absence much the same way that sickness is the absence of health and poverty is the absence of prosperity. It is true to say, then, that evil only exists because good exists first, and this is reflected in nature. We only see shadows because light first shines on some object. The shadow would not exist were it not for the light. Similarly, blindness is the result of a lack of sight,[6] and a hole in the ground is there

---
3   St. Thomas Aquinas, *De Malo* (*On Evil*), Notre Dame University Press: Notre Dame, IN. 1995, cf. I.1-3.
4   *Ibid.*, I.1.
5   *Ibid.*
6   *Ibid.*, I.2.

because it has been created by the removal of some material that was there before it. Many other examples could be added.

St. Thomas goes on to say that evil, while not existing as a thing in its own right, can however, exist *in particular creatures and things* because there are many ways and means to deprive us of the good. It is a matter of Catholic doctrine to recognize that the devil, like all angels, was created good.[7] By his own free will he chose to reject the true good and suffered the consequences of that choice. Hence, the devil can subsequently be considered the font of all evil in the world, not because evil has an independent existence in itself but because the highest angel who was the most sublime of all God's created beings chose to reject the good and thus became the greatest force in the world seducing the rest of creation to choose evil.[8]

2. What do we call the devil and why?

There are three common names by which most people describe the font of all evil: the devil, Satan and Lucifer; each of these names comes to English from a different language. The name "devil" comes from the Greek word διάβολος (diábolos), which literally means "one who throws things around" in the sense of creating the chaos for which he is so infamous. The name "Satan" comes from the Hebrew verb "to accuse" and is variously translated as "the accuser," "the tempter," "the persecutor," "the calumniator" or "the adversary." Not ironically, the Church, taking her cue from the Gospel of John, calls the Holy Spirit, "the Advocate," (i.e., defense lawyer) in order to remind us that the depredations and accusations of our principle enemy are always met with a more powerful Divine Person who takes our side when we are accused or attacked.

---
7 Cf. *The Catechism of the Catholic Church*, nn. 391-395; St. Thomas Aquinas, *Summa Theologica*, Christian Classics: Westminster, MD, 1948, cf. I.63.4.
8 *Summa Theologica*, I.63.8.

"Lucifer" is a name that derives from Latin and means "light-bearer," commonly understood as his God-given name before he fell from grace. This name is cited in St. Jerome's Vulgate translation of the Bible in Isaiah 14:12-15.[9] This potent creature has always been considered by the tradition of the Church as one of the most powerful angels that God created. Theology speculates that his name was "Light-Bearer," understanding him to be a Seraphim angel, the highest order of the angelic hierarchy. St. Thomas Aquinas quotes Pope St. Gregory in saying that Lucifer was "set over all the hosts of angels, surpassed them in brightness, and was by comparison, the most illustrious of them all."[10] Lucifer's fall from grace did not deprive him of his natural powers but rather corrupted those powers for the perverse work of undermining God's plan of salvation for men.

There are many references to this wretched being in the Bible. The New Testament alone refers to this origin of all wickedness nearly three hundred times to warn us of his presence and work. He is described in Rev 12:9 as "a huge dragon, the ancient serpent, known as the devil or Satan, the seducer of the whole world." However, the devil's most serious indictment came from our Blessed Lord Himself, who called him "a liar and the father of lies," and "a murderer from the beginning" (Jn 8:44).

3. What does the *Rite of Exorcism* call him?

The list of condemnatory names for the devil contained in the three prayers in the original 1614 *Rite of Exorcism*[11] (and its 1952

---

9 Isaiah 14:12-15. Quomodo cecidisti de caelo, Lucifer, fili aurorae? Deiectus es in terram, qui deiciebas gentes, qui dicebas in corde tuo: "In caelum conscendam, super astra Dei exaltabo solium meum, sedebo in monte convertus in lateribus aquilonis; ascendam super altitidunum nubium, similis ero Altissimo." Verumtamen ad infernum detractus es, in profundum laci. Cf. *Nova Vulgata, Bibliorum Sacrorum*, Libreria Editrice Vaticana, Typis Polyglottis Vaticanis ,1979.
10 St. Thomas Aquinas, *Summa Theologica*, I.65.7.
11 Weller, *Rituale*, p. 185.

revision) is nothing short of impressive. The inventive and aggressive terms that the Church uses to describe the fiend are not for show and even less for mockery; they are meant to expose his evil and thus to manifest the Church's power over him and break his pride. The use of condemnatory terms against a powerful adversary is also a kind of psychological warfare that helps the human exorcist gain an edge over a powerful spiritual being. Some of these names come from Scripture, while others are simply the fruit of the Church's long experience in fighting the ancient enemy of the human race. The names and terms listed below are all direct quotes from various parts of the ritual.[12]

<u>In the prelude to the first exorcism prayer</u>: fugitive and fallen tyrant, that spirit of evil, noonday demon, the beast that lays waste [the Lord's] vineyard, that reprobate dragon, unclean spirit, this cruel demon.

<u>In the first exorcism prayer</u>: the wicked enemy, and every phantom and diabolical legion, Satan, thou enemy of the faith, thou foe of the human race, the carrier of death and the robber of life, the shirker of justice and the root of all evil, fomenter of vice, seducer of men, traitor of the nations, the instigator of envy, the font of avarice, the source of discord, the exciter of sorrows, unclean spirit, the ancient enemy, the archenemy of the earth, the wicked tempter, the mighty adversary, evil spirit who hitherto terrorized over us.

<u>In the second exorcism prayer</u>: thou ancient serpent…along with thy ravaging followers, transgressor, seducer full of deceit and perfidy, enemy of virtue and persecutor of the innocent, horrible creature, monster, profligate dragon, the asp and the basi-

---

[12] All quotes are from the 1614 exorcism ritual. For the complete text of the ritual, see Appendices A, B and C.

lisk [i.e., two types of lethal serpents], the lion and the dragon, unclean spirits.

<u>In the third exorcism prayer</u>: every unclean spirit, every phantom, every encroachment of Satan, ye accursed, O evil one and…thy followers, thee and thine angels, the prince of accursed murder, author of lechery, leader in sacrilege, model of vileness, teacher of heretics, inventor of every obscenity, O evil one…accursed one.

<u>In Pope Leo XIII's exorcism (added to the ritual in 1925)</u>: the princes and powers…the rulers of this world's darkness, Satan's tyranny, the dragon, the ancient serpent, the demon, Satan, hostile powers, every unclean spirit, every devilish power, infernal adversary, legion, every diabolical group and sect, cunning serpent, accursed dragon and every diabolical legion, Satan, founder and master of falsity, enemy of mankind, accursed spirits, enemies of holy Church.

4. Who is Beelzebul then?

The name "Beelzebul" (in some ancient biblical texts he is called "Beelzebub") does not appear in the text of the exorcism ritual except in one of the optional readings from the Gospels. This name is a Hebrew term meaning "the lord (or god) of the flies." Jesus speaks of the demon Beelzebul in responding to the frightening pharisaical blasphemy against the Holy Spirit in which they attributed Jesus' exorcist powers to the prince of demons. As a Hebrew or Aramaic name, the Pharisees were more likely to use it than the Latin or Greek names for the devil, but it is interesting that they did not use the more common Hebrew name of Satan, which appears many times in the Hebrew Bible.

While it is not entirely clear from Scripture whether Beelzebul is actually the same as Satan, it is possible that

Beelzebul is another distinct and powerful demon in league with Satan. Beelzebul is called, "the prince of demons,"[13] but Jesus refers to Satan as "the prince of this world."[14] The distinction in terminology notes a possible distinction in demonic functions: Satan could be the overlord of the human and demonic world, while Beelzebul could be his commanding general of the army of demons. Just as there are many holy angels with distinct personalities and functions, so also the demonic world reflects certain distinctions of personality and function.

Common usage, however, identifies the two names as one entity. Popular literature usually identifies Beelzebul with Satan. Nobel prize-winning author William Golding's fascinating novel, *Lord of the Flies*, relates a fictional story of a group of children who are stranded alone on a deserted island where they are forced to survive and form their own make-shift community without any adult influence. One group of children begins to worship a rotted-out carcass of an animal that is covered with flies (shown so effectively in the Judas suicide scene of Mel Gibson's film, *The Passion of the Christ*). Over time they begin to follow the murderous dictates of the demon operating through the carcass. This novel shows both the disgusting nature of evil and the innate human tendency toward evil when deprived of human culture, God and religion. Beelzebul, the "Lord of the Flies," is, in this account, simply an image of Satan.

Fr. Gabriele Amorth, the former chief exorcist of the Diocese of Rome, mentions in his book, *An Exorcist Tells His Story*, that in the course of exorcisms, when a demon identifies himself with a biblical name, these are usually the most important demons[15]

---

13 Mt 12:24
14 Jn 12:31
15 Rev. Gabriele Amorth, *An Exorcist Tells His Story*, Ignatius Press: San Francisco, 1999, p. 116.

and therefore the most difficult to expel. It stands to reason that Holy Scripture would point out to us, or "expose" to the light of faith, the worst enemies of our souls even if it is difficult to know everything about them.

5. Which are the wickedest demons that may afflict humanity?

Demons with biblical names are always the "most important" and hence, the strongest and wickedest demons.[16] Their names have been revealed to us in the Scriptures or Tradition by the Lord who, in His Mercy, has warned us of their malice in a deliberate way. Father Amorth lists: Satan or Beelzebub, Lucifer, Asmodeus, Meridian and Zebulun as examples, the latter two being names from Tradition rather than Scripture. I would add Astarte or Ashteroth, Baal, Moloch, Lilith, Mephistopheles or any derivative of these names as other more common biblical and traditional names.

6. Was Jesus concerned about the devil?

Yes and no. The posture of Jesus towards the devil in the New Testament is as a superior who is concerned about but hardly threatened by a subordinate spiritual power. Jesus speaks relatively little about the devil in the Gospels, but His reticence about the devil is undoubtedly due to His all-consuming mission to tell us about His Father first. He never wavered in the slightest from His main mission of establishing His Father's Kingdom which would inevitably supplant the princedom of the devil and break the power of evil over men.

Our Lord's attitude toward the devil is thus paradigmatic for us: we ought to be concerned about the devil's desire to kill our souls and vigilant toward his real power, but we ought not to give him more attention than is his due. Nor should we be unduly

---
16 *Ibid.*

fearful of him who is so limited a spiritual force that he can only act with our consent. Our concern should always be first and foremost the fulfillment of God's Will.

7. What is the difference between angels and archangels?

There are two ways to reckon angels which are not incompatible, just different ways to assess the biblical data about these mysterious beings. The first description of angels comes from traditional theology and speaks about the splendorous angels arrayed in a hierarchy of nine "choirs,"[17] each with its own particular mission and character. This reckoning explains the functions of the angels in the order of the universe and the plan of salvation. The second reckoning divides all the angels into just two categories: angels and archangels, with the latter being the more exalted and powerful of the two. If the "choirs" of angels are actually understood as "armies" commanded by "the Lord of Hosts," then the archangels are the various grades of officers and the angels are the non-commissioned officers and the rank and file soldiers.[18]

In the angelic armies, there is perfect harmony in the ranks because they completely united in their duty to help man on his way to salvation. There is no jealousy of rank, authority, power or gifts.

---

17 The traditional patristic authority quoted in reference to the angelic hierarchy is the late-5th Century theologian, Pseudo-Dionysius, whose work, *The Celestial Hierarchy*, explains in full the nine choirs and their functions. Angelic music aside, it is better to imagine ranks of angelic "armies" rather than ranks of musicians whenever we think of angelic "choirs." St. Thomas Aquinas, in the 13th century, based most of his theology of angels on this source. Cf. *Pseudo-Dionysius: The Complete Works*, The Classics of Western Spirituality, tr. Colm Luibheid, Paulist Press: New York, 1987, pp. 143-191.

18 Jean Danielou, S.J., in his marvelous little work, *The Angels and their Mission According to the Fathers of the Church* (Christian Classics from Ave Maria Press: Notre Dame, IN, n.d.), cites Irenaeus saying: "In this place God, Creator of all things, had placed servants, each with his own particular office. A captain of a thousand men was in charge of this place and he was set at the head of his fellow soldiers. These soldiers were the angels, and the captain was an archangel...," p. 45.

Rather, angels are humble and zealous beings, and each is content with his place and in his duty that God has given him for our good. Dante, in *The Divine Comedy*, expresses it perfectly when he says: "From seat to seat throughout this realm, to all the realm is pleasing. For in his will, our hearts have found their peace."[19]

8. What is the difference between demons and devils?

The difference would be explained by the answer above concerning angels and archangels. Since demons are fallen angels, they retain their same nature and natural order among themselves. So correspondingly, demons are the lower fallen angels, and devils are the more powerful ones.[20] What was said about "harmony in the ranks" only applies to holy angels though because the fallen angels exist in a world of perpetual chaos, competition, hatred, game-playing, power plays and maliciousness. If they maintain their natural order or ranks at all they do so only by the imposition of the more powerful upon the less powerful. In other words, the demonic world is the epitome of an environment of pure Darwinian "survival of the fittest."

9. How are demons different from the devil?

The word "demon," δαίμων (dai-mōn), is found in the New Testament and refers to the fallen angels. New Testament writers also refer to them as "unclean spirits," πνεῦματοι ακαθάρτοι (pneúmatoi akahártoi). However, the term "devil," διάβολος (diábolos), is used almost exclusively in reference to Satan. The fallen angels are all, without exception, subordinate to *the* devil or Satan who is their master and overlord. Chapter 12 of the Book

---

19 Cited by Peter Kreeft in *Angels (and Demons) - What Do We Really Know About Them?* Ignatius Press: San Francisco, 1995, p. 60.
20 Jean Danielou, SJ, *The Angels and Their Mission According to the Fathers of the Church*, Christian Classics from Ave Maria Press: Notre Dame, IN, n.d., pp. 45-46.

natural world, their attributes and abilities are properly termed *preternatural*—more specifically, "beyond" the natural world and the normal powers of human beings.

11. Are demons male or female?

Devils and angels are spiritual beings so, strictly speaking, they cannot be males or females, i.e., natural differences which require a body. However, I fully agree with Peter Kreeft[22] that angelic beings can have gender, i.e., masculinity or femininity, because these are spiritual attributes not bound by matter. They can also afflict male bodies and female bodies in particular ways.[23]

For example, the devil, Satan, is univocally identified in Holy Scripture with masculine nouns and attributes; he is also assumed to be masculine because he is ferociously misogynistic and has a coldly logical, calculating, aggressive will to destroy all of the Heavenly Father's beloved children.

Males, however, don't have a monopoly on evil. There are other wicked feminine creatures identified in the Bible whose evil can sometimes put men to shame. Female fertility deities, witches, necromancers and evil seductresses of Palestine were always pulling the Israelites away from God as evidenced by such Old Testament female characters as Lilith, Ashteroth, Jezebel, Delilah, the Witch of Endor and others. Not to be outdone are the hateful feminine personages in the New Testament: Herodias

---

22 Peter Kreeft, *Angels (and Demons) – What Do We Really Know About Them?* Ignatius Press: San Francisco, CA, 1995, p. 76. Kreeft bases his insights on the thinking of C.S. Lewis.

23 Attempted "spiritual marriage" by demons is not uncommon, as is evidenced by the demon Asmodeus in the Book of Tobit. There is also a rather common experience throughout the ages that some demons, although incorporeal, attempt to have sexual relations with women (called incubus, plural incubi) and others with men (called succubus, plural sucubi). "Incubus" means "I lie on top" and derives from the Latin "in" (on top of) and "cubo" (I lie). Sucubus accordingly, means "I lie under" from sub-cubo. Cf. Wikipedia.

and her... the soothsayer in the Acts of the Apos... ...e Whore of Babylon,[27] both referred to in the bo... ...on.

12. What do demons look like?

Spiritual beings have no bodies and therefore cannot technically "look like" anything. They are invisible, but they can periodically take on or project appearances to be seen or experienced by human beings. Demons might make themselves known to the person through the faculty of sight or through the other senses of hearing, feeling, smelling and touching. Demons are generally more "felt" than seen by people, the most common form of demonic manifestation being the sensation of a malevolent *presence* in the same space as the person sensing them.

Aside from the popular image of the little red horned creature with a tail and a pitchfork, there are standard "forms" that demons have used to reveal themselves to humanity through the centuries. Popular horror movies, video games or mascots of heavy metal bands often show demonic images: goats with horns, centaurs, witches and warlocks, vampires, living skulls/skeletons, mummies, decayed human bodies that talk, vicious creatures with fangs and claws. *The Alien* movies featured a vicious, rapacious little creature that emerges out of the stomachs of people looking like a fetus transformed into a fang-toothed ravaging demon. Some believe that this movie represents the epitome of demonic glorification of abortion. Be that as it may, the devil's spawn are not hard to recognize. It's just too bad that most of our faith-deprived society thinks that they are only harmless "entertainment."

---

24 Mt 14:1-10.
25 Acts 16:16-18.
26 Rev 2:20.
27 The Book of Revelation, Chapter 18.

13. Is it possible for the devil or a demon to look beautiful?

St. Paul says that the devil and his associates can come dressed as an "angel of the light,"[28] so indeed it is possible for demons to take on an attractive appearance at times. I have even known the devil to falsify, in the mind of one of his victims, an image of the Virgin Mary for a time. However, the devil can never sustain a beautiful appearance for any length of time. Beauty militates against his nature, and he is disgusted by it. His "beautiful" appearance is more appropriately described as *seductive* like the androgynous image of the devil in Mel Gibson's *The Passion of the Christ*.

The devil's main way to use beauty is through his worldly servants who take God's many gifts with all their inherent beauty and use them to seduce men into sin. Sinful institutions such as pornography, drugs and some forms of music all misuse and pervert the beautiful things of this world for demonic purposes. "Whatever works" to drag souls to hell is his motto.

14. What is a demon's "personality" like?

Demons have personalities just as any human being has a personality. They are, after all, *persons*, except that they do not have bodies. We can know demonic personalities, and we can engage them in a battle precisely because they are personal beings, not impersonal forces of evil. This always becomes clear in situations where the demon uses the voice of the possessed individual to speak to the exorcist. The voice is the same as that of the human victim, but the *personality* behind the voice is different.

Each demon's personality is related somehow, mysteriously, to his function. A demon of anger will speak, well, angrily. Demons of pride will insult and mockingly laugh at the exorcist and blaspheme the things of God. I once heard a demon of

---

[28] 2 Cor 11:14

bigotry shout out obscene remarks about minorities and other races; a demon of retaliation once yelled at me vainly, "You'll pay for this!" A demon of profanity used strings of curse words; and most curious of all, a demon of greed once asked me, "What's your price" (i.e., to stop the exorcism)?

It is important to discern the personalities of the stronger demons carefully in an exorcism. Their particular concerns, their relationship with the victim, their phobias and hatreds will give the priest a good sense of what their "function" is and how then to attack them most effectively. The *Rite of Exorcism* traditionally advocates finding the thing that bothers the demon most and repeating it. However, an exorcist must not manifest interest in the demon's personality as such or indulge in questioning the demon out of curiosity. In fact, the *Rite of Exorcism* forbids it. The priest's only interest in a demonic personality is that he may more deeply understand the mystery of the possession in order to liberate the victim from the demon's power.

15. When the apostate angels rebelled, what happened to their hierarchy?

In Dante's *Inferno*,[29] when Dante and his guide Virgil reach the lowest circle of hell, they see Lucifer there. They climb down the back of the Prince of Evil through a trap door in the center of the earth and then make their way upward through the various circles of purgatory. There, Satan is not the exalted Seraphim angel, the brightest of the heavenly dwellers gazing upon the Magnificence of God any more; rather, he has fled farthest away from the Light and rules his kingdom of terror from the pit of hell, the lowest realm of creation. Although the fallen angels' rebellion from God resulted in utter chaos, their angelic order of being, intelligence and authority remained intact because it is an

---
29 Cf. Canto XXXVI.

order of nature; it just *inverted* to reflect the new power structure. The chart below suggests one view of the reversal of order among the apostate angels when they rebelled against God and in the ages since:

The Kingdom of God (order)	The Kingdom of Satan (inverted)
Angels	**Demons**
*Serve **God** and heaven*	*Prowl about the **material world** "seeking the ruin of souls"*
Seraphim	Demons
Cherubim	Fallen Archangels
Thrones	Fallen Principalities
Serve the universe	*Rule over earth, air, fire and water*
Dominions (Dominations)	Fallen Powers
Virtues	Fallen Virtues
Powers	Fallen Dominions (Dominations)
Serve humans and the material world	*Rule over hell*
Principalities	Fallen Thrones
Archangels	Fallen Cherubim
Angels	Lucifer and the other Fallen Seraphim
All holy angels serve **God and man**	All apostate angels serve **Lucifer**

16. Can demons repent after they sinned?

It is not possible for demons to repent after their sin. According to St. Thomas, the will of an angel cannot change after it has made a choice because the angel (or fallen angel) sees with much greater clarity the object of his choice and hence his decision about that thing is irrevocable.[30] Angels are mid-way between the immutable God, whose Mind and Will are unchangeable, and human beings, whose intellect and will are clouded by the flesh and therefore always changeable. Humans have to be trained to choose the right things over time but are still free to choose evil. Angels, however, don't have to be trained. Once they grasp something, they know it in its entirety and they cannot change their choice for good or for evil once they have chosen it. That is to say that their choice of evil is always a mortal sin because they always give a deliberate consent of the will with full knowledge about matters which are always grave, and because of their superior knowledge, they remain for all eternity obstinate in their sin.

17. What are the levels of the devil's activity against God's children?

There are many assessments of demonic activity, but the simplest scheme to describe the demon's work is the triad of temptation, oppression and obsession.[31] These three kinds of demonic activity go from the least intrusive to the most intrusive and represent differing degrees of loss of freedom for the afflicted person. Temptation is an *attempted "dialogue"* where the person's freedom remains intact, oppression is *an attack from the outside,* which limits but does not take away the person's freedom, and obsession is *an attack from the inside,* which severely restricts or harasses the individual's freedom. Possession is different from obsession only by degree; it is the highest degree of obsession, in

---

30 St. Thomas Aquinas, *Summa Theologica*, I.64.2; *De Malo (On Evil)*, 16.5.
31 Here, I have chosen to use the classic word "obsession," rather than the word "infestation" to describe the entrance of a demon into a body. Infestation, properly speaking, has to do with the entrance of a demon into the body of an animal or a locality.

which the person loses most or all of his freedom at any given time of attack.

We can liken the kinds of demonic activity to an enemy army that lays siege to a city:[32] *temptation* is like the enemy standing outside the city gates asking the occupants to come out and talk; *oppression* is like the enemy bombarding the city from the outside with shells and mortars; *obsession* is when the enemy breaches the walls and gets inside the city taking it block by block but is not yet in full control of it. This is sometimes called "partial possession." Finally, *full possession* is when the enemy is fully inside the city and has taken near or full control of the body. Although this state of full demonic control is rare, it is nonetheless real and extremely dangerous to the spiritual and bodily wellbeing of the individual.

18. Are good angels always stronger than demons?

St. Thomas Aquinas says that, even though it would seem logical that certain of the *higher demons* may seem to be superior to the *lower angels* due to their different natural powers even in a fallen state, it's not true, however, that demons are stronger than angels, ever. "An angel who is inferior in the natural order presides over demons, although these may be naturally superior," he says, "because the power of Divine justice to which the good angels cleave, is stronger than the natural power of the [demons]."[33] St. Thomas seems to apply that distinction to the whole angelic hierarchy: namely, that even the lowest angel is more powerful than the strongest demon.

---

32 Various forms of this analogy have been used by exorcists such as Fr. Gabriele Amorth, preachers such as Fr. John Corapi and saints like St. Ignatius Loyola.
33 St. Thomas Aquinas, *Summa Theologica*, I.109.4.ad3.

19. If a demon is not a material being, how can a demon be "in" a body?

Two simple analogies help explain this phenomenon based upon our understanding of angelic natures.

The first is the analogy of a container. A spiritual being cannot be technically contained "in" a space because only a material being can take up space or seemingly be confined to space. Rather, it is better to say that the demon *contains the space* within its malicious mind and will.[34] It is present there by its innate powers to think about its victim and the will to harm him. Peter Kreeft, citing the theology of St. Thomas, describes the demonic presence in a body or place like a stage upon which the demon acts.[35] The stage "contains" the play and so also does the demonic will "contain" the action of his persecution, but he is not contained by the body. The same can be said of angels for good, of course.

The second analogy is that of light. Sunlight can be seen everywhere on a bright day, sent to us in rays from an immense burning star that is 93 million miles away from the surface of the earth. In a sense, the world is contained "in" the sunlight, not the other way around, because the sun is coming to it from "beyond" and encompassing it. Yet, someone may take a magnifying glass and willfully focus the power and intensity of the light on some definite object within that overall scenery where the sun shines. If he focuses it long enough on a material surface, the intense focused beam may penetrate the object with great harm. That magnified light beam and its destructive power is similar to the intensity of the destructive demonic mind and will on his object.

---

34 Cf. St. Thomas Aquinas, *Summa Theologica*, I.52.1. What St. Thomas says of the angelic intellect and will applies of course to the demons.
35 Peter Kreeft, *Angels (and Demons): What Do We Really Know About Them?* Ignatius Press: San Francisco, CA, 1995, p. 69.

20. If the body is God's temple, how can a demon and the Holy Spirit co-exist in the same body?

Two physical bodies cannot be in the same place at the same time because of the laws of physics. Nor can two angels be together in one place at the same time, not because they have physical bodies, but because "an angel is said to be in a corporeal place by application of the angelic power in any manner."[36] This means that only one angel can apply his power to any place at any given time, and so if a fallen angel is in (control of) a body, another angel cannot also exercise his power there at the same time. This is not to say that good angels and demons cannot both be "present to" the same person in some way. It simply describes the power of angelic operation which is singular and exclusive in the way that a physical space is occupied by only one body at a time.

This analogy does not apply to the Holy Spirit, however, Who is present everywhere[37] and Who holds all creation in existence. The Holy Spirit's power is not limited by the presence or operation of a demon, no matter how powerful the demon may be. Therefore, it is still possible for a demon to act on and possess a body while at the same time the Holy Spirit is present and active there.

21. How much power does the devil have over us in normal circumstances?

In general, the devil or any demon has no power to possess or enter a person who lives in a state of grace, especially a person who actively pursues a life of charity. God's grace makes the soul into a spiritual stronghold that evil cannot penetrate save by the person's own free will allowing it to enter. Demonic evil can only operate on a person with the consent of the human will.

---

36 St. Thomas Aquinas, *Summa Theologica*, I.52.1.
37 *Ibid.*, I.52.2.

There are two exceptions to this general rule. One is when God in His Providence allows a person in a state of grace to be afflicted by a demon. The stories of God's permission for possession are not common in the history of the Church, but there are a few dramatic stories recounted by Fr. Amorth in his book, *An Exorcist: More Stories*,[38] which tell of the possession of St. John Bosco, St. Gemma Galgani and Blessed Giovanni Calabria. In each case, God allowed these saints to be possessed by the devil for their own sanctification; thus did God prove to the world that He can use the devil to accomplish His purposes.

The other exception to the rule is when an innocent person becomes the victim of a satanic curse or witchcraft of some sort.[39] Clearly there are innocent victims of occult evil, but even though the victims did nothing to bring the evil upon themselves through any personal consent, the evil act still involves the free will of some other human being cooperating with the powers of darkness.

22. Can a demon kill someone or make him commit suicide?

Once again, a demon is not given this power unless God grants it for some reason, but it is hard to imagine why God would do that. The highly unusual case of the exorcism of 23-year old Anneliese Michel[40] in Klingenburg, Germany, in 1976 may be taken under this rubric; she died of starvation in a possessed state after a year of exorcisms, but I doubt that the presence of the devil victimizing her is to be considered the actual cause of her death. There were various medical and spiritual factors that

---

38 *Op. cit.*, pp. 100-101.
39 This is discussed more at length in Chapter 7 and in the Afterword of Chapter 4 of this book.
40 For more details on this case, see Appendix H.

led to her demise, all of which are dealt with in the excellent book, *The Exorcism of Anneliese Michel*, by Felicitas Goodman.[41]

Fr. Gabriele Amorth of Rome says that it is highly unlikely that a person would commit suicide once he enters into the care of the Church. This spiritual agreement between a possessed person and the Church exerts a restraining force on the demons even before the exorcism formally takes place. The devil can certainly *tempt* people to suicide, however; he cannot *make* someone commit suicide. Jesus does not call him "a murderer from the beginning"[42] without reason, and certainly suicide is one of his tools; however, neither must we allow ourselves to believe that the devil has more power than he actually has.

23. Why does the devil possess people?

There are three main reasons why the devil tries to possess human bodies.

The first reason he possesses bodies is *malice*. Simply said, the devil enjoys causing people pain and sorrow, which is part of every demon's scheme of self-aggrandizement and control over humans. When a demon enters a person's body, he causes significant interior chaos, hoping to eventually cause the person to despair of God's Mercy and reject God's grace.

The second reason for possession is *envy*. Here, the devil attempts to play the part of the human soul to the body.[43] He is supremely jealous of God's love for man and seeks to ape the Incarnation of Christ. The New Testament writings of St. John witness that the Eternal Word united with human flesh and be-

---

[41] Felicitas D. Goodman, *The Exorcism of Anneliese Michel*, Resource Publications: Eugene, OR, 2005.
[42] Cf. Jn 8:44.
[43] Thomas B. Allen, *Possessed: The True Story of An Exorcism*, iUniverse.com, Inc.: New York, 2000, p. 59.

came visible to man.⁴⁴ The devil knows that the union of God with man is the central mystery of our Faith, and, in his envy, he tries to create his own false version of this union, as if to say, "I can be visible too."⁴⁵ However, the devil can never be truly united with flesh. He can penetrate it, pierce it and violate it, but he is incapable of uniting respectfully with the flesh of man in the way that God and His Holy Spirit can.

The third reason for possession is *pride*. Since the body is the Temple of the Holy Spirit,⁴⁶ the devil only wants to violate and pollute it and claim it for his own. The Holy Spirit rightfully "indwells" therein; so the devil, called a "transgressor" by the ritual, enters in and attempts to claim ownership to defile the holy temple where God dwells. When the devil was cast out of heaven, he wanted a temple of his own to glorify himself, but hell isn't much of a temple! He thus tries to steal something that belongs to God and make it his own. If God did not assign a guardian angel to each of us, perhaps no one's temple would ever be safe from the defiling presence of the devil.

24. Why does the devil possess some people and not others?

The definitive answer to this question will remain unknown until we see God face to face. Fr. Dennis McManus speculates that a demon's choice of his victim may be related to personality; that is, just as we gravitate toward certain people naturally, so do they.⁴⁷ It is a plausible explanation for a very mysterious phenomenon.

What is sure, however, is that there are many more possessed people than we will ever know. We speak here about the *freely*

---

44   Cf. Jn 1:14; 1 Jn 1:1-3
45   Fr. Dennis McManus, Mundelein conference.
46   Cf. 1 Cor 6:19.
47   *Ibid.*, Mundelein conference.

chosen possession of people who have given themselves over to devil worship. Such people do not exhibit satanic behaviors, appearance or tendencies in public, and no one would ever know they are possessed. They offer no resistance to the devil because they freely consent to his being in them. The Book of Wisdom talks about these in a frightening passage: "It was the wicked who with hands and words invited death, considered it a friend, and pined for it, and made a covenant with it, because they deserve to be in its possession."[48] We must always pray for the conversion of these people, but more than anything we should pray to be protected from them.

25. What is a state of "perfect possession"?

Following from the last question, "perfect possession" describes a state in which a person not only freely invites a demon to possess him, but also cooperates, with full consent of the mind and will, in the demon's malicious desire to destroy God's Kingdom and children. Some think that this type of human malevolence is not possible, but they are sorely mistaken. Of this frightening phenomenon, Malachi Martin writes:

> As the term implies, a victim of perfect possession is absolutely controlled by evil and gives no outward indication, no hint whatsoever, of the demonic residing within. He or she will not cringe, as others who are possessed will, at the sight of such religious symbols as a crucifix or a Rosary. The perfectly possessed will not bridle at the touch of Holy Water or hesitate to discuss religious topics with equanimity.[49]

We may never know why people so perfectly surrender themselves to the source of all evil, but the fact of the matter is that there are people whose lives are just as given over to the

---

48 Wis 1:16.
49 *Op. cit.*, p. xxiii.

promotion of the Kingdom of Darkness as ours are in promoting the Kingdom of Light.

26. What does a demon actually "possess," the body or the soul?

It is a common misconception that demons possess souls. They do not. The soul and its two spiritual faculties of mind and will are closed realms to the devil, and he cannot penetrate them. Demons, strictly speaking, "possess" only bodies. Demons can exercise a certain measure of control over mind and will, however. They can so "override" these faculties as to cause the person to lose both consciousness and freedom, sometimes completely, but this does not mean that they possess these faculties. They remain uniquely the property of their human owner, which is why it is possible for a person in a totally possessed state to remain without sin. There is always some realm of the person that the devil is not permitted access to.

What is most common, however, is the devil's penetration of the emotional and sensitive parts of the human soul, traditionally known as the memory or imagination. This is the realm of images, senses, passions and memories to which the devil can have access because they are more tied to the flesh than the other spiritual faculties of mind and will. The devil can attack and manipulate these sensitive parts of the human soul with experiences of severe nightmares, voices, unclean images, visions, etc. This is usually why people who are possessed or seriously obsessed suffer so much. They are attacked in the *sensitive* parts of the soul.

27. Can a person become possessed inadvertently?

The portrayal of possession in the movie *The Exorcism of Emily Rose* showed the devil stalking and forcibly entering the body of a pious girl in the middle of the night almost without notice. The film showed her totally normal one minute and totally possessed and paralyzed on the floor the next. Thankfully, possession does not happen that way.

Unfortunately, this and other movies give the impression that the devil has certain powers over the human person that he is simply not granted by God. The devil would *like* to act that way, but if God allowed the devil that kind of predatory access to the human person, no one on earth would survive! Aside from true victimization, the "standard" way the devil possesses people is through a process of subtle and perverse invitations to gain the person's free consent. There is no *inadvertent* possession. Demons usually come in through some sort of acquiescence of the human will. Malachi Martin described this interplay between a human will and demonic intent in a full possession very well in his book *Hostage to the Devil*:

> [The] process of possession ran as follows. First, the actual *entry point*, the point at which Evil Spirit enters an individual and a decision, however tenuous, is made by the victim to allow entry. Then, a stage of *erroneous judgments* by the possessed in vital matters, as a direct result of the allowed presence of the possessing spirit and apparently in preparation for the next stage. Third, the *voluntary yielding of control* by the possessed person to a force or presence he clearly feels is alien to himself and as a direct result of which the possessed loses control of his will, and so of his decisions and his actions.
>
> Once the third stage is secure, extended control proceeds and may potentially reach the point of completion—perfect possession. In any individual case, these four stages will dovetail and overlap differently. And, while the process may be swift, more often it seems to take years to accomplish (…)

At every new step, and during every moment of possession, the consent of the victim is necessary, or possession cannot be successful. The consent may be verbal, but always involves choice of action. Once initial consent has been given, its withdrawal becomes more and more difficult as time goes on.[50]

28. Can a demon possess a house or building? How about an animal?

Demons cannot "possess" localities because, strictly speaking, they can only possess *living* things. A house can be *infested* with demons that have mysteriously chosen that place or have been invited to that place by some evil or occult practice in its history. When demons focus on a human habitation or locality, they can cause much suffering and chaos. This is why a third section was added to the exorcism ritual in 1890 which contains the Exorcism of Pope Leo XIII, entitled Exorcism Against Satan and the Fallen Angels, which is an exorcism for places. This same prayer that appeared in print officially in the 1925 edition of the *Rituale Romanum*. It is important to note that public recitation of this prayer is restricted[51] and must be authorized by a bishop.

The bodies of animals, while living, are not considered temples of the Holy Spirit, and so they too cannot be possessed, strictly speaking, although they can be infested by demons, and in that state can do much harm. I do not agree with the very strange idea of Fr. Fortea that animals can only be freed of their obsessions by being killed—no! If a building can be freed of evil powers, all the more can these dear and innocent creatures of God be delivered of an infestation of demons.

---

50 *Op. cit.*, p. 436.
51 Congregation for the Doctrine of the Faith, *On the Current Norms Governing Exorcism* (*Inde Ab Aliquot Annis*), September 29, 1985.

29. Can one demon control another?

This is undoubtedly true. Demons are completely devoid of love or respect for anything, including their own kind. They have no ability to relate to each other or to the human world except through power and control. If they work together for some purpose, it is only out of the most inveterate sense of self-interest, not because they have any fraternity or common cause with one another. Their kingdom is strictly one of brute, loveless force which is maintained through a demonic game of survival of the fittest.

The demons' innate powers of intelligence and will make it possible for the stronger ones to dominate the weaker ones and even use them like slaves for their purposes. It is very common for an exorcist to come up against demons that work as a pack but who are always dominated by one principle demon that is the strongest intellect and will of the group. The challenge of the exorcist in these cases is to discern the identity of the individual demons, and to "divide and conquer" the band of demons. The weaker demons are usually cast out first with the strongest one going last. With perseverance and humility, demonic power can always be broken by the authority of the Church as long as it is correctly applied.

30. Will a person go to hell if he is possessed? What if he dies possessed?

Objectively speaking, a possessed person has about as much chance of going to hell as anyone else because both heaven and hell are a matter of an individual's free decision, and the individual can always make the choice for God, even while possessed. The devil cannot force a person to reject God. A possessed person, however, will labor under a much greater burden of choice because the demon inside his body incessantly tempts him to reject God in despair of salvation with an intensity that non-possessed people rarely understand.

If a person dies in a possessed state, he can be saved for the same reasons. Like any of us, his salvation depends on the decision of his free will which becomes fixed for all eternity at the time of death. God may allow the possession of bodies in order to purify the souls of his chosen ones. Therefore, while we never wish a person to die possessed, one who does so is not necessarily damned; death *can be* the definitive casting out of the demon from his body.

31. How much power does the Church actually have over demons?

Even the strongest demons cannot resist the authority of the Church when the Church acts in a formal way against them. Exorcism is, in a certain sense, an irresistible power for expulsion when it is used properly and when the victim cooperates with it. Exorcism cannot fail to have some salutary effect for the comfort or deliverance of the victim, even if in any given session the expulsion of the demon is not fully accomplished.

We must resist the false notions and Hollywood-generated perceptions that the Church is a beleaguered combatant against the devil in an exorcism. It is the other way around! Demons are bound by the Church's authority, and their only means of fighting back is to resist expulsion, if they can. Rarely do demons overtly attack the priest in an exorcism, because they are generally too busy defending themselves! Demons never trivialize the power of an exorcism; they flee it because they are always defeated by it. They have a particular spiritual power which must be respected, but it is no match for the spiritual power of the Church.

32. Do sacraments protect a person against evil?

Sacraments and sacramentals undoubtedly protect us from the power of evil but not because they are magic. They are, rather, spiritual fountains which confer grace, provided that the recipient of these marvelous gifts uses or receives them with faith. The "protection" of the Church's spiritual resources can be likened to an electrified fence around a house. The grace that flows into a person's life through these channels is like the electricity flowing through the wires of that fence. Without the electric current, the fence is still a barrier of sorts but with less protection against an invader. So also, without faith, the sacraments and sacramentals do very little to protect us from the power of evil spirits.

33. What is a state of grace?

A state of grace is the spiritual condition of an individual who has sanctifying grace in his soul; that is, he is free from mortal sin and seriously disordered inclinations to sin. Any "state" can be lost—i.e., a state of mind, a state of euphoria, a state of favor with another person—and the state of grace can be lost simply by the commission of one mortal sin. Venial sin denigrates and weakens the state of grace but does not technically destroy it in the soul. It cannot be said enough that the state of grace, and the attempt to live an authentic life of faith, are the greatest protections from evil for everyone, even those not of our faith.

34. How powerful is St. Michael the Archangel against the devil's action?

St. Michael, the great prince of the heavenly host, is the most feared of all the angels by the demons because he was commissioned by God to expel Satan and his minions from heaven. His deed is recorded in the Book of Revelation, Chapter 12. He is an exorcist angel, and when we are in need, he commands the army of angels for the expulsion of demons.

Michael, of a lower order of angels (Archangels) in the heavenly hierarchy, defeated the proud Seraphim angel, Lucifer, and cast him out of heaven when he rebelled. Michael, full of grace and authority, assists the Church Militant in its ministry of exorcism. He is ever at the side of those who call upon him and has innumerable angels at his disposal to fight the battles that flesh and blood cannot win. Even the strongest demons can never under any circumstances match the power of this iron-clad angel whose force over them is irrepressible and immediate. St. Michael just waits for our call to enter the spiritual battle on our behalf.

35. Can an exorcist permit a demon to leave one body and go to another?

No, the exorcist must never permit this even though the demon may beg for it or promise to leave a person in peace if he is just allowed to go into another person. There is absolutely no negotiation with spiritual terrorists. For an exorcist to allow this would be a great sin against the next person who became possessed because of the permission he gave to the demon.

Neither must any person ever naively invite the devil into himself in order to get him off the original victim, as was portrayed vividly in the movie *The Exorcist*. The naïve young priest did that and subsequently threw himself out the window to his death. Such a thing is never to be done! This misguided act would just end up creating two possessed persons and not alleviate the problem of the first victim. *The Exorcist* movie incorrectly portrayed the priest's invitation as freeing the girl from her demon—that never happens.

Only Jesus has the authority to allow a demon to leave a body and go elsewhere in this world. He permitted the demons to go into the swine (as in the case of Legion[52]) for the purpose of evangelizing the pagans in the region of the Ten Cities. Human beings can never give that permission. The Church only sends the demons to one place—Calvary, the place of the devil's ultimate defeat. There Jesus judges them and assigns them to where their presence may best serve the interests of the Kingdom of God.

36. How does God use the devil and demons in His Providence?

In the divine plan, all demons have a part to play in assisting the saints on their way to heaven. Demons are allowed by God to roam the world "looking for someone to devour"[53] with the mysterious purpose of using their rebellion to test the people of God and bring them to salvation. In the Book of Job, God clearly allowed Satan to tempt and harass the righteous Job for some larger purpose not immediately apparent to him or his friends.

Demonic temptation can accomplish many purposes if one looks at it with the eyes of faith: it can show us our sinfulness, teach us how to choose the things of God more resolutely and strengthen our minds and wills in His service. Spiritual combat, likewise, often urges us on to a greater heroism in our rejection of evil and growth in virtue. In fact, the fiercest adversaries in sports are the stronger players who challenge us to use our talents to the fullest and to be better athletes. It is in this way that God "uses" the demons for our personal sanctification and can even use the sad reality of a full possession to bring a person to conversion of heart, moral rectitude and strong religious practice.

---

52 Cf. Mk 5:1-20
53 1 Pt 5:8.

The same can be said for the universal Church, whom the devil promised to "sift as wheat"[54] the night before Jesus died. The Church is purified by the persecutions of the devil and his servants as she makes her way to heaven. The famous phrase of Tertullian, "In the blood of the **martyrs** lies the seed of the Church,"[55] is relevant in every day and age. The Church only grows and flourishes through persecution, and thereby, God uses the devil for His ultimate purposes of advancing the Kingdom of God and leading souls to Him.

37. Is there really a Church of Satan?

You bet there is. The Church of Satan was established in April of 1966 and founded by Anton Szandor LaVey (1930-1997), who featured as the devil in the movie *Rosemary's Baby*. He is the author of five books, including *The Satanic Bible, The Satanic Ritual* and *Satan Speaks!* as well as dozens of movies and media interviews. Ironically, he died at St. Mary's Hospital in San Francisco in October of 1997, two days short of Halloween.

This "church" moved its central administrative offices to the Hell's Kitchen section of New York City in recent years and is a religion in every sense of the word: worship, rituals, priesthood, scriptures, membership, doctrines, codes of conduct, etc. It has attracted many members, some of whom would not cause surprise, like the hideous entertainer, Marilyn Manson, and others who would raise an eyebrow, such as Sammy Davis, Jr. who received an "honorary membership."

Strangely, the Church of Satan does not actually purport to worship Satan as such, whom it believes is just a legend. It teaches its adherents to worship self and indulge in the pleasures of this

---

54 Lk 22:31. Note that, in this passage, the "you" that Jesus refers to in speaking to Peter is plural.
55 Tertullian, *Apologeticum*, 1, (cf. J.-P. Migne, *Patrologia Latina*, II, Parish, 1844-64.)

world. Its doctrine is atheism and complete materialism, nothing more, nothing less. Its website, which I do not recommend anyone to view, carries links to every major satanic group in the world.

Afterword to Chapter 2
The Psychology of Demons

(Adapted from a talk given by Fr. Dennis McManus on August 15, 2007 at a conference on deliverance and healing.)

A commentary on the story of the Gerasene demoniac in Mark 5:1-20.

Description

The Gerasene demoniac's state of possession shows him to be isolated and living "among the tombs," a place of death, with no normal cycles of life; it says he was in this state "day and night." Furthermore, he exhibited superhuman strength since he tore his chains to shreds and was violent towards others. He also exhibited severely self-destructive behavior, i.e., "gashing himself with stones."

When Jesus came, the man possessed by Legion ran toward Him, fell on his knees and asked Jesus to stop torturing him.[56]

---

[56] English exorcist, Fr. Jeremy Davies, has a magnificent interpretation of this action from the possessed man's point of view: "The Gadarene [i.e., Gerasene] demoniac had probably, in the past, committed grave sin. He was almost completely possessed, raving and dangerous; but when he saw Jesus from afar, he saw his one hope and used his last mite of freedom to run to the Lord and fall down in worship before him—though the words which came out of his mouth were demonic, he himself was dumbly crying out to the Savior—who knew his heart and heard his cry and set him free. Even in the depths of his affliction, the spiritual state of the demoniac had been better than that of the respectable citizens of Gadara and he went on to become their evangelist!" *Exorcism: Understanding Exorcism in Scripture and Practice*, The Incorporated Catholic Truth Society, London: England, 2008, p. 15.

The demon screamed with anxiety and was forced to reveal his name ("Legion") to the Lord, whereupon he was commanded to leave. The Lord allowed him to enter the herd of swine as a witness to the people of that region of His authority over evil. The infested swine threw themselves into the abyss, and Jesus told the liberated man to go home to his family and tell them of all that God did for him.

Analysis

Many elements of a demonic "psychology" can be understood from this story.

1. <u>Fascination with death</u>: having abandoned the Source of Life before time began, demons fled to the farthest corner of the universe to create a place of death for themselves. The Lord called the devil "a murderer from the beginning,"[57] and, subsequently, all demons have as their singular focus the intent to maim, kill and destroy God's children. So it is that the possessing demon in this story drove the poor man to live among the death chambers and manifested through him all kinds of self-destructive tendencies, which may have led to his death had he not met the Lord of Life.

2. <u>Isolation and violence</u>: the possessed man was completely unable to live in community and had apparently lost all meaningful contact with the human family. All attempts by others to help or even restrain him were met with violence, the anti-sacrament to true solidarity with others. His human family was *replaced* by a demonic cohort inside of him. Isolation is a typical tactic of demons when they wish to possess a human being. They first isolate, then they possess, and when they possess, they separate the person from

---

57 Jn 8:44

those who can potentially help him. Nakedness was a further sign of his social isolation.

3. <u>Gang existence</u>: while each demon is a unique individual, demons usually operate in a coagulated horde for greater effect;[58] they live and work in colonies or gangs united with a single-focused will to carry out their destructive plan. The group of thousands of demons in the biblical story had a collective "code name" of *Legion* by which all were known and by which they were overpowered by Jesus once they revealed it to Him. Their identity as individuals is of less importance than that of the group.

4. <u>Preoccupation with names</u>: names are very important to demons. As intelligent creatures, they have an intense desire to know the nature of things and people, and this necessarily involves the act of *naming* things and learning names. In the story, they immediately screamed His Name loudly, "Jesus, son of the Most High God," because saying a name *can* bestow some measure of power over the person. However, Jesus allowed no control and turned the table on them, forcing *Legion* to reveal his name. Demons also have an intense dread that their own dark names will come to light, because they do not want to *be* controlled or cast out by a greater authority.

5. <u>Paranoia</u>: being dispossessed from heaven, demons have a powerful fear of being thrown out of their "homes" in possessed persons. They live in this fear. They rejected the

---

[58] Those who may have watched the third segment of the movie trilogy, *The Matrix*, saw what could be interpreted as a demonic attack on the "City of Zion." When the "sentinels," very evil squid-like machines, first breached the City enclosure, they were coming in individually to attack and kill anyone they saw. After awhile, these same creatures coagulated into a kind of stream of slithering evil that was much more difficult to defend against due to its cumulative force. It was a perfect pop-culture depiction of how demons band together for harm.

inheritance of the children of the light, and they fear and hate God's benevolence toward humans and want to deprive them of it. There is no peace in the demonic kingdom. *Legion* shrieked in desperation and could not run away since Jesus was commanding him to come out. The existence of some holy force of love and authority is a threat to these creatures that live in fear and loathing of all that is good. They cannot be neutral toward it.

6. <u>Territoriality:</u> a great victory for a demon is to become "incarnate" in a deliberate way in the world of material existence. Demons desire to identify themselves with things (occult objects and rituals), places and animals (infestations), and human beings (possession). It is ironic that these bodiless creatures, who in the beginning, proudly rejected God's own identification with human flesh, now obsess about finding a body! The process of expulsion shown in this story explains how the "incarnation" of a demon is undone through a deliberate step-down process of reversing the possession: Legion leaves the human temple of the Holy Spirit and enters into animals; these precipitate themselves with their demons into the abyss; at the death of the swine, the demons presumably rush into the water and out of the world. Thus, they were "sent back" whence they came and lost their "territory" definitively.

7. <u>Eternal despair:</u> the reason why the demon speaks to Jesus with such absolute anguish is that he knows he can never, throughout all eternity, break this cycle of trying to possess and being cast back into the abyss. The demon must go through this again and again and again—it is the very definition of hell. He is not damned by God; rather, he has doomed himself to this eternal hopelessness by his original decision to reject God. There is no possibility of his repen-

tance, only a painful regret and unmitigated wailing and gnashing of teeth at his decision. Demons are the most miserable creatures in existence: eternally frustrated, eternally envious of something they can't have because they have rejected it, eternally hating others who have it, hating themselves and eternally choosing this state of existence that they hate. They also live in desperation about the reconciliation of all things in Christ because, as the Book of Revelation says, they "know that [their] time is short."[59]

The antidote to demonic possession: family

The inner life of demons is illustrated very clearly in this scriptural narrative, but we must not miss the most important and telling line of the whole narrative, namely, the advice of Jesus to the man to "go home to your family and tell them what God in His goodness has done for you." Family life, despite all its problems, is the antidote to the devil's depredations and hopelessness.

Demonic possession *does indeed* happen "in a vacuum." Namely, the vacuous state that is the pre-condition to demonic possession is found when people are deprived of the benefits that family offers. Family life is a divine and human institution given for the wellbeing of man and is natural protective force against the negativities of the demonic world. It is the antidote to the above seven points: it is the source of our natural life (vs. number 1 above) and, when lived according to even minimum standards of upright living, a place of belonging and human affirmation (vs. 2). Family is the primary cohesive unit of any society and is organized for the provision of basic human essentials like education, economic productivity, training in social behavior and the communication of civic and religious values, etc. (vs. 3). Families

---
59 Rev 12:12

bestow meaning on individuals by providing them with names, relationships and dignity (vs. 4), and they provide a basic sense of security against the vicissitudes of the world (vs. 5). Families, and family homes, are safe havens protected by law as sacred spaces (vs. 6) and are the last source of refuge and strength in times of crisis, illness, disaster, despair and death (vs. 7).

Demonic possession usually starts through a certain vulnerability in human relationships. No bonding equals "no meaning." Family fills the void of the world's meaninglessness and cruelty, especially for the young. Conversely, the failure of family life in any society creates a dangerous void and opening for demonic activity. It is not hard to see why the devil so viciously attacks marriage, family and innocent human life in any society. The enemy of our human nature has understood the truth that good, holy families are the best rampart that human beings have to stand against the destructive force of the devil and all his works and all his empty promises.

Chapter 3
Exorcism and Church Authority

Jesus said to Peter, "I for my part declare to you, you are 'Rock,' and on this rock I will build my Church, and the jaws of death shall not prevail against it. I will entrust to you the keys of the Kingdom of Heaven. Whatever you declare bound on earth shall be bound in heaven; whatever you declare loosed on earth shall be loosed in heaven." (Mt 16:18-19)

God the Father commands + thee, God the Son commands + thee, God the Holy Spirit commands + thee! The mystery of the Cross commands + thee! The faith of the holy Apostles Peter and Paul and all the other saints commands + thee! The blood of the martyrs commands + thee! The constancy of the confessors commands + thee! The devout intercession of all holy men and women commands + thee! The power of the mysteries of the Christian faith commands + thee!... I adjure thee, therefore, thou profligate dragon, in the name of the spotless + Lamb,...depart from this man +, depart from the Church of God +. (Roman Ritual, *Rite of Exorcism*, n. 4)[1]

---

1   Weller, *Rituale*, p. 189.

1. How do we define exorcism? Is it a sacrament?

Exorcism is a potent prayer of the Church and a spiritual work of mercy calling down the power of God to free an individual who is possessed by demons. *The Catechism of the Catholic Church* defines exorcism in this way: "Exorcism is directed at the expulsion of demons or the liberation from demonic possession through the spiritual authority which Jesus entrusted to his Church."[2] Exorcism is thus a public act of blessing which requires (in the Latin Church and in some Eastern Churches) explicit authorization from those who have the power of governance in the Church, namely, the bishops.

Exorcism is not a sacrament. It is a sacramental: that is, some prayer or devotional item that communicates actual grace to men's souls. Exorcisms do not work "automatically" like the sacraments. Rather, an exorcism is always a process and always requires faith and perseverance, sometimes heroic, to free a person of demonic possession.

2. What other ways does the Church understand exorcism?

There are at least four other ways that the Church understands exorcism:

- *As spiritual warfare:* an exorcism is a confrontation between the spiritual authority of the Church and demons of great strength who have possessed a human body or infested a locality. For this reason, the Church restricts the ministry of exorcism to ordained priests whose religious consecration seals and prepares them for this battle.[3]

---

[2] *Op. cit.*, par.1673
[3] Private conversation with Neal Lozano, August 15, 2007.

- *As spiritual healing:* the possession of a person's body by demons is a form of spiritual sickness, and exorcism is the healing of that sickness by ejecting the entities that cause it. While exorcism works through expulsion rather than surgical excision,[4] nonetheless, the person is healed when the spiritual sickness is gone.

- *As an eschatological sign:* the Church also understands exorcism as an affirmation and a proclamation of Christ's ultimate victory over evil. Here the focus is not on the demon, as if the Church were in the business of demon-hunting. Rather, exorcism serves to draw attention to the awesome power and authority of Christ who has already conquered the devil and will consummate that victory at the end of time when He frees all who believe in Him from the power of sin, death and the devil.

- *As a means of evangelization and conversion:* the exorcist functions *in persona Christi* as a catechist of sorts in the process of freeing people from the grip of the devil. The person who enters into the spiritual care of the Church through exorcism receives a much deeper understanding of the authentic Christian faith: the Church's authority, community, liturgy, doctrines and gifts of the Holy Spirit. The focus is not so much on fighting the demon but on the sanctification and salvation of the individual soul who has, culpably or not, fallen prey to the power of evil and has turned to the Church for help. It is the common experience of exorcists that some people who go through exorcism become truly holy through their struggle and purification of faith in the process.

---

4 This analogy is explained further in Chapter 6, Question 2.

3. What is exorcism *not*?

Exorcism is *not psychological counseling*, although the priest who does it certainly offers counsel to the afflicted person. It is *not therapy* although the procedure must often be repeated like therapy for results to be seen. *Neither is it spiritual direction,* in a technical sense, which is directed to a healthy individual's growth in faith and discernment of God's Will. It is *not a form of spiritual friendship* even though the priest will often have great esteem, even friendship, with the person he assists. It is certainly *not a group intervention* where concerned people confront addictive behavior, although it always involves people who are concerned about the person's wellbeing.

4. Why do we need exorcism?

Exorcism is needed because the devil is active in the world and seeks to prohibit souls from entering eternal life. Once thrown down from heaven, the devil became "the prince of this world,"[5] as Jesus called him three times in the Gospel of John. The devil entered God's created world as a transgressor on another's property; he dominates it in a very real way and declares it to be his own kingdom. The devil's ultimate objective is to annihilate the beauty, truth and goodness of the Holy Trinity as it is reflected in creation, and especially in the human person who is created in the "image and likeness of God."[6]

Exorcism aims to re-establish the order of the universe over against the devil's plan to destroy it. Nothing will fully restore the order of the universe this side of the Last Judgment, but exorcism, as a pastoral ministry, seeks to help at least some individual souls re-create that order in their own lives. The Church's

---

5 Jn 12:31
6 Gen 1:26

exorcists thus act like St. Michael and the holy angels in casting out the demons who afflict humanity day and night.

5. Where does the word "exorcism" come from?

The word "exorcism" comes from the Greek verb εξορκιζειν (egzorkeézein), meaning to "adjure," or more literally, "to put (someone) under oath." Exorcism is a sort of judicial process in which the Church puts the devil "under oath" in a formal way. Through this process, the Church calls the devil to account for his crimes against God and man. An exorcism is like the prosecution of a criminal, adjuring any evil spirit to answer before the Tribunal of the Lord.

Indeed the 1614[7] *Rite of Exorcism* expresses this sentiment perfectly in its second exorcism prayer addressed to the demon: *"Thou art guilty before the almighty God, Whose laws thou hast transgressed. Thou art guilty before His Son, our Lord Jesus Christ, Whom thou didst presume to tempt, Whom thou wast emboldened to nail to the Cross. Thou art guilty before the human race, for through thy blandishments thou didst proffer it the poisoned cup of death."* This tough indictment puts the spiritual criminal in question—the demon—under oath, the ultimate aim of which is to convict the criminal and remove his ability to harm human society, i.e., souls.

6. Who may authorize an exorcism?

In the Latin Church, the power to authorize an exorcism was limited to the one called by the 1983 *Code of Canon Law* the "local Ordinary," that is generally, the bishop of a diocese or others who have executive power with him. The appropriate canon of the *Code of Canon Law* is 1172 §1 which reads: "No one may lawfully exorcise the possessed without the special and express

---

[7] Which was slightly revised in 1925 and again in 1952.

permission of the local Ordinary."[8] However, with the promulgation of the 1999 *Rite of Exorcism*, the law seems to specifically limit this permissive authority only to certain Ordinaries, namely, "diocesan bishops" and those priests or bishops who are canonically equal to them according to Canon 368 (i.e., territorial prelates and abbots, vicars and prefects apostolic, and apostolic administrators). It also seems that those who govern the local church while a diocese is vacant or impeded (cc. 413, 419-421) have such authority, after consultation with the College of Consultors.

A vicar general or episcopal vicar (i.e., priests or auxiliary bishops who also have some form of executive power in the running of dioceses; cf. Canons 475-476) must now receive a specific mandate by the diocesan bishop (or his equivalent) to authorize priests—whether one-time or in an ongoing manner—for exorcism, except in case of urgent necessity when the appropriate authority is unavailable.[9] Likewise, others who govern the local church while a diocese is vacant or impeded (excepting those mentioned in Canon 368, above, who already possess this authority) seem to have the authority to authorize priests to exorcise, but only after informing the College of Consultors.

In the Eastern Catholic Churches, there are no general canons requiring a priest to seek authorization to perform an exorcism. As was often the case in the early Church, both East and West, the priest may properly exercise this office at his own discretion. In some cases, however, the canons of the local eparchy (diocese) may require the priest to receive the bishop's permission, as in the practice of the Latin Church.

---

8 Cf. John P. Beal, James A, Coriden, and Thomas J Green, eds. *New Commentary on the Code of Canon Law*, New York/Mahwah, NJ: Paulist Press, 2000, p. 1405.
9 *Ibid.*

7. Who has the authority to perform an exorcism?

The Vicar of Christ may perform an exorcism anywhere and at any time. More commonly, bishops have the proper authority to exorcise in their own dioceses because they bear the actual authority of the Apostles to whom Jesus Christ explicitly entrusted power to "bind and loose" on earth. However, as stated above, bishops usually give permission for exorcism to a qualified priest, rather than taking cases themselves. The second section of Canon 1172 states that "this permission is to be granted by the local Ordinary only to a priest who is endowed with piety, knowledge, prudence and integrity of life." Therefore, only a priest authorized by a bishop may perform an exorcism, and he must manifest to some degree the qualities indicated in the canon.

8. May a lay person ever perform a solemn exorcism?

According to the current norms of the Catholic Church, it is not possible for a lay person to perform a solemn exorcism. That is strictly limited to priests. Here we must recognize a distinct historical development of the *solemn* rite of exorcism that limited the practice of public exorcism to the ministry of the ordained clergy. From the primitive Church onward, the solemn, public practice of exorcism was the purview of those who acted in the name of the Church to heal the possessed. The Fourth Council of Carthage in the year 398 prescribed a rite of ordination for exorcists, and as early as 251, references to exorcists can be found in the letters of Pope St. Cornelius.[10] These were always and exclusively clerics who were under the watchful oversight of the Church's authorities.

---

10 Deborah Danielski, "Troublesome demons still on the Church's hit list?" *Our Sunday Visitor*, February 28, 1999.

Various rituals and texts from the earliest centuries also bear witness to the fact that official prayers for the casting out of demons was a matter of a liturgical rite performed by clerics both in the Catechumenate and in a solemn way for the healing of the possessed. In fact the testimony of saints, Fathers of the Church and early theologians on the performance of exorcism in the liturgical rites of the Church is impressive.[11] Also, there is a long history regarding the development of the exorcism ritual that dates back to documents and rituals of ancient use.[12] This, of course, culminated in the 1983 *Code of Canon Law* which restricted the conduct of a solemn exorcism to priests.

The solemn *Rite of Exorcism* must, however, be distinguished from the spontaneous prayer of blessing and/or petition which seeks to free someone who is not possessed but who may have diabolic problems of one sort or another. The Church has always distinguished between a private act of blessing, whereby a person prays on behalf of his or her own faith, and a public act, whereby the person prays on behalf of the Church. All Christians exercise a certain power over the devil by virtue of their baptism. As we have been delivered from the power of darkness, so the spiritual power to bless and combat the works of the devil is inherent in the priesthood of the faithful. Such an authority is acknowledged by the Lord's Prayer when we pray, "Deliver us from evil."

Indeed, many saints in the life of the Church have wielded enormous spiritual power over the devil because of their holiness. It is said that St. Catherine of Siena in the 14th century was so holy that priest exorcists who could not expel demons usually brought the afflicted persons to her to be immediately freed of

---

11   Rev. Paul Turner, "Scrutinies Scrutinized," *Liturgical Ministry* 8 (Spring, 1999), pp. 68-77.
12   Rev. Jeffrey S. Grob, *A Major Revision of the Discipline on Exorcism: A Comparative Study of the Liturgical Laws in the 1614 and 1998 Rites of Exorcism*, Archdiocese of Chicago: unpublished doctoral thesis, 2006, pp. 60-104.

their demons![13] There is no reason why the laity cannot exercise holiness in a similar way in the modern day.

9. How many exorcists are there?

Fr. Jeffrey Grob of the Archdiocese of Chicago, who wrote his doctoral dissertation on the history of the exorcism rite, addresses this question. He says, with some sadness, "It is staggering to realize that there are no more than seventeen officially appointed exorcists working in the United States. Seven dioceses have exorcists appointed on a stable basis and approximately ten exorcists work on a case by case basis in various parts of the country."[14] The harvest is great but the laborers are few, but thankfully, there is a growing interest among priests in the ministry of exorcism and deliverance. May the Lord inspire many priests to take up this difficult but very rewarding ministry.

10. Why aren't there more exorcists?

Although the trend is changing, it is regrettable that more priests and bishops do not receive training in this important ministry of healing which the Lord entrusted to His disciples.[15] There are various reasons for this:

- *Lack of faith:* some clerics simply do not believe that the devil exists and so feel no need to fight him;

- *Lack of pastoral concern or involvement:* some priests and bishops do not understand the nature of spiritual afflictions and do not see the need to minister to spiritually-afflicted individuals;

---

13 Fr. Gabriele Amorth, *An Exorcist: More Stories*, Ignatius: San Francisco, 2002, pp. 92-93.
14 Grob, *op. cit.*, p. 175.
15 Mt 10:1, Mk 6:7, Lk 9:1

- *Lack of moral courage:* there are good priests and bishops whose theological understanding of evil is accurate but who lack the courage that it takes to confront demons; also, some are afraid of making mistakes, adverse publicity or lawsuits and so never enter into the field of battle;

- *Lack of vision:* spiritual healing receives relatively little attention among the priorities of a diocese because of the great number of seemingly more pressing needs; a mature pastoral vision should not only include the corporal works of mercy but also the spiritual works of mercy, which certainly include exorcism and spiritual healing;

- *Lack of understanding:* many clerics believe that demonic manifestations can be explained by psychiatry and should be treated as such; they may believe in the devil theoretically but not appreciate the range of his power in the daily lives of their own flocks;

- *Lack of training:* there is little or no training for the practice of exorcism in seminaries; there are, however, more opportunities for training in the Church today;

- *Lack of mentoring:* there are many good priests who would be willing to take the training but simply lack another more experienced priest to teach them; when a diocese has no priest who is familiar with the ministry, it is less likely that a willing priest would find the necessary hands-on training for this work;

- *Lack of perseverance:* priests can sometimes be interested in this ministry, but when they find that it is very difficult, they abandon it too easily; proper mentoring would help them develop the requisite habits and skills to give them success and reasons to persevere.

11. How may a priest become a qualified exorcist?

A priest must first and foremost discern a calling to this type of ministry because, like any specialized ministry, it demands a certain interest and anointing. If the Holy Spirit calls a priest to this ministry, it is for the fruitful exercise of the charism for the building up of the Body of Christ. The decision on whether a priest can officially exercise this ministry rests in the hands of the local bishop.

The skill for exorcism, like any pastoral ministry, is acquired through both book learning and practice. Thankfully, today there are an increasing number of reputable and easily-accessible resources from experts in the fields of exorcism, healing and deliverance (see Bibliography), and the priest must become familiar with all the learning available on the topic. He may then inquire in his local diocese to see if there is an established exorcist by whom he may be mentored through a period of training. Lacking that, there may be an established exorcist in a neighboring diocese.

It is a hopeful sign that there are growing associations of exorcists who have regular conferences and are attempting to disseminate greater knowledge and pastoral skill so that more priests may get involved in this ministry. The International Association of Exorcists (IAE), based in Rome, is the most obvious example, but there are local associations of exorcists in Italy, Poland and Mexico as well. There have been several unofficial conferences dealing with the subject of exorcism and deliverance ministry in the US in the past four years, and it is likely that some interested priests will establish a branch of the IAE in the United States soon.

12. Isn't the identity of an exorcist supposed to be kept secret?

There is no rule about this in canon law or church teaching other than the rule of prudence. There are several reasons for discretion in publicizing that one is an exorcist: he may potentially be the target of attacks by Satanists or others involved in the occult; his reputation as an exorcist may draw an overwhelming flood of requests that will be difficult to manage in his already busy pastoral schedule; and he may also want to protect the reputations and identities of the people he works with who might be suspected of being possessed if they were seen regularly seeking his help.

On a more personal level, the priest should be extremely modest about his exorcism work and guard against taking pride in the title "exorcist." Given the nature of the subject matter, the priest could easily get caught in other people's fascination with his work or his experiences. He must also deal with the temptation of telling stories about extraordinary things that happen in exorcisms just to satisfy people's curiosity. If an exorcist wishes to strengthen people's faith through talking about spiritual warfare, he must do so with humility of heart, with no desire for personal gain and always for the good of souls. The teachings in this book would be an example of this pastoral desire of a priest to strengthen the faith of others and get more priests involved in this very important ministry.

13. Does an exorcist ever charge for his services?

An exorcist does not charge for his services because spiritual things are not bought and sold. However, he may accept hospitality and reasonable compensation for the services that he provides, as long as it is in keeping with the custom of the local church for regular priestly ministry. In the event that the person or family is particularly insistent upon offering a significant token of gratitude, in order not to offend them, the priest may suggest a worthy charity to receive their gift on his behalf.

14. How common is exorcism?

Since full possession is rare, so also are solemn exorcisms rare. However, as mentioned in the Introduction to this book, I believe that this will undoubtedly change dramatically within the next decade. The amount of serious mortal sin, the growing pernicious occultism and the systematic rejection of God that is common in the modern world will lead to increasing numbers of people becoming demonically obsessed and fully possessed. Exorcist priests will be needed more than ever to heal the ravages of the culture of death and the effects of the aggressive pagan culture that is spreading the darkness of the Evil One's kingdom far and wide.

15. What is the difference between a "minor" and a "major" exorcism?

The *Catechism of the Catholic Church* uses the adjectives "minor" and "major" to describe exorcism.[16] A "major" exorcism is one that is always authorized by a bishop and performed by a priest. It is also called a *solemn* exorcism in today's language and is reserved for cases of true demonic possession. "Minor" exorcisms, according to the Church, are the exorcisms that take place in the baptism of children and those that occur during the Scrutinies which are found in the *Rite of Christian Initiation of Adults*. These are all official and public acts of the Church involving some liturgical ritual.

There is also a well-recognized tradition in the Church of priests praying "minor exorcisms" over people. These are understood as prayers *from the ritual* itself or spontaneous commands

---

16 *Op. cit.*, paragraph 1673.

prayed in private and often in secret,[17] such as those that St. Alphonsus Liguori recommends to pray in the confessional when the priest suspects some demonic attachment related to a sin.[18] These types of prayers, while not solemn or liturgical exorcisms, are perfectly consistent with the nature of the priesthood and the power to bless which the priest receives by virtue of his ordination.[19] Accordingly, there has always been a strong consensus of spiritual and moral theologians (such as St. Alphonsus Liguori and Tanquerey, etc.), manualists (in the Jesuit, Redemptorist and Dominican traditions, etc.), canonists, demonologists and exorcists (e.g., Balducci, Rodewyk, Amorth, Davies, etc.) who all recognize this distinction.

16. Was there a change in the regulations concerning exorcism in the new 1983 *Code of Canon Law*?

There was little change in the 1983 *Code of Canon Law* from the previous *Code* in 1917. The 1917 *Code* contained basically the

---

17 Fr. Jeremy Davies, in his *Exorcism* booklet cited above, correctly states that "the reservation of Major Exorcism to the Bishop's permission...clearly leaves unbroken the tradition of priests doing minor exorcisms of the obsessed.... For every possessed person needing a major exorcism, there are many more who could be helped by a minor exorcism," p. 41.
18 "If someone, however, wretchedly falls in these temptations or seeks rather than flees the occasions of them, the cure of this one is very difficult; for sinners of this kind, who have intercourse with the devil, are with the greatest difficulty converted from the heart. For on the one hand the devil gains a certain dominion over their wills, and on the other hand they remain exceedingly weak in resisting sin; they may need an extraordinary grace from God, but God usually grants this grace to wicked people of this sort only with the greatest difficulty. Nevertheless let the confessor not lose confidence if one of them has come to him, but let him take care to show him the utmost charity, and to encourage him by saying that where there is no will, there is no sin; hence, if he resists with his will, he does not sin at all. In these cases, above all, let the confessor send out in advance at least a private exorcism against the demon, which is certainly licit in this manner: 'I, as the minister of God, command you, or you all, unclean spirits, to withdraw from this creature of God.'" St. Alphonsus Liguori, *Praxis confesarii*, trans. Rev. James Mercer.
19 Jordan Aumann, O.P., *Spiritual Theology*, Sheed and Ward: London, 1980, p. 411.

same provisions requiring "special and express permission" from the Ordinary for a priest to exorcise, and it was required that the priest be distinguished by "piety, prudence and integrity"—to which the new *Code* added "knowledge." Nowadays priests have to be much more familiar with the complexities of psychological, mental and spiritual disorders in order to make a judgment about a state of possession. The new *Code* altered the canon about those who can authorize exorcisms from the "Ordinary" to the "local Ordinary" and the 1999 revision of the *Rite of Exorcism* specifies even further that permission is to be given by the "diocesan bishop" and his assigns.

The old *Code* had two additional canons related to exorcisms, which the new *Code* did not reproduce: one canon pointed out that exorcisms could be performed on non-Catholics and even on excommunicated persons if necessary (c. 1152). This seemed unnecessary to re-state since this situation is technically included under the canons relating to the reception of sacramentals. Another canon specified that simple exorcisms related to baptisms, consecrations and blessings may be performed by any of the regular ministers of these sacraments or sacramentals (c. 1153). These too seemed obvious and so were not repeated in the 1983 *Code*.

17. Other than the *Code of Canon Law*, what else has the Holy See said about exorcism in recent times?

The Magisterium of our Church has not been silent about this pastoral need of the faithful, which hews so closely to the mission of saving souls. In the past forty years alone there have been numerous documents that reaffirm the Holy See's total support of the ministry of exorcism—including several references to exorcism and deliverance in the documents of the Second Vatican

Council. The following are relatively recent Church documents on this matter:

June 25, 1975—*Christian Faith and Demonology* (commissioned and authorized by the Congregation for the Doctrine of the Faith): This excellent document explains the Church's longstanding teaching on the existence of demons and their negative effects on souls. It details the Church's fight against heresies and errors about the devil over the centuries and emphasizes basic Christian teachings about good and evil: namely, that the devil and his minions were created good before they rebelled, that Christ came to put an end to the kingdom of Satan, and that, while the devil is the instigator of all sin, every man is responsible for his own sin and salvation.[20]

September 29, 1985—*Letter to Bishops Concerning Exorcism* (Latin, *Inde Ab Aliquot Annis*, also from the Congregation for the Doctrine of the Faith): This short letter from then-Cardinal Joseph Ratzinger to all the bishops of the world was sent as a response to the problem of lay people conducting unauthorized exorcisms. The letter reiterated the provision in Canon 1172 and specified that deliverance services must be supervised by priests and conducted with the utmost care for the souls of the participants. Cardinal Ratzinger further stated that no person may use the exorcism prayer of Pope Leo XIII in a public way without authorization of the bishop. A final paragraph clarifies that, despite this official limitation, the laity are indeed encouraged by the Church to pray for deliverance from evil spirits and engage in spiritual warfare for souls.[21]

---

20 Congregation for the Doctrine of the Faith, *Christian Faith and Demonology*, 1975. (See *Vatican Council II: Conciliar and Post-Conciliar Documents, New Revised Edition*, ed., Austin Flannery, OP, Costello Publishing Company, Inc., Northport, NY, 1992.)
21 Congregation for the Doctrine of the Faith, *On the Current Norms Governing Exorcism* (*Inde Ab Aliquot Annis*), 1985.

November 22, 1998 (published in 1999)—*De Exorcismis et Supplicationibus Quibusdam* (from the Congregation for Divine Worship and the Discipline of the Sacraments): This is the revised *Rite of Exorcism* approved by Pope John Paul II. The preliminary notes (or *Praenotanda*) specify a number of adjustments or augmentations to previously established practice and applicable canon law.[22] It is the opinion of many exorcists, as well as my own, that the 1999 revision of the *Rite of Exorcism* was both unnecessary and poorly done.[23]

There have been many other statements of recent popes and Vatican dicasteries regarding the devil, the occult and healing. Fr. Gabriele Amorth notes that Pope Paul VI gave three general audiences on the topic of the devil, the most famous one being the "smoke of Satan" locution on June 29, 1972. Pope John Paul II gave as many as twenty-two public addresses on evil or the devil, and the Second Vatican Council referred to the devil on eighteen different occasions.[24] Pope Benedict gave his blessing to a group of exorcists who attended his papal audience in September 2005 and encouraged them to "carry on their important work in the service of the Church."[25] Two other related Vatican statements are the *Instruction on Prayers for Healing* from the Congregation of the Doctrine of the Faith in 2000

---

[22] Congregation for Divine Worship and the Sacraments, *De Exorcismis et Supplicationibus Quibusdam*, 1999, *Praenotanda*, n. 19. This specific prohibition concerning media exposure for exorcisms may have been due to the unusual April 5th, 1991 broadcast of an exorcism in the Diocese of Palm Beach, Florida on ABC's prime-time magazine show *20/20*.
[23] For further commentary on this matter please see my article, "The 1999 Revision of the Rite of Exorcism: The Devil Is In The Details," published in *Latin Mass Magazine*, Advent/Christmas, 2006.
[24] Fr. Gabriele Amorth, *An Exorcist: More Stories*, Ignatius: San Francisco, 2002, p. 57.
[25] General Audience, September 14th, 2005. "Saluto poi i partecipanti al convegno nazionale degli Esorcisti italiani, e li incoraggio a proseguire nel loro importante ministero a servizio della Chiesa, sostenuti dalla vigile attenzione dei loro Vescovi e dalla incessante preghiera della Comunità cristiana."

and the 2003 document on the "New Age" from The Pontifical Councils for Culture and Interreligious Dialogue.[26]

18. Wasn't there an "order of exorcist" prior to Vatican II? What was that?

Yes, there was such an "order" prior to Vatican II, and it was one step toward receiving the Sacrament of Holy Orders in the Latin Church before the liturgical reform ordered by the Council. The Sacrament of Holy Orders, properly speaking, at that time consisted of three different degrees (bishop, priest and deacon). The "major order" of subdeacon and the four non-clerical "minor orders" of porter (or "doorkeeper"), exorcist, lector and acolyte were stages of preparation for receiving Holy Orders. Each had its own rite of installation.

The minor orders were offices connected with the ministry of public worship, especially the Eucharistic Liturgy. However, the exercise of the specific offices of porter and exorcist had disappeared during the early Middle Ages, despite the fact that these minor orders were still being received *as a stage of preparation for the priesthood* into the decade following Vatican II. The minor orders as such, including the "order of exorcist," were casualties of the revision of the liturgical books and offices following the Council, and ceased to exist in 1972 when the Motu Proprio *Ministeria Quaedam* went into effect. This decree mandated the abolition of tonsure, the subdiaconate, and the minor orders except for lector and acolyte, which were reconstituted as "instituted ministries."[27]

---

[26] Congregation for the Doctrine of the Faith, *Instruction on Prayers for Healing*, 2000; The Pontifical Council for Culture and The Pontifical Council for Interreligious Dialogue, *Jesus Christ, The Bearer of the Water of Life: A Christian reflection on the "New Age,"* 2003

[27] *Loc. cit.*, Pope Paul VI, Apostolic Letter (*motu proprio*), August 15, 1972.

Thus, it is important to be clear that the "order of exorcist" was never a "religious order" and, since the Middle Ages, was not a stage of clerical life that allowed one to perform solemn exorcisms. (As already mentioned, solemn exorcisms since the earliest centuries have been limited in the West to *priests*, and later, priests with the express authorization of a bishop.) Even when the minor order of exorcist was exercised in antiquity, it was restricted to the exorcism of *catechumens* (pagans wishing to enter the Church) in preparation for baptism. It had become, in effect, more of a ceremonial title with no actual functions, except as a step toward priesthood.[28]

It is interesting to note that the document *Ministeria Quaedam*, which technically abolished the minor orders, also allowed for the possible establishment of a minor order or ministry of exorcist by the local conference of bishops if the local conference should deem such a ministry necessary for the local church. It is conceivable that such an order could have the function of performing exorcisms of places, deliverance prayers, or other new models of this ministry, even if it were not granted full faculties for performing solemn exorcisms on the possessed.[29]

---

28 Even centuries after most of the minor orders ceased to be exercised by those who held them, they reflected in some way aspects of the liturgy that the man would perform when he became a fully-ordained priest, thus retaining a symbolic and spiritual value.

29 "In addition to the offices universal in the Latin Church, the conferences of bishops may request others of the Apostolic See, if they judge the establishment of such offices in their region to be necessary or very useful because of special reasons. To these belong, for example, the ministries of porter, exorcist, catechist, as well as others to be conferred on those who are dedicated to works of charity, where this ministry had not been assigned to deacons." Motu Proprio, *Ministeria Quaedam*, August 15th, 1972.

19. Must each diocese have an appointed exorcist?

The 1983 *Code of Canon Law* does not strictly oblige the appointment of an "official" exorcist in a diocese, but it does not prohibit it either, and, given the immense need that the modern world has for spiritual healing, it should be considered a pastoral necessity today. In canon law it is technically the priest who petitions the bishop for permission to exorcise,[30] yet this falls short of reinforcing the responsibility of bishops to provide for the extreme spiritual needs of possessed persons in the way that they would provide for any other pastoral need in their diocese. In fact, Cardinal Medina Estevez, Prefect of the Congregation for Divine Worship and the Sacraments at the time of the promulgation of the new *Rite of Exorcism* in 1999, spoke of the need for exorcism as an urgent pastoral need of the Church.[31]

20. What if a bishop denies a priest the authority to exorcise when there is a real need?

If the bishop denies permission for a solemn exorcism in his diocese, a priest must never disobey his bishop even if he disagrees with his decision. The priest can still pray private deliverance prayers over a presumably obsessed or possessed person as long as the diocese has not forbidden him to do so. He must take care that any persons involved in the deliverance process know the difference between solemn exorcism and deliverance so as not to give the impression that the priest is being disobedient.

If the priest truly believes that the individual in question is possessed and needs the help of an exorcism, he can petition a different bishop for permission to perform a solemn exorcism in

---

30 Rev. Pellegrino Ernetti, OSB, *La Catechesi di Satana*, Edizioni Segno:Udine, 1992, p. 249.
31 *Presentación oficial del Cardenal Jorge A. Medina Estévez, Prefecto de la Congregación para el Culto Divino y La Disciplina de Los Sacramentos en la sala de Prensa de la Santa Sede, 26 de enero de 1999.*

the physical confines of another diocese. Permission for solemn exorcism is territorially-bound, and there is no canonical prohibition for a visiting priest to perform an exorcism in another diocese as long as the permission of the local bishop is obtained. Lacking permission of another bishop, he can only pray private deliverance prayers for that person which, over time, may have the same effect. The possessed person or his family also has the right, according to canon law,[32] to seek this pastoral service from another diocese.

21. Does the Church keep records or recordings of exorcisms?

Not usually. One exorcist in a large archdiocese told me that he did an extensive search of diocesan records and found only one documented case of an actual exorcism performed throughout the 150-year history of the archdiocese! That does not mean that no other exorcisms were performed in that period of time; it is just more likely that no records were kept.

Policies may vary from diocese to diocese, and even among exorcists, and there is a debate as to whether sensitive information of this sort should be kept either in electronic or written form. Some exorcists tape record and/or video tape exorcisms, if that can be arranged, because they believe that these recordings can assist others in training for this ministry. Others see too much liability for a diocese or for a client in keeping these records. As far as I am concerned, records of exorcisms, in any format, become classified records treated the same way as any other profession would treat them, shrouded with confidentiality and legal rights, for the good of the patients or clients.

I am not personally in favor of electronically recording exorcisms, but I do believe that an exorcist should take notes about

---

32 Canon 213.

his prayer sessions with people in order to help him remember the many details of exorcism sessions and related matters. A process may last for many sessions over many months, and professional notes will assist his ongoing care of the person's soul.

22. Does the Church allow exorcisms for non-Catholics?

Yes, the Catholic Church can technically perform an exorcism on any person who is demonically possessed and who requests it. A person does not have to be Catholic to receive the spiritual benefits of an exorcism because the *Church's faith* in Jesus is what gives strength to the act, even if the individual has not reached the stage of explicit faith in Christ. The Church cannot, however, change its ritual in order to exorcise a non-Catholic, and the priest must never agree to omit the Name of Jesus to accommodate the sensitivities of someone who does not believe in Jesus. The demons would love nothing more than to have Christ's Name omitted from an exorcism. In actual fact, the Church's immense power over demons is a witness to the truth and can be seen as an opportunity for evangelization and conversion of those who do not share our faith.[33]

There are two stipulations to keep in mind, however. First, the priest in question is still obligated to receive the authorization of the bishop to perform the exorcism, even if the person is not Catholic. Second, conversion to the Catholic Church is not a *condition* for undergoing an exorcism. People sometimes promise to convert to Catholicism if only a priest will perform an exorcism on them or their loved ones, but people in such stressful situations are not able to make a free decision about something so important, and so any discussion of conversion to the Faith

---

33 Christopher Neil-Smith, *The Exorcist and the Possessed: The Truth About Exorcism*, James Pike, Ltd., St. Ives, Cornwall: 1974, pp. 88-89.

is to be had when the person is of sound mind and free of all demonic influences.

23. Does a person have to officially consent to an exorcism?

Yes, in principle, a person must consent to an exorcism in much the same way that a person must consent to medical treatment. Most dioceses require the signing of a release/consent form prior to a solemn exorcism. There are cases, however, when a person is so afflicted or overcome by demonic power as to be unable to make a free decision to receive treatment. This is rare. In such an event, a concerned family member or caretaker may give consent. Usually, though, even a severely afflicted person is aware of the problem and is able to give consent for the Church's help in moments of lucidity. It goes without saying that a person can never be forced to receive an exorcism. In the case of a minor child who cannot decide for himself, the consent of a parent is absolutely necessary.

24. Can Protestants do exorcisms?

Catholicism teaches that the Protestant churches and denominations share elements of the true Faith and worship of Jesus Christ with our Church. Their union to us through baptism and true faith in Christ can be used against demons effectively. They do not conduct solemn exorcisms as we define them, but there are many Protestants whose deliverance ministries are effective in delivering souls from the power of evil, not because their churches share in the Apostolic Succession, but because they are authentic men and women of faith. As mentioned in the last chapter, in all warfare, spiritual or otherwise, what matters most is the potency of the weaponry and the faith with which it is used. The Catholic Church has the greatest power over evil because it has the greatest weaponry and wisdom of the ages passed down in the ritual and practice of exorcism; nevertheless, others with lesser weaponry, but great faith, can also drive out demons.

25. Who wrote the exorcism ritual?

The *Church* wrote the exorcism ritual over the course of centuries. The prayers of exorcism for the Latin Church are found currently in its official ritual text promulgated by the Vatican's Congregation for Divine Worship and the Discipline of the Sacraments.

The post-Tridentine *Rite of Exorcism* appeared as a standard part of the *Roman Ritual* in 1614 and consisted only of two parts: the Notes for exorcists and the Prayers. In 1890 the longer prayer to St. Michael the Archangel, written by Pope Leo XIII, was added to the ritual as a third part. The *Rite* was very slightly revised in 1925 and again 1952. In 1999, the *Rite* was completely revised in both text and format (along with some other minor alterations in 2000). It was the last of the liturgical revisions mandated by Vatican II; however, with the promulgation of the Motu Proprio, *Summorum Pontificum*, which freed up the Roman Ritual for universal use in the Church, the 1614 *Rite of Exorcism* no longer needs permission of a bishop for use in exorcism.[34]

The 1614 *Rite*, especially, is a compilation of prayers which have been handed down by the Church throughout many centuries. Some of the prayers date back to the ninth century, having been compiled by the famous French Benedictine abbot, Alcuin. The most time-tested of these prayers have been handed down to us in a standard ritual used since the seventeenth century. The Church wrote the ritual out of the abundance of experience in battling the devil and his minions throughout the centuries.

---

34   Rev. John Zuhlsdorf, *What Does The Prayer Really Say*, weblog <www.wdtprs.com>, "The Rite of Exorcism," December 28, 2007.

26. How is the *Rite of Exorcism* organized?

The 1614 ritual is held by many as more effective against the devil than the 1999 revision due to its structure and content; hence, we limit this discussion to the 1614 *Rite of Exorcism* which is divided into three distinct parts totaling approximately 17 single-spaced type-written pages. The texts of the exorcisms can be recited from beginning to end without interruption in about twenty minutes.[35]

Part I consists of a series of introductory notes that explain how an exorcist is to conduct the exorcism. These are twenty-one short paragraphs on the reality of demonic possession, discernment techniques to determine the presence of demons, rules of engagement and pitfalls that the exorcist is to avoid in his confrontation with demons. There are also a few items on the follow-up care of the person who has been liberated from demonic possession.

Part II is the exorcism ritual proper which starts with a Litany of Saints followed by an imperative (commanding) prayer to the demon requiring his obedience and laying out the terms of warfare: namely, his submission to the Church and final expulsion. These are followed by three exorcism prayers of different lengths. Each of these is preceded by a prayer petitioning God for the deliverance of the afflicted person. There are also some biblical prayers, the Magnificat and the so-called Athanasian Creed (*Quicumque vult*) that follow the exorcisms as prayers of thanksgiving when a person has been liberated.

Part III is an exorcism of place (Exorcism Against Satan and the Fallen Angels[36]) written by Pope Leo XIII who personally wrote the original, longer prayer to St. Michael the Archangel.

---
35 Malachi Martin, *Hostage to the Devil*, Harper, San Francisco, 1992, p. 17.
36 Cf. Appendix C for the complete text.

Part III was added permanently to the exorcism ritual in 1890 and codified in the 1925 revision, as stated above.

27. Must the priest always use the words of the ritual in an exorcism?

The priest's conduct of an exorcism is not limited to the written words in the ritual, but he must recognize that the efficacy of his prayer is tied in some way to the "official" prayer of the Church. He may address the demon directly in his own words and take actions that go beyond the standard formulae in the book, but it is recommended that he return again and again to the ritual even in the midst of the many ups and downs of an exorcism. The priest must always recognize, in humility, that the Church's warfare in expelling demons is always more powerful than his own. An exorcee once wrote me the following beautiful testimony after an exorcism:

> *Sometimes during the exorcism you would ask me what bothered the demon the most. It was always the prayers [i.e., of the ritual]. And I wanted to say that for me the prayers were like hearing just the music without the words and I really liked hearing that. I was not always conscious of it, but when I was, I liked hearing the prayers. It was like having music played perfectly and just for me.*[37]

The Church's ritual prayer is a *tour de force* against demonic creatures of any type. Demons often yell and scream in horror when the Church's ritual is addressed to them; and judging from this reaction, we must have the greatest possible faith in the power of the Church's prayer to weaken and expel demons, because it carries the authority of Christ Himself in a very direct way.

---

37 Used with permission.

28. Must a priest conduct the exorcism in Latin or may he use another language?

The demons understand and speak all human languages.[38] Although Latin was also used by pagan societies for centuries, it is now almost exclusively the Church's own sacred language in the West and seems to have greater efficacy against evil spirits because it has passed out of secular use in the modern era. Biblical Greek or Hebrew would likely have the same effect on demons if one were able to actually speak or pronounce blessings in these languages.

Oftentimes however, the priest is less familiar with Latin and there is a danger of him losing concentration in his confrontation with the evil spirit while attempting to manage the Latin text. Lacking familiarity with the Latin text, an exorcist may use an approved translation into his native language. However, Latin is clearly more odious to the demon and therefore more effective in weakening and expelling him, and a serious exorcist will familiarize himself with at least the basic Latin prayers of the *Rite*. Objectively speaking, Latin is a more effective instrument of warfare. Most exorcists I have spoken to have had the same experience.

What is significantly more effective than words, however, is the faith of the priest who pronounces them. The same can be said for the faith of the prayer partners who participate in the exorcism and that of the person receiving the prayer. "Your faith has made you well,"[39] the observation of Jesus when He healed people, remains the standard measure of effectiveness for any healing, spiritual or otherwise.

---

38 Lawrence LeBlanc and José Antonio Fortea, *Anneliese Michel: The True Story of a Case of Demonic Possession*, unpublished manuscript, 2007, p. 47.
39 E.g., Mt 9:22, Mk 5:34, Mk 10:52, Lk 17:19, etc.

29. Can a priest ever do an exorcism in secret?

Yes, but not a solemn exorcism. A priest can say exorcism *prayers* "in secret" if he suspects that a person is demonized but is not able or willing to accept the fact that he has some demonic problem. It is particularly recommended by St. Alphonsus Liguori (see Question 15 above) that a priest can recite silent prayers of this type in the confessional if he suspects that the person needs deliverance from a demon that is the source of a pernicious pattern of sin. He need not recite these prayers out loud: the devil, if he is truly present in the interior of the victim, will certainly hear them!

30. What are some of the deceptions that a demon may employ in an exorcism?

The priest and all helpers must remember that the devil is a "liar and the father of lies"[40] and will do everything he can to throw them off the track of getting information that will be used to cast him out. The ritual states: *"[The exorcist] will be on his guard against the arts and subterfuges which the evil spirits are wont to use in deceiving the exorcist. For oftentimes they give deceptive answers and make it difficult to understand them, so that the exorcist might tire and give up, or so it might appear that the afflicted one is in no wise possessed by the devil."*[41]

It is possible for a demon *to cause distractions* in the course of an exorcism by making things break, move, make noises, tear, disintegrate and generally disorient the people involved. I remember one exorcism session in which three telephones rang in succession with the most distracting of ring tones. Two participants had forgotten to turn their cell phones off before the ses-

---

40 Jn 8:44
41 *The Rite of Exorcism*, n. 5 (Weller, p. 168).

sion began and then when these were turned off we could hear another phone ringing loudly outside the chapel!

A demon will often try to *hide* during the exorcism and afterwards in order to deceive the person or the exorcist about his departure. This takes a great deal of discernment, and perhaps even obedience, on the part of the individual if the exorcist determines that he has not gotten a sufficiently clear sign of departure from the demon.

Verbal deception is the most common method of derailing the exorcism because all demons are liars and manipulators. It is necessary for the exorcist to command the demons to tell the truth with no trickery or obfuscation in order to be assured that the information coming forth is truthful. Even then, great discernment is needed to find the full truth. Once, in an exorcism, a demon used the person's actual voice to attempt to throw me off the track. The person said to me in her natural voice, "I think he's gone, Father. No, I am sure he is gone, I feel so much better."[42] I suspected that it was the demon speaking, so I commanded the person to recite the Hail Mary, and when the person refused, I knew whose the voice was. There are many other ways demons attempt to deceive the exorcist: half truths, mumbling, vague or symbolic answers, etc. Demons are like the most inveterate criminals under interrogation who will not give information except under the greatest duress.

Finally, demons will not hesitate to resort to *threats and intimidations* when these are expedient. A common experience among exorcists is that the demons say they will kill the priest or the victim—which of course never happens. Once I even heard a demon threaten to kill the bishop who authorized the exorcism!

---

[42] Malachi Martin calls that the stage of "Pretense" in his book, *Hostage to the Devil: The Possession and Exorcism of Five Americans,* HarperSanFrancisco, ed.: San Francisco, CA, 1992, pp. 18-19.

The exorcist must not enter into a contest of egos or be drawn into mind games with a demon—battles he can never win. He must keep his wits about him and tell the demon that it is not by our power or virtue that he will be cast out but by the power of Christ operating through the Church. This usually silences the demons.

31. How do you define success in an exorcism?

Total "success" is easy to define in an exorcism: namely, the victim is liberated from the demonic influence and is restored to spiritual health. The person must experience a profound sense of enduring peace over a long period of time for an exorcism to be considered entirely successful.

Short of the actual expulsion of the demon, however, there may be other ways to define "success" in an exorcism:

- The growth of faith, hope and charity that occurs in the victim through the arduous process;

- The victim's increasing relief from demonic persecution;

- Insight gained into the source of the affliction or behaviors and influences that sustain it;

- The formation of a prayer team and the involvement of people of good will in the process of spiritual healing; and

- The offering of one's suffering for the sake of the Kingdom, etc.

The growth in faith of the team and the victim is one of the most tangible and positive signs of success of the exorcism process. The exorcism process actually trains them to "see" the deeper dimension of God's grace that is operative in their lives, which in some mysterious way provides for spiritual growth and the advancement of Christ's Kingdom. They will inevitably understand St. Paul's wisdom in a more experiential way: "Where sin abounds grace abounds all the more."[43] Because of this dynamic of grace, sometimes people who go through this rigorous testing of their faith can turn out to be the holiest people we meet in ministry.

32. How do you define failure in an exorcism?

"Failure" may be harder to define. A trained exorcist is supposed to be a man of "piety, knowledge, prudence and integrity of life"[44] according to canon law, but he can make mistakes as all professionals do from time to time. "Ineffectiveness" is perhaps the better term to use. There are many reasons why an exorcism might be ineffective:

- Mistaken judgments by the exorcist in the heat of the battle;
- Loss of control of the process;
- Lack of true preparation and discernment; and
- Falling into "traps" set by the demonic intelligence.

There are other elements of weakness in the conduct of an exorcism which will delay or undermine the expulsion of a demon:

- The priest may not have conducted a thorough enough investigation of the person's case to discern the sources of the demonic problem;

---

43 Rom 5:20
44 Canon 1172.

- He may not have trained his team well or have good prayer support;

- He may not ask the correct questions of the demons, prosecute them forcefully enough when they are weak, or sufficiently persevere in commanding and praying until the demon is totally vanquished;

- He may declare victory too early;

- He may fail to get definitive signs of departure to be assured of the demon's exit; and

- He may also fail to ascertain whether there are other demons still remaining.

An exorcism may also "fail" because of the victim's inability, through fear or inadvertence, to cooperate sufficiently with the exorcism. He may be "attached" to the demon for some reason or have a deep-seated fear of changing his life in order to take away the demon's foothold. The experienced exorcist will be proficient at identifying these bondages and helping the person to withdraw the demon's "legal right"[45] to be in his body.

Finally, an exorcism would certainly be a failure if it succeeded in casting out a demon who then returned "with seven demons more wicked than itself."[46] This would be a total travesty.

33. Does the devil attack exorcists?

In a recent deliverance I conducted, the unclean spirit yelled out, "I hate priests!" but he had no power to harm me or the two

---

45   This is a common term in exorcism and deliverance ministry to designate the "permission" that a demon has to stay inside the body of a person. The exorcist or deliverance minister will use great diligence and discernment to help the victim to identify the reasons why he or she may inadvertently wish the demon to remain.

46   Lk 11:26

other priests in attendance. The devil cannot effectively harm the exorcist who endeavors to live in a state of grace and fortifies himself against the wiles of the devil, as both St. Paul and St. Peter admonish us in their writings.[47] A priest can be harmed, however, if he is imprudent or inattentive to his enemy. For example, the first exorcism done on the boy whose case formed the basis of the movie, *The Exorcist*, was performed by a young priest whose arm was gashed from the shoulder to the wrist by the demon wielding a sharp piece of metal he had pulled out of the bed spring. The wound required more than one hundred stitches.[48] This was the case of an inexperienced priest attempting to exorcise a very powerful demon. The exorcism was unsuccessful, and the priest eventually handed the case on to another priest.

More common are the relatively minor harassments that exorcists and their helpers experience from time to time before and after exorcisms. These usually amount to inconveniences and minor disruptions or persecutions of a superficial character rather than catastrophic problems. These "attacks" can usually be avoided and often nullified if the priest is personally vigilant against them. Personally, I have experienced a multitude of disruptions in my life including sudden illness, pipes bursting, mechanical failures, a stolen credit card number, and once, at the end of an exorcism session, a totally dead car battery. When such things happen, especially within a short time of an exorcism, one can often interpret them as harassments, but it is necessary to approach these situations with firm faith and an increase of prayer in order to limit their power to harm. If one remains in a state of grace and practices his faith diligently, then the devil has extremely limited powers to bring any damage or pain.

---

47 See especially Eph 6:10-17 and 1 Pet 5:9
48 Thomas B. Allen, *Possessed: The True Story of An Exorcism*, iUniverse.com, Inc. Lincoln, 2000, p. 37.

34. Can an exorcist be deceived by the devil and end up in spiritual trouble?

This is always possible but, hopefully, rare. The most important virtue to have as an exorcist is not intelligence, but humility. For a priest to be most protected from deceit and spiritual danger, he must not think too much about himself; he must depend completely on God. Spiritual direction, good habits of discernment and a profound spirit of prayer will also help the priest maintain his spiritual integrity.

Readers may know the case of the infamous Catholic archbishop from Zambia, Emmanuel Milingo, who was an exorcist and conducted huge exorcism ceremonies in the 80s and 90s before he was brought to Rome for closer scrutiny. His exorcism services were marred by excessive emotionalism and chaos. He continued these practices even in Italy under the Vatican's watchful eye, but somewhere along the line he got seduced by the devil into thinking that he could do exorcisms without the aid of grace or the protection of the Church.

In 2001, the Archbishop actually joined the Moonies,[49] participated in a massive marriage ceremony in a stadium—himself "marrying" a Korean woman—and for a time left the Catholic Church altogether. He was briefly reconciled to the Church but then relapsed into his Moonie state and re-established concubinage with the Korean woman. He is now going around advocating optional celibacy for priests. When he unlawfully ordained

---

49 "The Unification Church is a new religious movement founded by Korean religious leader Sun Myung Moon. In 1954, the Unification Church was formally and legally established in Seoul, South Korea. In the English speaking world, church members are sometimes referred to as 'Moonies.' Unification Church beliefs … include belief in a universal God; in striving toward the creation of a literal Kingdom of God on earth; in the universal salvation of all people, good and evil, living and dead.…Members of the Unification Church believe [the] Messiah is Sun Myung Moon." (Cf. Wikipedia)

a bishop for (former Catholic priest) George Stallings' African American Catholic Congregation in Washington in 2006, he was excommunicated.[50] This very sad case shows that even a full archbishop, with experience in exorcism, is not outside the grasp and seductions of a demon. Humility optimally expresses itself in a spirit of obedience to Truth and to religious authority.

35. What did Pope John Paul II say about the devil? Did he really do an exorcism as Pope?

Let's start with the last question first. Yes, Pope John Paul II in fact performed three exorcisms during his tenure as pope. The first was in 1978, the second in 1982 and the third one was in September of the year 2000 at the end of a papal audience. Apparently, the latter occurred when a 19-year-old Italian woman who had a history of demonic problems and had had an exorcism the previous day was in the papal audience and began to scream with a demonic voice as the Pope left the audience. The Holy Father prayed over her for half an hour and ordered the devil to leave, unsuccessfully. Another priest spent two more hours with her that day, also unsuccessfully, but of course, as has been noted many times in this book, an exorcism is not an "event"—even if a pope is performing it. It is always a process. Allegedly, the young woman continues under the care of an exorcist in Rome.

In his life as a priest, Pope John Paul was undoubtedly familiar with the work of the devil and spoke frequently in his audiences and public speeches about the devil and the Christian response to him. John Paul II gave a catechesis in his Wednesday audiences in July and August of 1996 on the Angels.[51] The August 13, 1996 segment on "The Fall of the Rebellious Angels"

---
50 In 2009, Archbishop Milingo was dismissed from the clerical state by the Vatican.
51 John Paul II, General Audience of August 13, 1986.

is a marvelous, clearly-reasoned and doctrinal explanation on the apostasy of the devil and his angels in which he explains the freedom of the angels to rebel and our need to battle them. It is worth the time to read.[52]

36. Is Freemasonry still forbidden by the Catholic Church?

Official Church teachings have always taken the most severe stance toward Freemasonry due to the irreconcilable nature of its teachings and systems. Freemasonry is a false religion that requires absolute secrecy for its members and draws them through a system of ever-tightening strictures in order for them to advance in the order. It is based upon a relativistic value system that sees no moral absolutes and recognizes no eternal destiny of the human soul. As a false religion which stands opposed to and even attacks the Church that Christ founded, Freemasonry is pernicious to the salvation of those who adhere to it.

After the publication of the 1983 *Code of Canon Law* in which the direct reference to Freemasonry was removed, the Congregation for the Doctrine of the Faith was asked whether the Church's teaching on Freemasonry had changed. Then-Cardinal Joseph Ratzinger responded: "The Church's negative judgment in regard to Masonic association remains unchanged, since their principles have always been considered irreconcilable with the doctrine of the Church and therefore membership in them remains forbidden. The faithful who enroll in Masonic associations are in a state of grave sin and may not receive Holy Communion."[53] The Church's teaching about this false religion has therefore not changed. In fact, since Pope Clement VII's decree, *In Eminente*, in 1738, there have been more than a dozen official condemnations of Freemasonry by the universal teaching

---
52 Cf. Appendix G.
53 Congregation for the Doctrine of the Faith, *Declaration on Masonic Associations*, November 26th, 1983.

Magisterium of the Church,[54] not to mention the numerous instances of local pastoral letters concerning the same.

Afterword to Chapter 3
Practical Advice for Petitioning an Exorcism

Any priest may use the following approach to petition authorization from a diocese to perform an exorcism.

Basic insights about diocesan officials:

- With some exceptions, most pastors of souls have good will toward the needs of those who suffer, including obsessed and possessed people.

- While bishops and chancery officials want to avoid legal liability and negative publicity about "demonic problems" in their diocese, they are justified in taking a cautious approach and "testing all spirits" when people petition exorcism.

- Most bishops and chancery officials are willing to let an interested and competent priest handle this pastoral need, provided there is accountability.

- These matters are best handled priest-to-priest rather than priest-to-bishop; the proper diocesan official will bring the matter to the bishop's attention when all appropriate measures have first been taken.

- In the vast majority of cases, the professional investigation and presentation of a case by a competent priest, using

---

54 R.H. Goldsborough, *Masonry, Root of Modern Apostasy*, Goldsborough and Associates: Baltimore, MD, 2003.

solid pastoral judgment, will obtain the needed permission from the diocese for exorcism.

To petition a diocese for the authority to exorcise, a priest should:

1. First meet the afflicted person and conduct a thorough initial investigation of the case before any mention of the matter is made to the Chancery.

2. A "thorough initial investigation" generally means personal (and family) interviews, assessment of any relevant medical and psychological history and, if possible, prayer with the person.

3. Contact the diocesan exorcist or Vicar General in charge of Pastoral Services to inform him that you have been asked to assist in a case that may need exorcism. Assure the official(s) that you are only in the assessment stage and are not at this time requesting exorcism and that you will submit a report on your findings within several days. Also assure him of total confidentiality.

4. After initial contact with the diocese, write a short (2-3 single-spaced pages) report with the following elements: a personal profile, a brief history, a description of the investigation efforts and your initial assessment of the case.

5. Conduct more prayer sessions with the person and continue to gain more personal experience of both the person and the facts of the case.

6. Maintain contact with the chancery official during this time and assure him that you are continuing to assist the person and will submit a second report to confirm or augment your initial findings.

7. Send the second report within a week to ten days of the first report if possible. This time, add any relevant documentation from medical professionals to confirm your assessment.

8. In this second report, include a section detailing the direct evidence of the signs of possession either outlined by the General Rules Concerning Exorcism[55] of the 1614 *Rite of Exorcism* or the common experience of other exorcists and established cases.

9. In this second report make a formal request for exorcism on behalf of the person. The report should indicate that you have been asked by the person and/or family to make the request, and that you agree that it is appropriate.

10. No more written reports are necessary at this stage, but the diocese may ask for further professional evaluations prior to granting the request for exorcism. Prepare the person and family to comply strictly with all diocesan requests.

11. If permission is granted, follow all the proper procedures for a solemn exorcism and make periodic progress reports to the chancery official who is your contact with the bishop. Inform the diocese directly when the case is terminated through mutual agreement or definitive liberation.

Other caveats and bits of advice to priests:

1. Take what is told to you by the afflicted person at face value, but vigorously *verify* every claim of demonic activity personally and through professional assessment if necessary.

---

55 Cf. Appendix A for the complete text of the General Rules Concerning Exorcism.

2. Do not make a diagnosis of "possession" too easily. While it is true that no one can be hurt by an "unnecessary exorcism," at the same time, do not cheapen the notion of exorcism by applying it to every case of suspected demonic problems or by crying wolf when there is no solid evidence of possession.

3. Do not unduly promise exorcism to the afflicted person or the family before you have verified what the actual spiritual state of the individual is. It is also best to dampen any expectations for quick action from the diocese.

4. At the same time, strive to be a Good Shepherd to the afflicted person and family, always presuming good will and offering plenty of pastoral guidance and authentic kindness, even if their need is not as serious as they think it is. They will likely have been treated roughly by others already.

5. Do not bring this request *directly* to the bishop and do not mention exorcism when in casual conversations or settings with the bishop. There is a place and time to address these concerns and a chain of command for these matters at the Chancery; follow it. Bringing sensitive matters like this up over dinner when the bishop comes for Confirmation is not good protocol.

6. Do not go to a bishop or diocesan official to ask for *emergency authority for exorcism*—the bishop will not give it, nor should he. The Church should not be forced into action on matters that need great discernment. Rather, calmly apply every spiritual remedy that the Church has in her immense spiritual arsenal prior to gaining permission for a solemn exorcism.

7. Always presume that the chancery will ask about psychological or psychiatric evaluations, and be prepared to satisfy these concerns. While the opinions of psychiatrists should never be considered definitive in spiritual matters, nonetheless, they may carry a great deal of weight for ruling out other possibilities.

8. Do not quote the most recent book on exorcism (including this one) when making a case for possession; give the diocese, rather, your own independent and theologically-sound judgment of the matter with proper consultation of professionals and other exorcists when possible.

Chapter 4
Discernment Issues[1]

Beloved, do not trust every spirit, but put the spirits to a test to see if they belong to God, because many false prophets have appeared in the world. This is how you can recognize God's Spirit: every spirit that acknowledges Jesus Christ come in the flesh belongs to God, while every spirit that fails to acknowledge him does not belong to God. (1 Jn 4:1-2)

Especially, he [the exorcist] should not too readily believe that a person is possessed by an evil spirit; but he ought to ascertain the signs by which a person possessed can be distinguished from one who is suffering from melancholy or some other illness. Signs of possession are the following: ability to speak with some facility in a strange tongue or to understand it when spoken by another; the faculty of divulging future and hidden events; display of powers which are beyond the subject's age and natural condition; and various other indications which, when taken together as a whole, pile up the evidence. (Roman Ritual, *Rite of Exorcism*, General Rules Concerning Exorcism, n. 3)[2]

---

[1] **AUTHOR'S NOTE:** Please refer to the companion edition to this book, entitled *Discernment Manual for Exorcists and Pastoral Ministers*, projected to be published in the Fall of 2010, for a fuller treatment of this subject for those involved with demonically-afflicted individuals. Since the primary audience of this book is priests, the answers in the present chapter are mainly directed toward priests and those who work with them in spiritual healing.

[2] Weller, *Rituale*, p. 169.

✠

1. Why should an exorcist be concerned about discernment?

An exorcist must be most concerned and diligent about discernment because of the very nature of demons: they are deceivers. Good discernment is necessary both to sort out the truth from deception and to distinguish natural causes of things from spiritual causes. There is no other skill quite as necessary in exorcism work as discernment.

By virtue of ordination a priest naturally acts in various discernment capacities in his care of souls (*cura animarum*). First, he is a *counselor* as his discerning listening skills aid a person in his faith journey of better understanding God's will. He also acts like a *true shepherd* whose "rod and staff"[3] (protective prayers and sacramentals) give courage to afflicted persons and help them to see the true nature of their affliction. Finally, the priest acts like a *doctor of souls* who assists people in healing their spiritual wounds, which also leads to self-understanding, spiritual growth and sanctification.

2. What forms of discernment may a team employ to understand more about demonic presence and actions?

There are four tools that may be employed by priests and deliverance ministers in the discernment process: prayer, discernment of spirits, medical science and common sense.

Prayer itself provides perhaps the best opportunity to discern the extent and nature of a spiritual affliction, and to test the spirits.[4] The spiritual light brought by prayer may reveal things

---

3   Ps 23:4
4   1 Jn 4:1—"Beloved, do not trust every spirit, but put the spirits to a test to see if they belong to God...."

that are not clear during an interview process. For example, in a prayer session, a demon may speak his name (identity or mission) or may manifest some sign that indicates why he is there. The victims themselves may gain insight into their own memories or behaviors which could unlock the mystery of their inner state. Furthermore, the prayer of the Church will oftentimes cause demons to "come to the surface" like the dross that is being purified from precious metal in a crucible. Prayer itself is perhaps the most effective form of discernment of both the presence and identity of demons.

The classical Rules for Discernment of Spirits in the *Spiritual Exercises* of St. Ignatius of Loyola are also helpful tools in understanding the dynamics of spiritual "consolation" (caused by God) and spiritual "desolation" (caused by evil spirits). While these rules are generally meant for spiritually healthy people who are seeking a greater knowledge of God's will in their lives, they can also be extremely helpful as a primer for understanding the actions of demons and how to navigate the mysterious world of spiritual signs. The priest and helpers should be thoroughly schooled in these time-tested rules for discernment.

Added to this is the *charismatic gift of discernment of spirits,* where an exorcist or pastoral minister can accurately tell what spirits are operative in any given situation by a special spiritual faculty of discernment. As has been said before, all charismatic and spiritual gifts, if they are to authentically serve the Church's care of souls, must be tested and proven true over time and ultimately must manifest a sincere humility and obedience to the Church's authority.

The priest may also consult the expertise of the *modern medical and psychological sciences* for discernment. He is careful to maintain a healthy detachment from all claims of possession, but he must attempt to evaluate the possible causes of problems that the person claims are demonic in origin. There may be multiple causes for what looks like a single problem in a person's life, and science may be able to shed light on the nature of a person's problems, and at the very least, rule out causes by a process of elimination. It is also the common experience of exorcists that the vast majority of spiritual problems are attached to or the result of unresolved human woundedness. Modern psychological sciences are very helpful in treating the human pre-conditions for spiritual infestation, and exorcists should be very diligent in seeking out competent professionals to assist in the overall healing of the person.

A diagnostic process should not be made more complex than is necessary. *Common sense* also plays a crucial role in discerning demonic activity. For example, if a person with no personal or family history of psychiatric problems admits that he participated in a séance, played with a Ouija board, or consorted with a witch and *from that time on* he began to experience intense personal problems, pain and great destruction in his life, then common sense tells us that his problem is probably one of a spiritual nature.

St. Paul says that we see "darkly as in a mirror."[5] That is true, but through a combination of professional expertise, discernment rules, prayer, and common sense, we can usually arrive at great insight about the problems of an individual and weaken or totally break the demon's dark power over God's beloved children.

---

5 1 Cor 13: 12

3. In discerning demonic presences what "types" of demons are there?

People involved in deliverance and healing ministries usually distinguish four general "types" of demons that can afflict us: demons of the occult, demons of sin, demons of trauma/sickness and generational spirits.[6] These names indicate more the mode of entry and affliction rather than the "strength" of the demon. There is a general hierarchy of wickedness in this list: that is, the demons of the occult are usually stronger than the demons of sin, and demons of sin are usually stronger than demons of trauma, etc.; but it is not automatic or easy to predict.[7]

Occult demons are the most difficult to expel due to their mode of infestation. They generally come in through a person's participation in or contact with occult things or people, even if the person thought that he was just playing a game. The devil "disguises himself as an angel of light,"[8] so it is no surprise that people are deceived when they engage in occult activities. Occult demons are sometimes "locked" into the person by some iniquity such as curses, satanic consecrations, hexes, spells, black magic, etc., and in order to expel them there must be an act of repentance and some form of renunciation on the part of the individual. All close contact with persons in the occult business must be broken. Then the person needs the help of the Church through restoring his relationship with Christ and prayers of deliverance or exorcism for the evil to be cast out.

Demons of sin can enter a person through long habits of seriously sinful behavior, or they can enter when a person has

---

[6] Francis MacNutt, *Deliverance from Evil Spirits*, Chosen Books: Grand Rapids, MI, 1995, pp. 182-222; and Christian Healing Ministries, Inc., *School of Healing Prayer tape series, Level II*, "Deliverance," 1998.
[7] See the Afterword to this chapter for a fuller treatment of this topic.
[8] 2 Cor 11:14

been in the presence of a particularly traumatic sin like murder. These unclean spirits often bear the names of their particular sins, "Lust," "Idolatry," "Greed," "Fornication," "Avarice," and so forth. The range of these spirits is the whole panoply of human sinfulness, and demons of this type delight in seducing weak human beings into behaviors which can enslave them. They require profound repentance and a break with any sinful lifestyles, a renunciation of the sin by name and a re-establishment of the person's relationship with Jesus Christ. The prayer of the Church will assist the individual to be open to God's grace for expulsion of the demons and inner healing. In some cases a person can self-deliver if his repentance and conversion is deep enough.

Demons of trauma enter through the doorway of traumatic experiences or "inner wounds" created by trauma; experiences such as grief, rejection, sadness, depression, fear, abuse, etc. Demons can "attach" to these experiences of trauma or abuse and enter the body *like an infection* enters a physical wound. These, like the effects of Original Sin, can afflict those who are not personally guilty of sin and did nothing to "invite" the demon in. However, to be freed of these demons, such a person must sincerely forgive anyone who may have caused the particular trauma and receive deliverance prayer or prayer for inner healing.[9] This can be a long or short process depending upon the inner woundedness of the person, but renewing or strengthening the person's relationship with Jesus is always the best form of healing and liberation.

The fourth category of demons, *generational spirits*, are also called familial or ancestral demons. These refer to demonic entities that seem to flow down through family lines or are attached to whole families in a deliberate way through curses or some other occult force. Sometimes they are demons attached to sinful human behaviors and the long-term effects of sin in much

---

[9] MacNutt, *Deliverance*, p. 186.

the same way that an addictive behavior in an adult may create a propensity for that addiction in the child. Scripture makes it clear that we cannot pass *personal guilt* on to future generations as each person bears the guilt of his own sin,[10] but certainly the effects of sin and occult activity can be passed on to others as punishment "down to the third and fourth generation."[11] This is of course consistent with the Catholic doctrine of Original Sin. These afflictions are commonly related to medical diseases, negative feelings, attitudes and addictions, etc.[12] To free a person or family of these demons, deliverance prayer must be done for the individual, or prayers of healing must be done for the family tree[13] after a careful investigation into the nature of the demonic affliction.

4. What is the difference between demons and ghosts?

Most pagan societies believe in the separation of the soul from the body and an afterlife. This includes the idea that souls may "linger" after death due to "unfinished business" such as unbroken attachments to the earth, to unreconciled relationships or to the affairs of men that supposedly last beyond the grave. In this view, the souls can be benign or malicious; often pagan traditions of ancestor worship or appeasement of the dead are the result of these beliefs.

The Roman Catholic belief is categorically different from these pagan beliefs, however. The theological tradition concerning souls in purgatory is based on the belief that bodily death

---

10 Cf. Dt 24:16
11 Cf. Ex 20:5 and 34:7, Num 14:18, Ex 18:20.
12 Kenneth McAll, *A Guide to Healing the Family Tree*, Queenship Publishing Company: Goleta, CA, 1996, pp. v-vii. McCall relates that even psychological pioneer Carl Jung believed that some of his patients were controlled by ancestral spirits, p. 203.
13 For many years there has been a growing interest in "healing the family tree;" see Fr. John Hampsch, CMF, *Healing Your Family Tree*, Queenship Publishing Company: Goleta, CA, 1989.

constitutes a *definitive* entrance into an afterlife which is either a temporal purification followed by heaven, or an eternal damnation. Thus, for Catholics there is no such a thing as a "lingering" or "wandering" soul who has "not cut the bonds of this earthly life." For Catholics, there is another way to explain these things than the standard pagan reasoning.

A strong *theological tradition* recognizes that deceased human souls can and do visit the living after death for various reasons and in various modes.[14] It is clear that this is only done "according to the disposition of Divine providence" and not as a common occurrence. St. Thomas Aquinas says that "separated souls sometimes come forth from their abode and appear to men…", and this can be both for "intimidation" (i.e., damned souls) or for "instruction" (i.e., redeemed souls). He also claims that souls may appear to others "in order to seek our suffrages" (i.e., souls in purgatory).[15] Such apparitions can also be due to a special intervention into the human sphere by a demon creating a deception or an angel appearing in human form to communicate a message.[16]

Some people call these various apparitions "ghosts."[17] In light of the tradition above, these can be either disembodied human

---

14 Rev. Herbert Thurston, S.J., *Ghosts and Poltergeists*, Henry Regnery, Co.: Chicago, 1954, p. 205. Thurston says that "God might permit souls from purgatory to revisit the earth to ask for prayers, though the shapes which they assumed were phantasmal and not solid."
15 St. Thomas Aquinas, *Summa Theologica*, Suppl.69.3. "Whether the souls who are in heaven or hell are able to go from thence?"
16 Hospers, John, "Is the Notion of Disembodied Existence Intelligible?" In *Immortality*, Paul Edwards (ed.), Macmillan: New York, 1992, pp. 279-281; St. Thomas Aquinas, *ibid.*, Suppl.69.3.ad6.
17 Peter Kreeft, *Everything You Ever Wanted to Know About Heaven*, Ignatius Press: San Francisco, 1990, pp. 33-35. Kreeft describes three types of "ghosts," only one of which he claims are souls in the midst of purgatorial purifications. The other categories are the demonic and those "bright, happy spirits" of family and friends, i.e., redeemed souls that God allows to return to the earth to give messages. Kreeft, it should

souls or evil spirits. In Catholic thought, however, if such appearances happen, they are always limited and marked by truth, simplicity and utter clarity to distinguish a holy apparition from a demonic one, which is always marked by confusion, discord, chaos, fear and anxiety. Thus, there is no strictly theological basis for believing that there are souls "wandering" around in the world communicating with loved ones, or "haunting" places, but Catholics do believe that the deceased can appear after death in a strictly limited fashion and only with God's permission for some greater reason.

What has been absolutely forbidden by the Church from the beginning is the attempt to conjure deceased souls from the grave or to communicate with the dead, a dark art known as necromancy. This prohibition is from Scripture.[18] In the Christian tradition, we honor the dead and pray for them—we even consider ourselves in communion with them—but we do not conjure them up or attempt to dialogue with them. All such practices open us up to demonic deception and infestation.

5. Can damned human souls possess or torment people?

Whether damned human souls can actually possess living persons is an open question still debated even by experienced exorcists, but the classical view is against the idea. Notwithstanding what was mentioned above about "separated souls," it is hard to see how a damned human soul would be released from hell to *independently* possess or haunt another human being. This is first of all based upon the biblical image of the "chasm between us and you" of the parable of Lazarus and the Rich Man.[19] A damned

---

be noted, here bases his observations mostly on anecdotal evidence and not on doctrinal teachings: "That there are all three kinds of ghosts is enormously likely," he says.
18   Lev 19:31, 20:6; Deut 18:11, 12. Leviticus 20:27 even considers necromancy a crime punishable by death.
19   Cf. Lk 16:19-31

soul would not have the spiritual power over nature to return to torment humans as a demon would and, being separated from the body, would not likely be able to manifest itself in the world with any great power that would be needed for an actual possession. If a damned soul were somehow "attached" to a demon roaming the world, such a soul would be entirely controlled by the stronger demon and *theoretically* participate vicariously in the demon's haunting, harassing, frightening or possession of the living human person but not be able to do those same activities on its own. This however, is pure speculation and not defined doctrinally. Biblically and theologically, it is most accurate to presume that damned human souls do not possess or torment other human beings.

6. How does a person know he needs an exorcism?

Generally speaking, when a person suffers deep and prolonged emotional or even physical pain and can't find the origin of it or alleviation from it through natural means, he may have a spiritual problem. It is important that, after having exhausted the standard means of healing through natural/scientific means, such a person seek spiritual help and not attempt to diagnose himself as possessed just because he feels he has a spiritual problem. Like any sick person, he is not capable of seeing fully his own symptoms and manifestations of illness, especially if they are spiritual in origin. He must humbly submit to the judgment of someone with more experience in this realm and follow the path to healing that is laid out for him.

This is especially important if the problem truly is demonic: humility is the necessary virtue for overcoming the pride of the devil. This is not to say that a person cannot know by deep intuition that he has a spiritual problem or may be possessed. It is just to say that he should not declare himself possessed without a definitive judgment of the spiritual authority. It is the common experience of exorcists that people claiming to be possessed and loudly demanding the help of the Church are usually not possessed, while those who are truly demonically afflicted and need spiritual help are suffering silently and often waiting for someone to assist them.

7. What if a person needs it but refuses to get an exorcism?

There are always people who are so overpowered by evil that *their demons* will do everything possible to keep them from going to a priest for spiritual healing. I recall a time when I performed one exorcism on a young woman who was quite mentally disturbed. I believed that her problem was truly demonic in origin. The demons gave very little reaction during the course of the exorcism that day, but I knew the prayer had a powerful effect on the demons. When she went to school the next day, she threatened suicide, and the authorities immediately called the police to put her in a mental institution where it was impossible to continue the exorcism ritual. The demon was therefore successful in keeping the person from the Church's help, but it was not really the person's fault. She was just powerfully controlled by the demon, and the demon acted through her to get her locked away from any significant spiritual help of the Church.

Sometimes people are uncooperative, rebellious or simply reject the Church's help, but there is no way that an exorcism can be forced upon someone. Therefore, in cases like this, the family or loved ones should always unite to pray for the person and bind the demons they suspect are there. They may also ask the person's guardian angel for assistance. This binding will have a powerful effect over the demons in time, and it is likely, though not always sure, that the person will reach a stage where he may be willing to submit to the Church's help. However, we must be very patient with the rebellious, just as God is patient with our rebellions against His Goodness.

8. How can a Christian have a demon?

There are three main reasons why someone who confesses the Name of Jesus may have a demon. First, Christians can be slothful in their practice of the faith or vulnerable to demons through unrepentant and unconfessed sin. Christ cannot fully protect even His followers who do not invoke His protection consciously. Second, the Lord allows Christians to suffer in this way to "test" or "prove" them in the fires of adversity. The devil is most effective in offering that kind of spiritual testing, and sometimes it comes as internal obsessions rather than merely external forms of persecution. Third, "God wishes to give us a true knowledge and understanding of ourselves" and show us how impossible it is to advance in His service without the aid of His grace.[20]

Some have wondered how it is possible for the devil to inhabit a body which St. Paul says is the "temple of the Holy Spirit."[21] It would seem that God and Belial cannot exist in the same place at the same time.[22] But an unclean spirit may enter and inhabit a body in the same way that a sin may enter and stain a soul: by the human will, which gives permission for its entrance. Or to use another analogy: a demon may enter a body in the same way a Satanist may enter a church building; either through a deliberate wicked action or a free invitation. The mere fact of God's Presence in a place does not prohibit the action

---

20 Cf. Rules I.9 of St. Ignatius' *Rules for the Discernment of Spirits*, which is one of the appendices of the *Spiritual Exercises* written in the 16th century but valid as a retreat and discernment guide to the present day. See Louis J. Puhl, S.J., Trans., *The Spiritual Exercises of St. Ignatius*, Loyola University Press, Chicago: IL, 1951, pp. 143-144.
21 I Cor 6:19
22 2 Cor 6:15

and activity of human or spiritual evil even though a place may be sacred.

9. How does the Church determine that a person is possessed?

The 1614 *Rite of Exorcism* gives several basic criteria for determining possession. The ritual states: *"Signs of possession may be the following: ability to speak with some facility in a strange tongue or to understand it when spoken by another; the faculty of divulging future and hidden events; display of powers which are beyond the subject's age and natural condition; and various other indications which, when taken together as a whole, build up the evidence."*[23] The most obvious sign of possession, however, which is presumed by these rules, is a distinct aversion to the sacred. Keep in mind that these criteria are not meant to be exhaustive or to diagnose demonic possession with absolute certainty. The rules say that the various signs are to be "taken together as a whole" in order to "build up the evidence" for making a judgment.

The criteria are, however, good indicators of possession because the phenomena noted here are quite rare, and it is hard to fake such things. I recall the case of a young man who was given a page of the Bible to read, and when he did so, he read it in a perfectly fluent middle-eastern-sounding language. English was the only language that this man could speak or understand. He would also recite intimate details of atrocities committed in the Nazi concentration camps to nurses in the psychiatric hospital where he was staying. There was no human way he could have known or invented that information. When these factors and others were *"taken together as a whole,"* it was not hard to assess that he was possessed.

---

23 Weller, *Rituale*, p. 168.

The ritual says further that the priest *"should not believe too readily that a person is possessed by an evil spirit; but he ought to ascertain the signs by which a person possessed can be distinguished from one who is suffering from some illness, especially one of a psychological nature."*[24] While there is always a danger of too easily assuming a diagnosis of possession where it does not exist, if anything, churchmen are usually overly cautious and seek too much certainty before they help a person with spiritual problems. A person can be fully possessed and yet exhibit none of the above criteria, so a priest must not necessarily wait to hear esoteric languages coming from an afflicted person before he offers help.

10. Can the exorcism prayers be used "diagnostically" even if a priest is not sure a person is possessed?

The following prefatory note of the 1614 ritual presumes that exorcism can and will be used to help "diagnose" the problem when it says, *"In order to understand these matters better, let him inquire of the person possessed, following one or the other act of exorcism, what the latter experienced in his body or soul while the exorcism was being performed,"* which means that there are times when the priest is not sure of what he is dealing with and can employ the ritual even in the investigation stage to have a more clear picture of both the presence and the extent of demonic evil in a person's body.

11. What other "symptoms" might the Church acknowledge as signs of possession?

There are so very many. The following list is not meant to be definitive, but the symptoms listed are generally indicative of possession. These "symptoms" will vary in intensity according to the strength of the affliction, and it is up to the priest to judge

---

24 *Ibid.*

whether they are signs of possession or just demonic affliction at a lesser level. He may need the advice of psychiatric professionals to help determine if some of the phenomena are simply expressions of mental illness. All possessed persons do not exhibit the same signs, but all the possessed have terrible internal problems and even agonizing pain due to the presence of aggressive and malicious spirits inside of them.

Possessed individuals have told me that they experience the following types of "symptoms:" as mentioned above, an overt repulsion in the presence of anything blessed or holy (this is common to all possessed people); horrible nightmares and vivid terrors that afflict them in or out of sleep; sometimes a fascination with occult and evil tendencies; terrible physical pains like migraines and/or stomach pains; emotional torments and tortures varying in intensity; experiences of being in a trance-like state or "disconnected" from reality; the distinct feeling of being covered by an evil "presence" or "shadow" of sorts; total loss or absence of energy; constant mental chatter or noise in their minds; voices that blaspheme God or threaten them with punishment; physical blockages to healing or subterfuge to any type of human progress in their lives or careers; the destruction of meaningful human relationships and isolation from the human community; constant temptations to suicide or to other crimes. Sometimes the possessed individual will even experience the presence of "someone" that is with him every day and harasses him without him knowing why or being able to explain it to anyone.

For such people, medical treatments and medications will generally give them little or no relief, much as the woman with the hemorrhage exhausted all her savings at the hands of doctors for a dozen years without effect.[25] They will often react ferociously to the recitation of prayers, placing of relics on their

---
25 Cf. Mk 5:26

body, sprinkling of holy water, use of holy images, etc., and when in a possessed state their eyes will roll up or down into the head showing only the whites. Their possessed state will sometimes be accompanied by a horrible stench in the room and/or a severe drop in temperature with no notable external change in the weather and the shouting of horrible obscenities. On rare occasions the person may levitate.

In short, people severely afflicted with demons live in a state of ongoing physical and mental torment which very few people can understand. They will often either be afraid to reveal these inner problems to another for fear that they will be labeled psychotic or because they think that no one will believe them or want to help them. When someone from the Church will actually listen to them and take them seriously, they are given hope.

12. How does the Church determine that a person has a demon but is not fully possessed?

Testing and discernment is needed by the priest and his team to assess whether a person has a serious enough demonic problem to warrant an appeal to the diocese for exorcism or whether the individual can be helped through deliverance prayer sessions. This is the great challenge of discernment, which, as I have mentioned, is the hardest part of deliverance and exorcism ministry. However, it is not impossible to make the distinctions between full possession and lesser forms of obsession. English exorcist Fr. Jeremy Davies has an insightful paragraph in his new booklet on exorcism regarding some of the things to look for as signs of obsession:

> Obsessions may be disturbances of the mind and heart (e.g., aversions, fixations, paranoias, depressions, fears, delusions, self-glorifications, complacencies, sloth and other temptations and trials); or they may be 'psychic'/'soulish' (e.g., hal-

lucinations, locutions, deductions, blows, a sense of an evil presence); or they may be physical (e.g., illnesses, as in *Luke* 4:39). The Devil commonly seeks to exploit our natural weaknesses and so the discernment of the demonic by no means rules out the co-existence of spiritual, moral and psychological factors.[26]

Authentic deliverance prayer deals with obsessions proper and is always seen as part of a process of evangelization and conversion, not just a process of fighting with or casting out demons. Deliverance from demonic presences also requires the full cooperation of the individual and is not just something the deliverance ministers do.

13. What types of demonic manifestations do we see in people who are obsessed and need only deliverance?

When demons have gained access to the person *to a lesser degree*, the most common manifestations (usually during prayer) are bodily shaking or agitation, discomfort in certain organs or parts of the body, mental confusion or hazy vision, pressure in the chest or heart, sometimes temporary nausea, etc. Usually the person will remain awake during the prayer, although his mind may be dulled somewhat, but he will be able to dialogue with those helping him and cooperate consciously with the prayer of deliverance. Afterwards, the person will often express an immediate sense of relief or the feeling that he has been "released" from a bondage of some sort.

Short of full possession, demons may be *more deeply rooted or powerful*, and in such cases the manifestations may be more intense or diverse: blanking out, screaming, at times snake-like movements of the body or writhing (which should be physi-

---

[26] Rev. Jeremy Davies, *Exorcism: Understanding Exorcism in Scripture and Practice*, The Incorporated Catholic Truth Society: London, England, 2008, p. 27.

cally controlled by the helpers), grimaces, retching or coughing, short-term severe agitation, severe discomfort in certain organs or parts of the body, and other such phenomena. However, if these types of more intense manifestations endure without any demons being cast out, they should be taken as signs of likely possession, and the priest or deliverance minister should refer the case to the diocese for exorcism.

14. What is the "line of demarcation" between deliverance and exorcism?

I believe that there are two ways to look at the difference between obsession and possession. Both ways attempt to quantify the strength of the demon by some sign or measure.

The first point of demarcation between exorcism and deliverance is usually when an independent spiritual entity begins to *speak* through the person's body. This is not an infallible sign of possession because many lesser demons speak also, but speaking usually indicates that a demon is more deeply rooted in the individual and has a greater measure of control.

The second point of demarcation, related in some way to the first, is the amount of actual visible control that the demon asserts over the individual. This can be assessed by whether or not the person can voluntarily cooperate in his own deliverance process and for how long, or whether the demon is so strong that he constantly "takes over" by overpowering the person's faculties, causing the person to go unconscious, etc. In such a case, it is likely that a higher-level demon is present that needs exorcism. Lower-level demons will have less control and will manifest their presences by various forms of persecution and harassments that do not reach the point of entirely controlling a person's body or faculties.

15. In general how does the Church distinguish between demonic influences and mental/psychological disorders?

The short answer to this question is that it is extremely difficult to distinguish the two at times. Demonic presences can coexist with and trigger or exacerbate the existing natural problems, while masking the spiritual problems underneath. Every exorcist knows that performing exorcisms is the simplest part of liberating a person from the power of the devil: the most difficult part of the exorcism process is the hard work of carefully discerning the root cause of a person's problem.

In very general terms, a person with a mental illness will be unable to remain connected to "reality" without the help of psychotropic drugs, and prayer will not help the person significantly. Likewise, if it is truly a case of psychological illness, it will get worse over time if it is not controlled with medication or therapy. Conversely, for persons with true demonic problems, medications and therapy will not work significantly but prayer will usually alleviate their pain and suffering in some way, at least temporarily. Beyond these general terms, it is difficult to explain where the line between mental/psychological and spiritual problems lies: it has to be discerned in each individual case.

Nowadays exorcists are much more inclined to work with competent healthcare officials in the healing of afflicted individuals, because the vast majority of people with demonic problems also have other human problems which should be treated by medical or psychological professionals. As has been stated before, where necessary, science and the Church should work together for the good of the whole person. When priests play psychologist and therapists play spiritual advisors, the true good of the person is not served.

16. What is a person to do if he suspects that he or a loved one suffers from demonic problems?

If someone suspects demonic problems in himself or a loved one, the first thing to do is to intensify the person's life of faith. This may not be possible due to persistent serious sin or some other personal dysfunction. People who live disordered lives often need true conversion of heart and reform of life more than they need an exorcism. However, it is the consistent experience of exorcists that most people need a much stronger faith life, which will go very far in diminishing the influence of the devil. There is no substitute for obeying the basic dictates of the Gospel.

If the problems persist, the person should seek some form of therapy and/or medical help as a means of ongoing discernment to "get to the root of things"[27] and to try to understand the underlying cause or causes of these problems. In time and with professional help, the person may gain great insight into his situation and find an appropriate treatment if the causes are natural.

Spiritual direction helps a great deal if one can find a competent priest or pastoral minister to give direction in situations like these. The vast majority of what are interpreted as demonic problems are resolved by short-term pastoral care, exhortation to conversion of heart and a bit of solid faith advice and prayer from a spiritual professional. Only after a serious analysis of the problem, deliverance prayer and a solid understanding of demonic possession should the priest present the case to the bishop for approval of exorcism.

Let us pray that the Lord will send more ministers of exorcism into His vineyard of souls who are suffering from demonic

---

27 My accompanying booklet to this work, called *Discernment Manual for Exorcists and Deliverance Ministers,* highlights "getting to the root of things" as the critical and main work of discernment. Please go to the website of Human Life International, www.hli.org, to order a copy.

persecution. The priestly ministry of comforting the spiritually sick is a vital part of *cura animarum*, the care of souls, for which we are ordained.

17. If demons can infest both persons or localities, how can you tell, in any given situation, whether a demonic problem is related to the person or the place?

In problems that seem to be located in places, if many people who inhabit the same place experience or observe the same demonic phenomena independent of each other, then, generally speaking, the problem is most likely related to the place itself. However, if the demonic problem "travels" with some afflicted person, or keeps showing up in different environments where the person is, then it is most likely *his* problem and not an infestation of some place. It can be difficult to tell which is which at times, especially in very complex or dysfunctional situations, but these two criteria generally apply. If it is not apparent at first whether a given situation is a personal or local infestation, then a greater emphasis on prayer and petitioning for understanding will always bring the matter to light.

Afterword to Chapter 4
Eight Degrees of Difficulty in Expelling Demons

As an aid to discernment, the list below describes the varying degrees of time and effort required to expel demons in different situations. The scenarios rank the degree of difficulty in ascending order from the "easiest" to the most difficult. They also describe briefly the means necessary and the optimal circumstances needed in the expulsion process. Since there are so many factors assisting or blocking liberation, this list is only meant as a reference point for discernment and not as an exact description of all possible scenarios of liberation.

Children—children can become possessed or obsessed primarily due to victimization by adults or direct curses. Because they are innocent and immature, the mind, emotions and will are not deeply bonded to the demons; and so the demons are generally the easiest to expel, as long as the victimization of the child is not enduring or related to Satanic Ritual Abuse, as will be described below. The expulsion process requires the faith-filled participation of caring adults close to the child, with the help of professionals where possible. All involved must express a profound love for the child and communicate an absolute assurance of safety in the prayer process. If the liberation requires multiple prayer sessions, it is very important to give ongoing explanations and solid catechesis to the child, helping him to call upon his guardian angel and his innate sensitivity to God as a help to liberation. In no way is the child to be held responsible for this problem; nor should the burden be placed on him to try to resolve it. A demonically-afflicted child is, by definition, a victim and must never be made to feel blamed for his affliction. All that a child usually needs for complete liberation from demons is a great deal of love, safety and persevering prayer on the part of loving adults.

Absorption—some persons have a frightful capacity to literally "absorb" demonic presences or curses through the senses, passions or faculties of the soul; this phenomenon is a fact of nature more than an artifice of demons. They would be described as "sensitives." This capacity represents a natural openness to the spiritual world which may not be mature or disciplined for good and, as such, turns into a vulnerability to evil. While technically speaking, such persons also have a strong potential for prayer and profound holiness, demons can take advantage of this innate receptivity to work their mischief. If such a person willfully (through sin or invitation) brings the direct invasion of unclean spirits on himself, the infestation can be serious and harmful. If the person picks up evil spirits by proximity to occult things and cursing, then the infestation is usually less serious but can still be harmful if it goes on long enough and is not addressed properly. Intrusions of this type are usually not deep and can be cleansed through deliverance prayer, even if it takes some time for the full number of demons to be revealed and expelled. These are not cases of full possession due to the superficial penetration of the evil, but the demons can cause a lot of pain while present. Such people can be helped with persevering prayer which aims to ferret out all unclean presences and admonishes the individual to strive for ongoing conversion and faith.

They should also be taught a serious prayer regimen and ways to reduce their own innate vulnerability to future demonic intrusions and persons who could harm them. They should have healing prayer to follow liberation.

Adolescents and Dabbling—young people make many mistakes and open themselves up to the power of unclean spirits, especially given the modern youth culture that is saturated with the occult. With cooperation, true repentance and a serious commitment to a life of faith, they can be liberated fairly quickly, due to the lack of deep penetration of the spirits into their lives, presuming that they are only dabblers and that the activity was not serious or sustained over years. Here it is important to distinguish the strength of the demon from the level of its penetration. Dabbling can open doors to more powerful demons, but it does not mean that the case is one of full possession, and the liberation of the person can be swift despite the power of the demon. In these cases, the fight is usually *furious* but of a shorter duration. Likewise, adults who "dabble" in occult things for entertainment or with very little intent to commit themselves to a life of evil can be liberated fairly quickly due to the superficiality of the attachment. Again, cooperation with grace, together with a serious desire to turn away from evil and "learn your lesson" is usually sufficient to expel these demons and give the person relief. The greatest determining factor for deliverance is usually the desire of the person to totally separate himself from evil and sin.

Childhood Trauma and Emotional Woundedness—I place these phenomena together since most serious emotional woundedness usually begins in childhood. I exclude here true cases of Satanic Ritual Abuse (see below). Emotional woundedness at any time in life can be a doorway to evil spirits, especially if the wounding experiences had some pernicious sin or occult forces behind them. The demons enter through wounds, traumas and abuses that people suffer and can be among the more difficult to expel because they are "attached" to traumatic events, memories and wounds that must be healed as part of the liberation process. Sometimes, but not always, the person gives unconscious permission for demons to stay. He may be afraid of the changes that will be required of him if the demon were to leave, or he may be unwilling to address some deep and painful wounds to which the demons are attached. Such deep, unconscious permissions must be uncovered and withdrawn in order for the demon to be expelled. *Spiritual healing alone* will not be sufficient to expel these demons because of the level of their attachment to emotional woundedness. Generally speaking, the longer the person has lived in this state, the more "impacted" or "intertwined" the demon is with the personality and therefore the more difficult it is to resolve. Here, it is best to have a prayer team (strictly spiritual) work in conjunction with serious therapy (by a trained professional) to achieve full healing, which usually takes a great deal of time. The liberation process is tied to the growth process.

In such cases there is always hope that the unclean spirits can be expelled in full, given the willingness of the patient to grow and the proper application of the dual process of healing.

Psychological and Mental Problems—demons take advantage of human weaknesses such as actual mental and emotional defects and can attach themselves to these defects in a way that makes them very difficult to dislodge. In situations of distinct psychiatric problems that have evil spirits attached, the healing process is similar to the above (professional and spiritual help together) but may be very difficult to undo if the natural problem is very severe. Discernment is needed to sort out what elements of the problem are spiritual and what are natural, and so the cooperation of professionals is necessary here. Since the possibility of deception and self-deception is greater in psychiatric cases, these situations require much patience and much effort, often yielding few results. Even where the expulsion of a demon is achieved, the natural problem may still remain and must be addressed professionally. However, nothing is impossible with God, and the person's cooperation with grace can bring full liberation from demonic forces if he has the right healing team and a great deal of patience.

Addictions—addictions add an extra element to the previous categories of emotional and psychiatric woundedness and can be healed in the same way, except that the addiction must receive a special focus of the healing program. Many of these cases can be pernicious and irresolvable due to the nature of an addiction, which enslaves and isolates a person. It is unwise to attribute all addictions to demons, but sometimes a demon is responsible for an addiction, and when the demon is expelled, the addiction may disappear. This is rare however. More often than not, the addiction has a natural cause but may have a demon that gives it extra force. It has to be treated then with something like a 12-step program or a major effort at renouncing the addiction in order for the spiritual and emotional healing to take place. Demons of addiction are difficult to expel due to the level of slavery of the will, deception of the mind and life dysfunction. Even the best 12-step programs have small success and high recidivism rates, so it is best to demand that the person have a true desire to overcome the addictive impulses and bind himself to complete accountability for his sobriety. Unless a person is willing to get rid of his addiction, the exorcist should not waste time on him and should treat him like the 12-step programs treat those who are not serious about recovery. These situations need a great deal of coordination with helping teams and loved ones, and require a great deal of patience.

Deep Occult Involvement—when a person has been deeply involved in occult activities such as New Age, witchcraft and Satanism, the key factor in healing is always the level of repentance of the person and the degree to which he is willing to purify his life and turn to Christ. While there may be deep emotional wounds or satanic abuse that were the origin of the possession, these can be healed in the ways described in this chapter, but the will of the person needs to be purified and converted to God. This is never easy since for such persons there always remains a temptation toward the dark side, even when liberated. Here we are dealing with people who made a commitment to the occult or sold their souls to the Evil One and invited or experienced a penetration of spirits that goes beyond the mere dabbler. These are technically the "professionals" in the practice of evil, and the liberation will be more difficult because the demonic enslavement was or is greater. Such persons may have been perpetrators of horrible evils on others, which make it more difficult for them to "get out" of their evil associations and bonds; or perhaps the devil has too much of a claim on them, or they are too seduced by the thirst for power to let go of their demons. Even when someone *in the depths of his heart* wishes to be free, he may not desire it enough to make a sufficient act of will to ask for it. However, the Lord offers everyone, even the most confirmed Satanist, sufficient grace for conversion, and such persons can, with time and persistent application of prayer, be healed. One caution, however: the exorcist is never, under any circumstances, to trust a former Satanist or allow him to take any position in the Church unless and until the conversion process is long-standing and complete. Only in rare cases has the Church ever seen such a complete victory over Satanism. The history of Blessed Bartolo Longo (1841-1926) who was at one time the high priest of a Satanic cult and was converted by the Rosary, is by all accounts, an exception. Exorcists must, however, be willing to help those who wish to convert from a life of such darkness and slavery.

Satanic Ritual Abuse—children born into witchcraft covens or Satanic cult families are initiated into the respective cult groups through satanic rituals and consecrations. They are the most difficult to heal. The physical and emotional trauma of the rituals, inflicted from the earliest childhood, even from the womb, is so extreme that it fractures the personality and deliberately hands the child over to complete possession and ownership by the demons of the cult. These seriously wounded individuals are complete victims in every sense of the word and undoubtedly need the compassionate pastoral care of the Church. They cannot, however, be healed by exorcism *alone*. Here we have individuals who are profoundly emotionally-wounded, mind-controlled by the cult and have virulent spiritual forces inside them that resist any healing process. Such persons need several elements working together for a full healing to take place. First, they need to make a total separation from all cult activity and persons actively involved in their abuse. Second, they need a skilled therapist who is knowledgeable in treating Dissociative Identity Disorder (DID, formerly known as Multiple Personality Disorder). They also need a skilled exorcist, regular prayer sessions and a support team that will apply the full range of the Church's spiritual resources to their case. The purpose of a designated support team is to re-initiate the individual into a healthy community of strong, loving relationships and tangible support that comes from true Christian fraternity. They have a long healing journey ahead of them and need as much support and affirmation as possible. As with all demonic afflictions, healing is only possible with God's grace and with the full cooperation of the individual. Full healing can take years of hard work by all involved, but it is truly possible.

A Final Word about "Perfect Possession"

Malachi Martin's description of "perfect possession" in Chapter 2, Question 25 accurately describes this state. In essence, the term describes a person who has made the intentional decision to subjugate his will to the devil and who lives in a state of total possession by a controlling spirit or spirits. Furthermore, he is a person who is perfectly aware of the eternal consequences of his decision and perseveres in that state with full knowledge and consent of the will. Perfectly possessed people look like "normal" human beings and may often be well-respected members of the community, often wielding great power and influence, even if on a smaller scale. These individuals are the walking damned, and they cannot be helped, nor will they come for help from the exorcist, except perhaps to test him or persecute him. Exorcists will do well to "test" all spirits in turn when they suspect that they are in the presence of such a person and dismiss all such insidious individuals as soon as they are exposed for what they are. While our Church recognizes that every human being is free to choose his own salvation even up to the very last moment of bodily life, such people don't want to be saved. An exorcist should not have any illusion that he can "save" them but should leave these servants of the devil in the hands of Almighty God and pray to the Holy Spirit for their conversion. Beyond that, there is nothing that can be done for them, and no one should be so foolish as to try.

Chapter 5
Healing and Deliverance

Finally, draw your strength from the Lord and his mighty power. Put on the armor of God so that you may be able to stand firm against the tactics of the devil. Our battle is not against human forces but against the principalities and powers, the rulers of this world of darkness, the evil spirits in regions above. You must put on the armor of God if you are to resist on the evil day; do all that your duty requires, and hold your ground. (Eph 6:10-13)

Not only did wondrous healings confirm the power of the Gospel proclamation in Apostolic times, but the New Testament refers also to Jesus' real and proper transmission of the power to heal illnesses to his Apostles and to the first preachers of the Gospel. In the call of the Twelve to their first mission, according to the accounts of Matthew and Luke, the Lord gave them "the power to drive out unclean spirits and to cure every disease and illness" (Mt 10:1; cf. Lk 9:1).... The power to heal, therefore, is given within a missionary context, not for their own exaltation, but to confirm their mission. (Congregation for the Doctrine of the Faith, *Instruction on Prayers for Healing*, 2000.)[1]

---

1 *Op. cit.*, September 14th, 2000.

✣

1. What is the Church's concept of healing?

The Church understands healing not only as a medical process which seeks the physical healing of sickness or injury. That is the proper role of medical science. The Church understands healing in a more comprehensive way, namely, as an expression of Christ's liberation of man from the grip of evil. Our Lord manifested power over Satan's kingdom through His authority over natural forces and demonic spirits; other signs of Christ's Kingdom were His power to heal and forgive sins, powers which He granted to His Church. Healing, then, can be spiritual, emotional or physical[2] in accord with the three dimensions of the human person, "spirit, soul and body."[3]

2. What is the Church's concept of deliverance?

Power to cast out demons is one of the "signs" that accompanies those who profess Christian faith. The Church sees deliverance from evil spirits as an action or a ministry which aims at the liberation of an individual from the influence of *demons of lesser strength*. Deliverance is an exercise of Christian authority that is rooted in Baptism. Someone who prays for another person to be delivered from the presence or activity of evil spirits is simply acting in his baptismal capacity as spiritual "priest, prophet and king," which bestows on baptized persons a certain authority over evil. This authority has its origin in Jesus' Will for all of His followers: "Signs like these will accompany those who have professed their faith: they will use my name to expel demons...."[4] Indeed, the Lord's Prayer concludes with a deliverance prayer asking the Father that He might "deliver us from

---
2   Francis MacNutt, *Healing*, Ave Maria Press: Notre Dame, IN, 1999, pp. 129 ff.
3   1 Thes 5:23
4   Mk 16:17-18

evil." Deliverance, then, is any spiritual victory over sin, death and demons.

The concept of "deliverance from evil" presumes that hostile spiritual forces are arrayed against souls to keep them from entering into the blessedness of heaven. The Church's saints and the long tradition of mystical and ascetical works bear constant witness to the need for deliverance from the three forces that separate us from God: the world, the flesh and the devil. Here we can cite the desert fathers symbolized by St. Anthony and his battle with demons; the mystical Carmelite tradition symbolized by St. John of the Cross and St. Theresa of Avila; such ascetical and spiritual classics as *The Ladder of Divine Ascent*, *The Cloud of Unknowing*, the *Spiritual Exercises*, and *The Imitation of Christ*, not to mention the writings and other works of countless saints. In other words, Church history shows that one need not be an exorcist priest to pray deliverance prayers: one need only be on a serious journey to heaven.

3. Why does the Church have two forms of dealing with demonic entities, exorcism and deliverance?

The priest receives a certain spiritual power to bless at his ordination. The power to bless is intrinsic to the Sacrament of Holy Orders. He may exercise that power in the solemn liturgical rite of exorcism, which is reserved only for cases of certified demonic possession. However, if solemn exorcism were the only way he could help people overcome the power of evil, then he would not be much of a help to the vast majority who need it! He may also exercise his power to bless in a more spontaneous way through deliverance and healing prayers. Most people with demonic problems have not reached the state of possession, and so the priest's priestly power to bless is helpful to them without the need to seek formal authorization from the bishop. The two types of demonic situations are just two different ways for him to express his priestly power to bless. The authority to pray for deliverance is inherent in the "priesthood of the faithful" as well, as has been mentioned.[5]

4. Which is more common: deliverance or exorcism?

Deliverance is a much more common pastoral practice due to the nature of the devil's influence on human beings. The devil is only allowed to work on people with their permission. He works by deception and stealth and eventually causes great pain and chaos in the lives of his victims. They wake up to him eventually and either repent or seek help. Even when a demon has the person's cooperation in the works of evil, it usually takes a great deal of time for him and his minions to gain a foothold or to build a stronghold in a person that grows to the level of full possession. While there are cases of people becoming seriously possessed through rather minimal contact with great spiritual evil, in most cases, it requires time for them to cede that much power and control over their interior lives to the demon. Virtually all exorcists will categorize the majority of their work as deliverance rather than exorcism.

5. What priority did healing have in the Public Ministry of Jesus?

Even the most superficial reading of the Gospels will show that Jesus constantly healed people of their physical infirmities, even to the point of personal exhaustion. He was often aware that "healing went out of him"[6] and spent whole days doing nothing but healing the sick. Healing, together with casting out demons and announcing the Good News of the Kingdom of God, was among the first "signs" of His power to bring people to salvation

---

5 Cf. Chapter 3, Question 8.
6 Mk 5:30

and so had the highest priority in His Public Ministry. In fact, the last miracle He performed before He was put to death was the healing of the severed ear of the soldier who came to imprison Him.[7] After the Resurrection, His disciples pointed out that "He went about doing good works and healing all who were in the grip of the devil."[8] Thus, His healing power was manifested in varied ways: by the forgiveness of sins, the call to conversion, the curing of bodies and the casting out of demons.

6. How do we know that He handed on the healing ministry to His Church?

The will of the Lord to hand on the ministry of healing to His Church is manifested from the very beginning of the proclamation of the Good News by the Apostles, even before His death. Above all, the Gospel says that the Lord commanded His disciples to heal. When He sent the seventy-two out on mission, He said to them, "Into whatever city you go, after they welcome you, eat what they set before you, and cure the sick there."[9] The disciples followed His directive, anointed the sick with oil and "worked many cures."[10]

After the Ascension, the Apostles manifested a prodigious ministry of healing, always "in the Name of Jesus." The princes of the Apostles, Peter and Paul, are healers in the Acts of the Apostles: both cured a lame man;[11] both cured bed-ridden men with severe infirmities;[12] the personal presence or touch of each

---

7 Lk 22:50-51
8 Acts 10:38
9 Lk 10:8-9
10 Mk 6:13
11 Acts 3:1 ff. and 14:8 ff.
12 Acts 9:32 ff. and 28:7 ff.

was healing;[13] crowds came to be healed by them,[14] and both raised someone from the dead.[15]

The ministry of healing soon took on a sacramental dimension in the life of the Church and is manifested in the two sacraments called by the *Catechism of the Catholic Church* the Sacraments of Healing: Penance[16] and Anointing of the Sick.[17] It is important to note, however, that Christian healing is not limited to priests, nor to these Sacraments; it is a command and prerogative of all the faithful. Many today, particularly in the Charismatic Renewal, continue the healing work of Christ in the Church through spiritual healing and deliverance ministries.

Finally, it is important to note that the Church has always considered suffering, when accepted in faith, to be a means for the sanctification of souls. This does not mean, however, that God wishes people to suffer with a positive Will. Rather, Christians accept it as redemptive and as part of the economy of salvation and at the same time see healing from suffering and sickness as a part of the proclamation of the good news of hope for the world.[18]

---

13 Acts 5:12 ff. and 19:11 ff.
14 Acts 5:16 and 28:9
15 Acts 9:36 ff. and 20:7 ff. and MacNutt, *Healing.*, pp. 44-45.
16 Jn 20:21-23
17 The following passage from the Epistle of James (5: 14-26a) is perhaps the most famous reference to healing in the New Testament: "Is there anyone sick among you? He should ask for the presbyters of the church. They in turn are to pray over him, anointing him with oil in the Name of the Lord. This prayer uttered in faith will reclaim the one who is ill, and the Lord will restore him to health. If he has committed any sins, forgiveness will be his. Hence, declare your sins to one another, and pray for one another, that you may find healing."
18 Congregation for the Doctrine of the Faith, *Instruction on Prayers for Healing*, September 14, 2000, I.1.

7. What are the four types of prayer needed to heal body, soul and spirit?

"Faith healing" has a negative connotation in the modern age due to some of its practitioners who give it a bad name, but, in reality, faith is the greatest resource for all types of healing. Christ came to save the whole person—body, soul and spirit—from the grip of the devil.[19] There are four types of prayers for healing:

Spiritual sickness falls into two categories: sin and demonic infestation. Prayer can help the spiritually sick person to be healed. The prayer needed to liberate someone from sin is *prayer of repentance*. The person himself can pray or others can pray for his repentance from sin. For demonic infestation, the prayer needed to set a person free is *prayer of deliverance* (or exorcism depending upon the severity of the demonic problem).

Emotional sickness, whether psychological or mental, can be healed through *prayers for inner healing*. This prayer is oriented toward healing of inner distressed states and memories related to them or memories of traumatic experiences. Prayer of this type can be of great advantage when accompanied by Christian therapy. Priests and deliverance ministers should have both a minimum knowledge of some of the more serious disorders as well as access to trusted professionals for a complete program of healing.

Physical sickness can sometimes be healed through *prayers for physical healing*. Even today many people are healed of their physical infirmities through faith healings of one type or another.

While it is true that sickness can be a cross we carry in life, we must not just *presume* that God wants us to suffer with in-

---
[19] MacNutt, *Healing*, p. 130.

ternal or external pain. He came to set us free from such afflictions. St. Matthew quotes Isaiah in giving us the true character of Christ's compassionate love for His people: "He expelled the spirits by a simple command and cured all who were afflicted, thereby fulfilling what had been said through Isaiah the prophet: 'It was our infirmities he bore, our sufferings he endured.'"[20]

8. What are healing services?

These are prayer services that bring the healing power of Jesus Christ to the brokenness of the human condition, and they can be large or small in scale. The most common form of healing services today is charismatic prayer meetings where people gather to sing, listen to Scripture and preaching, pray intensely for the needs of those present, sometimes anoint persons with oil (distinct from the Sacrament of the Sick which can only be administered by a priest) and discern the Will of God for individuals and for communities.

In recent years, non-charismatic-style healing services and retreats are being conducted for women (and men) going through post-abortion healing programs. The pioneer in post-abortion healing is the one-on-one counseling offered through the Project Rachel program, but there are also retreat experiences that attempt to release the person from any demons that are attached to the experience of abortion trauma and heal the profound wounds that are caused by that demonic industry. Many have experienced a sort of deliverance from evil spirits in these retreats. Once again, the deliverance from an evil spirit is distinct from the healing of the wounds caused by the evil presence, but deliverance and healing often go together in the same post-abortion "healing service."

---

20 Mt 8:17

9. Does the Church have any regulations regarding healing services?

Yes. Building on the 1985 document from the Congregation for the Doctrine of the Faith, clarifying the limits of exorcism in public prayer services,[21] the same Congregation released an *Instruction on Prayers for Healing* on September 14th, 2000 as a way to curb abuses that had accrued in the practice of charismatic healing services since the 1970s. It is an excellent document which recognizes the Church's legitimate ministry of healing as a sign of Christ's ongoing healing presence in the world and gives ten guidelines for the discipline of this ministry. The ten disciplinary norms for healing services[22] show the Church's desire to regulate this practice in order to avoid abuses and to unleash the true healing potential of the Church.

10. How are deliverance prayers prayed?

Deliverance prayer is any spontaneous prayer pronounced by a trained lay person, group or priest which attempts to free another person of some lesser demonic influence than full demonic possession. Deliverance prayers are always prayed "in the Name of Jesus," Who is the true source of authority behind any deliverance from evil.[23] We are all familiar with the Lord's Prayer asking that God may "deliver us from evil,"[24] and that is the paradigm for deliverance prayers as such. God is the one who delivers us from evil. The "deliverance ministers" are those who bring that authority to bear over the life of an afflicted individual in the Name of Jesus.

---

21 Congregation for the Doctrine of the Faith, *Inde Ab Aliquot Annis*, September 29, 1985.
22 Cf. Appendix F.
23 Cf. Mk 16:17-18
24 Mt 6:13

We cannot ignore the fact that the individual must always be a willing and faithful participant in these types of prayers. The individual's participation is not just passive, as if the deliverance ministers or priest were there to wave a magic wand and dissipate all the problems in a person's life. The afflicted person is required to go through a sometimes difficult process of conversion in which he must humbly repent of sin, forgive those who may have harmed him, exercise certain Christian virtues like humility and perseverance, and deepen his life of faith. Deliverance is not Christian magic: it is fundamentally a process of conversion and growth in holiness by confronting the evils of this world and of an individual's life, all in the context of prayer.

11. What is the "pastoral approach" to deliverance ministry?

There are several models of deliverance prayer which fit into what may be described as a "pastoral approach" to this important ministry. All of these models have several things in common: prayer and discernment with teams; the emphasis placed on the person himself as the main proponent of his own deliverance; and the focus on identifying the sources of bondage and addressing them with the tools of the Christian faith. These methods seek to remove the "legal" basis by which a demon may have entered a person's body or life. In the process, the person learns ways to take authority over his own life and rectify the distortions that led to or allow a demonic presence to remain.

The important difference from the ministry of exorcism is the emphasis on personal responsibility and active involvement in the process of liberation from an evil spirit. This process has much more to do with Christian evangelization, personal conversion of heart and sanctification than it does with freeing a victim of an aggressive evil force. Deliverance ministry here is conceived of as a sort of spiritual therapy or spiritual medication rather than as major surgery, which is one of the main analogies for exorcism. While a person's consent is necessary to conduct an exorcism, nonetheless, it is understood that the person will be less able to free himself from a true possession in the way that can be done in deliverance.

12. Does the Church forbid lay people from commanding demons directly?

The Church forbids lay people from conducting exorcisms,[25] but it is not easy to give a black and white answer to the above question since Church documents leave gaps and ambiguities. There are several ways to evaluate this question: first let us look at it *theologically* and *scripturally*.

Theologically, there does not seem to be any *absolute* restriction on believing Christians from commanding (and, by extension, entering into conflict with and expelling) demons: the Gospel of Mark says the ability to cast out demons in His Name is a sign of discipleship,[26] and it does not limit that to the ordained clergy. The Greek phrase used in the passage in Mark about the disciples, i.e., "those who believe," literally says that "they will expel demons" (δαιμόνια εκβαλοῦσιν, daimónia ekbaloúsin). In the early church there is evidence that the laity performed exorcisms in the Name of Jesus as a charismatic ministry that was unrestricted as to title and office.[27] As emphasized above, the authority to pray for deliverance from evil spirits is rooted in Baptism and exercised by virtue of the person's own individual faith in Jesus, not on behalf of the Church as a solemn rite.

---

25 Cf. Chapter 3, Question 8.
26 Mk 16:17
27 Fr. Jeffrey S. Grob, *A Major Revision of the Discipline on Exorcism: A Comparative Study of the Liturgical Laws in the 1614 and 1998 Rites of Exorcism*, Archdiocese of Chicago: unpublished doctoral thesis, 2006, p. 55.

A scriptural distinction may give us a more precise understanding of this, though. Luke 9:1-2, and its related passages in Matthew (10:1) and Mark (6:7), show the Lord sending out "the Twelve" with the mission to preach, to heal, and "to have authority over demons [or 'unclean spirits']." All three passages use the term "authority" (εξουσία, exousía) to describe the Apostles' mode of dealing with demons. The passage in Matthew actually uses the term "to expel" (εκβάλειν, ekbálein), and Luke says the Lord gave them "power" (δύναμις, dúnamis) as well as "authority." Then, the next chapter in Luke (10:1) shows the Lord sending out "a further seventy-two" to preach and to heal like the Twelve. In that case, however, the commission to *take authority* over demons is not expressly given to the mass of disciples.

In other words, a divine commission to take authority over (i.e., to command) the powers of hell seems to have been given specifically to "the Twelve" and not to the rest of His disciples as such. The expulsion of demons at the end of Mark's Gospel is noted by the evangelist as a "sign" that accompanies those who believe, but not as a specific commission by the Lord to all disciples. These passages may be the theological basis for the recognition that lay people can indeed enter into combat with demons but that they do not have the *full authority* that the Lord had given to the Twelve for spiritual combat.

It is interesting to note that the 1999 revision of the *Rite of Exorcism* contains a novelty that does not appear in the 1614 ritual. An appendix of private prayers was added that could be used "by the faithful" (*a fidelibus*) in their "wrestling against the powers of darkness" (*in colluctatione contra potestates tenebrarum*). This is pretty amazing! They are all prayers and litanies to God that are not direct commands to demons, but the fact that this collection of ten prayers was added to the official exorcism ritual of the Church may be seen as something very positive.

13. What specific restrictions does the Church put on the laity, then?

Looking at the question *pastorally* and *canonically*, we may gain some greater understanding about the role of the laity versus the ordained clergy in the field of deliverance.

Because the Church has a long history of care of souls, the ministry of exorcism began to be gradually systematized into a stable "order of exorcist" beginning in the third and fourth centuries for various reasons, not the least of which was to curb abuses.[28] Indeed, Church authority always has the responsibility to make prudential judgments about how charisms will be channeled into ministries and how these gifts will be "officially" exercised in the life of the Church for their greatest spiritual fruitfulness. The Church can thus restrict, for pastoral and canonical reasons, the practice of its solemn rites. Note that here we speak of the Western (i.e., Roman Catholic) Church only, since most Eastern Churches consider the practice of exorcism to be a charismatic gift and do not regulate it canonically.[29]

The one constraint to the laity that is entirely clear is the canonical restriction of solemn exorcism to ordained priests who have authorization from the diocesan bishop.[30] Since priests share in the power to "bind and loose"[31] through ordination, they can exercise that spiritual power in ways that lay people cannot: for example, through sacraments such as Confession and Anointing

---

28 Grob, *op. cit.*, pp. 56-59. Fr. Grob says that another likely reason for the limitation of the ministry was the Church's regular habit of standardizing and institutionalizing ministries as the centuries passed. I do not share the almost scathing opinion of Francis MacNutt that Church authorities virtually stamped out the healing and exorcistic charisms of the Holy Spirit in order to assert more control over people. That opinion ignores the Church's right and duty to protect people from spiritual harm by regulating the use of sacraments and sacramentals.
29 *Ibid.*, pp. 57-58.
30 Canon 1372 in the 1983 *Code of Canon Law*.
31 Cf. Mt 16:19

of the Sick and through sacramentals such as solemn exorcisms and other private adjurations and commands to unclean spirits.

Other documents seem to place further restrictions on the public practice of exorcism/deliverance. The 1985 instruction from the Congregation of the Doctrine of the Faith, *Inde Ab Aliquot Annis*, prohibits "those who lack the required power"[32] (i.e., untrained persons without some kind of Church mandate) from leading public "assemblies" and interacting with demons in such a way that the demons are "directly disturbed and an attempt is made to determine their identity."[33] This type of confrontation is reserved to the exorcism rite or the realm of private deliverances with trained ministers. The instruction concerns only public prayer services in which deliverance and exorcism is practiced. The 2000 document of the same Congregation, mentioned in Question 8, *Instruction on Prayers for Healing*, offered a necessary clarification—not necessarily a further restriction—that exorcisms and deliverances were never to be practiced in the context of a Catholic Mass or other prayer service.

While these restrictions exist for the sake of protecting good order and the spiritual welfare of the faithful,[34] Christians may make certain acts of *one-way commanding, binding and rebuking* of demons as a way of spiritually protecting persons from demonic influences, as will be described in the next question.

14. What are examples of deliverance prayers and commands?

There are many types of legitimate deliverance prayers that any disciple of Jesus Christ may practice:

---

32 *Op cit.*, n. 3.
33 *Ibid.*
34 Cf. Congregation for the Doctrine of the Faith, *On the Current Norms Governing Exorcism* (*Inde Ab Aliquot Annis*), 1985 and *Instruction on Prayers for Healing*, 2000.

Deprecative (i.e., petitioning) prayers: These are prayers to the Lord asking Him to intervene to help loose someone from the power of evil. The cry of the human heart at times shouts, "Lord, deliver us from evil!" It is also the foundation of our humility before God; we recognize that we cannot save ourselves. When we ask Him to free another person from the power of evil, we act like the friends who opened a hole in the roof and let down the paralytic on a mat before Jesus.[35] Jesus sees our faith and answers our prayer in some way. Any prayer of this sort can be addressed to God the Father, God the Son, God the Holy Spirit or the Most Holy Trinity.

> *Sample prayer: Come Lord Jesus, come, and deliver us from evil. Free Jean of the power of the curse which is oppressing her and causing her to lose faith, hope and charity in her time of need. Give her the strength and courage to fight this influence of evil and fill her with your peace which surpasses all understanding. Amen.*

Prayers asking the intercession of the angels and saints: It is well known that certain saints and angels are considered adept at liberation in particular areas of spiritual bondage. Some saints are known for their patronage in the fight against evil. The Virgin Mary is supreme because She is the New Eve who crushes the head of the serpent; St. Joseph is known in his litany as the "Terror of Demons;" the intercession (and medallion) of St. Benedict is known to be particularly powerful in freeing people from spiritual maladies; other saints either fought with the devil or had special powers of driving evil spirits out of people: St. Juliana (the Roman Martyr), St. Martin of Tours, St. Anthony of the Desert, St. Catherine of Siena, St. John Vianney and in our modern day, St. Padre Pio, a mighty spiritual warrior for deliverance.

---

35 Mk 2:4

Sample prayer: Come, St. Joseph, and free our brother John of the power of the demon of anger (arrogance, confusion, envy, fear, etc.); ask the Lord to bring His mighty power to restore our brother to peace and strength once again. We ask this in the Name of Jesus the Lord. Amen

Prayers of repentance: Repentance is the first command the Lord gave when He began His Public Ministry,[36] and all disciples must repent of their sins in order to be forgiven and to be freed of the internal devastation of sin. This personal renunciation of any fault, sin or attachment to the act of sin is foundational for all the prayers and commands that follow. Without repentance, one cannot enter the Kingdom of God.

Sample prayer: Lord Jesus Christ, Son of the Living God, I sincerely repent of all my sins, past and present; I repent of having ever offended You, and I pray that you will grant me the grace of true self-knowledge and recuperation so that I may serve You in holiness all the days of my life. I ask this through Your divine mercy and in Your holy Name. Amen.

Prayers of forgiveness: This is a simple prayer directed toward forgiving others and self if needed. In order to deprive a demon of its legal right to be there, the disciple must sincerely forgive in Christ any person who has hurt him and release any resentment that remains in his heart. Lack of forgiveness acts like an anchor for unclean spirits and must be let loose in order for the spirit to leave. The sincerity of forgiveness is not easy to arrive at, but in most cases, it is an absolute fundamental condition for liberation from the evil spirit.

---

36 Mk 1:15

Sample prayer: Dear Lord Jesus, in the fullness of Your divine mercy, I sincerely forgive anyone who has hurt me, especially _____, and I release all negative emotions, resentment and anger associated with any violation of my person in any way. I wish to forgive as You have commanded Your followers to do so that I will also receive mercy on the Day of Judgment. Amen.

Prayers of renunciation: As in the pastoral deliverance models mentioned above, the individual identifies the particular type of bondage that personally afflicts him, and in an authoritative act of sonship, renounces his attachment to it and its control over him. This prayer may need deeper work over time so that the renunciation may penetrate into the very depths of his mind, emotions and will and reach into the unconscious mind through repetition and prayer.

Sample prayer: In the powerful Name of Jesus, I renounce any occult spirits picked up through occult practices that continue to harm and control me; I refuse to live under their power any longer and command them to go directly to the Foot of the Cross in the Name of Jesus. Amen.

Commands of loosing: Similar to renunciation, a loosing command addresses the ties and bonds that chain people to the power of darkness; "loosing" (or breaking) evil is an element of the *spiritual authority* that Christ gave to His Church. We can pray them for ourselves or others. Loosing commands dissolve demonic bonds and liberate those who are under some kind of spiritual constraint. These prayers may even loose us from wrong beliefs, habits, ideas and influences. In this prayer we may call down the Blood of Christ upon us or our loved ones to dissolve negative spiritual bonds that bind us. St. Paul says that Christ's Blood is what "breaks down the barrier of hostility."[37]

---

[37] Eph 2:13-14

Prayers/commands of loosing may also involve the breaking of less powerful curses or soul ties that were caused by contact with occult practitioners. When there has been serious involvement in occult activity, the person must also renounce, specifically and forcefully, any participation he had in these activities in order to "undo" the work of evil in his mind, emotions and will.

> *The person's prayer of renunciation should come first: I renounce in the Name of Jesus, any participation I had in the Ouija board (tarot cards, séances, any other specific evil or sin, etc.). I repudiate any and all contact with and participation in occult influences, rituals and practices, and I reject Satan and all his works and all his empty promises. I ask Jesus the Lord to come and save me and free me from all these bonds. Amen.*

> *Sample prayer: May the Blood of Christ flow down upon William and release him from the power of any and all demonic attachments, ties, bonds, seals, blockages, curses, vows or pacts. I cover him with the Precious Blood of Jesus Christ so that he may be purified of all unclean attachments of evil and freed for the service and freedom of the children of God. I pray this in the Name of Jesus Christ our Lord. Amen.*

Commands of binding: The passage about "binding the strong man"[38] is particularly relevant here, as well as the promise of the Lord that the Church's authority over evil is manifested in the act of "binding."[39] They can be prayed for ourselves or others and are prayed without directly confronting or interacting with a demon. Any moral or spiritual evil can be bound by a prayer of faith: alcoholism, sexual immorality, drugs, pornography, occult attractions, greed or any of the Seven Deadly Sins, spirits of di-

---

[38] Mt 12:29
[39] Mt 16:17-18

vision, gossip, backbiting, lust, even depression if it has demonic roots. Binding prayers are not magic and must be repeated regularly—and with genuine faith—to have an effect. Their only purpose is to restrain the power and scope of evil spirits in our lives.

Sample prayer: In the Name of Jesus, I bind the power of the spirit of division that is operative in this place (or over this person), and I forbid this spirit to work any evil design for destruction, disruption or chaos here. Amen.

Rebukes: This is a direct prayer against a specific evil influence over a person in a moment of crisis with the intent of forcefully stopping its ability to do evil. It is usually applied by the person himself when he is feeling threatened or put upon by some malevolent force. A rebuke is *one-way communication* and is not a magical formula or an attempt at dialogue with an unclean spirit. For example, a pro-life woman told me she was once threatened with violence by a large man at an abortion mill. As he approached her she said, "I rebuke you in the Name of Jesus!" and the powerful man immediately lost his bravado and went away without doing her any harm. The rebuke had a direct effect on the unclean spirit of violence that was motivating the man, and when freed of it, he lost his ability to harass her.

Sometimes the rebuke is to protect a loved one in a situation of crisis. An elderly woman once told me of the time her son was being rapidly drawn into a bad group of friends and addictive behaviors. One night her son came home in a drugged state, and when she saw him at the door in that condition, she addressed a rebuke *to the demon*: "Spirit of drug abuse, leave my son alone and be gone!" The son staggered back as if hit by a ton of bricks and left the house. When he returned three days later, he was free of his addiction and demon. The mother took her Christian authority over her son seriously. It is to be noted however, that a stiff rebuke usually has effect only with demons that are superficially-rooted in the person. More powerful or infiltrated demons need deliverance or exorcism.

Sample prayer: In the Name of Jesus, I rebuke the spirit of violence (or lust, or revelry, or mockery, etc.) that is present at this place; evil spirit, I rebuke you, in the Name of Jesus! Be gone!

Imperative (i.e., commanding) prayers: These prayers are commands proper which have as their goal the casting out of demons from some place or person. They can either be done in private or formally in a deliverance setting.

Sample prayer: I command you, foul spirit, to leave this place (person) and go to the Foot of the Cross, now! Stop harassing the Church of God and His children. I forbid you to harm anyone or anything here, in the Name of Jesus! Go, now, to the Cross!

Rejection of evil: The Baptismal Promises are the best example of this type of deliverance prayer where the godparents (if the one to be baptized is an infant) or the catechumen himself pronounce the formula of rejection, *"I reject Satan, and all his works, and all his empty promises."* This formula is also recited by the congregation at Masses after Easter to reaffirm our baptismal commitment to Christ. A rejection of the devil and his minions is not to be done as a matter of spite or out of personal hatred. Rather, rejecting the devil and all his influences is a rational and calculated declaration of war and a condition for living as a member of the Kingdom of God.

15. When and where are deliverances to be performed?

Deliverances may be performed whenever it is suspected that a person is truly afflicted by an evil spirit. Deliverance prayer is usually prayed *in groups* rather than in individual sessions, but group prayer is usually preceded by some measure of private spiritual counseling and discernment. Deliverance may also be done one-on-one in private. If there is a question of a serious confrontation with the forces of evil, it is prudent not to conduct a private deliverance without assistance unless in the most extreme and urgent of circumstances; a wise deliverance minister will not allow himself to become a mere crisis counselor. His role is spiritual healer, not spiritual paramedic. The admonition, in the exorcism ritual, that priests should not perform an exorcism on a woman without another woman present[40] certainly applies to deliverances as well.

A sacristy or church where the Blessed Sacrament is reserved is the best place for deliverance prayer, although it is not always possible to conduct such services in churches due to lack of privacy. The person's home is another natural place for these prayer services, as is the privacy of a counselor's office. Whatever the place, deliverances should always be done in an area that offers assurance that the persons prayed over will not be subject to others' curiosity or any type of public embarrassment.

16. How can a deliverance go wrong?

There are several ways a deliverance can go wrong: first, if an individual or group practices deliverance without humility. Humility as a Christian virtue is primarily expressed as *accountability* to the local church. Without that virtue of submission to the oversight of ecclesiastical authority, a deliverance ministry is bound to fail in time. Also, arrogance, self-will, personal aggrandizement or grandstanding, self-absorption and vice are all invitations for demonic mischief to enter into a prayer ministry.

---

40 Weller, *Rituale*, I, n. 19, p. 173.

While good leadership is important in any group, deliverance ministry should not revolve around any charismatic personalities; it's only focus is the Person of Jesus Christ. Well-established prayer ministries can fall under the influence of a powerful, "charismatic" personality who purports to be a powerful deliverer or an exorcist but who does not have the virtue of humility. I have seen charismatic leaders of prayer groups become deluded by demons into thinking that they are operating in holiness and then seduce whole groups of people into terrible behaviors and practices that end up leaving a trail of pain and destruction in their wake. The humility of submitting a prayer ministry to the oversight of the legitimate church authorities is something that the devil profoundly hates.

Secondly, deliverances can go wrong if there is not a strong commitment to discernment in the group. The discernment tools listed in Chapter 4, Question 2 are available to anyone who takes the initiative to learn and use them. There is nothing more dangerous than groups or individuals with misguided zeal that enter into the lives of vulnerable individuals to "cure" them. The priests with oversight of such groups should never allow anyone to become a member of a deliverance team who is not schooled in the basics of spiritual discernment and tested in virtue.

Finally, things can go wrong in a deliverance team if the group loses its spirit of prayer and gets overly emotional. The actual practice of deliverance should be a profound faith event, which is not without its appropriate emotion but is always dominated by rational people who think on their feet, keep emotions in their proper place and have no personal interest in the work other than the salvation and sanctification of souls.

17. What is the most necessary quality for a person who wants to do deliverance ministry?

While personal holiness and humility are necessary virtues in the work of deliverance from evil spirits, I very much agree with the Spanish exorcist, Fr. José Antonio Fortea, that the best quality for an exorcist or deliverance minister to have is faith-filled common sense.[41] Any process of deliverance or exorcism needs hard-headed logic for it to come off successfully: investigating and discerning the root spiritual problem, setting up the circumstances of a person's prayer sessions, forming and training a prayer team, educating the person about his spiritual life and problems, calling the person to conversion of heart, conducting the prayer sessions, thinking on his feet in the midst of the prayer, tracking the progress of the person, guiding a true healing process afterward, etc. At every stage of spiritual warfare, prudence and practical common sense are needed to assist the true care of souls.

Afterword to Chapter 5
Case Study of a Successful Deliverance[42]

The following case is fairly typical of a person with a demonic obsession that did not reach the level of full possession. The vast majority of an exorcist's work concerns people with lesser demonic problems` which nonetheless cause people distress, anxiety and sometimes severe physical pain. As has been noted in this chapter, cases of full possession normally require solemn exorcism while other cases of lesser afflictions can be dealt with through faith,

---
41 Fortea, p. 98.
42 The name and details of the story have been modified to protect the identity and dignity of the person involved.

prayer and deliverance techniques, some of which may be seen in the following story.

A concerned friend asked me to assist a young Hispanic man with what appeared to be a true demonic problem. It should be noted from the start that the man wanted to be free of his problem, was fully cooperative with the healing process and actively practiced his faith to the extent that he was able. Furthermore, he had renounced any connection with previous occult activities.

This man, Mario (not his real name), had grown up in a broken family with an absent father and a mother who had friends who were witches. Apparently, the mother had dabbled in witchcraft herself. Mario had memories of incense, prayers, incantations and images in the home that were clearly demonic. He also took the death of his grandfather in his adolescent years very hard, and it may have been through that experience of trauma that he got infested. His grandfather was like a father to him.

In his adult life he admitted to have engaged in many types of sinful behaviors and had fallen prey to several addictions which he dealt with manfully and was free from at the time I met him. He did, however, suffer from a pernicious anxiety that, despite medication and psychiatric assistance, he was never able to shake. Prior to his conversion, he participated in some New Age and Native American occult rituals which only increased his demonic problems. Furthermore, he felt constant pain in several areas of his body that no medical diagnosis could ever explain and no medicine could heal.

After the interview, I was not sure if we were dealing with a possession, but it was obvious that he was suffering from real demonic affliction, so we made an appointment for deliverance prayer with a three-person prayer team. The prayer occurred in four sessions, three on a Saturday evening and one on the following Sunday morning. Since the man was Catholic, we began both days with Mass and prayed in a chapel with the Eucharist exposed in a monstrance on the altar.

Session one: The team of three lay people began by praying deeply over Mario, asking God to free him from the power of all evil influences, and at about the half hour mark of our prayer, Mario began to shake his head back and forth, up and down, and his facial features severely contorted. The demon tried to shield itself from the power of prayer by lurching backward in the chair at the mention of the Name of Jesus or the imposition of the crucifix on his head, but the helpers were there to immobilize Mario. There were no violent gestures, just attempts of the demon to get away from the prayer. The demonic entity did not like the stole of the priest being put on his neck or the blowing on the face (i.e., the *insufflatio* which symbolizes the breath of the Spirit.) When commanded, it said its name and mumbled some indecipherable syllables.

I commanded it to leave Mario and to go to Jesus without hurting him or anyone else, and within about ten minutes, the demon's strength reached a breaking point. The demon then shook the man who then went limp. Mario sort of "woke up" at that point and told me that he thought the demon was gone. Immediately he felt a tremendous sense of emotional relief, a lifting of some great weight off his shoulders, and he was smiling again.

Session two: After a break of about ten minutes we began the prayer again, and there was another manifestation of the same sort almost immediately. The demonic entity this time was a mute spirit that had bound Mario's tongue so he was not able to utter clear sentences. Nevertheless when commanded, he muttered some type of name which I then used, as I understood it, to command the demon to leave. This one hissed and shook and also left in a similar fashion to the previous one. The reaction from Mario was the same: convulsion, relief and tremendous peace. Then we took a break for dinner and returned in the evening for another session.

Session three: The third session was a virtual repeat of the first two sessions except that the demonic entity that manifested this time had a distinct name and personality from the others. It seemed to be a demon that entered the man when he was participating in the Native American rituals; it made some howling noises similar to American Indian chanting, the very things Mario had heard in the rituals. I commanded it to leave and again, Mario went limp when the entity left. He felt a tremendous sense of relief afterward, yet, he did not feel that he was totally free.

I anointed Mario with the Sacrament of the Sick, prayed prayers of healing and sealing for him so that no demon would "return with seven demons worse than himself,"[43] and the team retired for the evening. All of us stayed in the same facility that night so that we could continue with the prayer the next day.

Session four: Sometimes dreams are part of the discernment process. Before the team gathered for Mass the next morning, Mario told me of a nightmare he had had that night. He saw himself in a fight with his brother when they were younger, and in the dream, he actually killed his brother. It must be noted that Mario is on good terms with his brother who is still very much alive, but the dream revealed something about the *demon* which we did not understand until the deliverance was over.

---

43 Mt 12:45

That morning we celebrated Mass and went into the deliverance session the same way we did the previous three sessions. This time, a demon manifested quickly and said his name was "Cain," which was obviously a biblical spirit of fratricide: that certainly explained the dream of Mario killing his brother the night before. This was the particular mission of the demon which may have been picked up in the family home where the witchcraft was practiced. This demon too was expelled within about half an hour to 45 minutes and then Mario was free.

Assessment: When we decided to pray with Mario, it was not clear the extent of the demonic problem. Rarely is a demonic infestation fully clear until one enters into prayer. Deliverance prayer helped us understand the nature of the problem. Once it was clear that Mario had weaker demons that could be overcome by the spiritual force of simple deliverance prayer, we continued on that path since we saw that we were making progress. As it turned out, all demons obediently revealed their names and clearly departed as commanded. At the end of each session Mario felt an authentic sense of relief, clarity and joy. His case was, thus, one of serious internal obsession, but it did not need to be brought to the attention of the diocese because, through the faith of Mario himself and a small group of loving people, he was freed by Christ from years of demonic oppression and pain.

Follow-up: As has been noted in previous chapters, the ultimate proof of departure is a sense of enduring peace felt by the person himself. As it turns out, Mario felt immediately liberated from the power of these demons that had afflicted him for so many years. We understood them to be demons picked up from the occult rituals he had participated in. His peace did not, however, endure, and after some time (perhaps two years), he was able to come again for deliverance prayer and at least several more demons were cast out in exactly the same way as the first group. Deep peace followed, and he has had no further demonic problems. It seems likely that this peace will endure. However, I remain in contact with him to monitor his ongoing healing.

Chapter 6
The Conduct of an Exorcism

The seventy-two returned in jubilation saying, "Master, even the demons are subject to us in your name." He said in reply, "I watched Satan fall from the sky like lightning. See what I have done; I have given you power to tread on snakes and scorpions and all the forces of the enemy, and nothing shall ever injure you. Nevertheless, do not rejoice so much in the fact that the devils are subject to you as that your names are inscribed in heaven." (Lk 10:18)

As the evangelist Luke testifies, when the disciples returned to the Master full of joy at the fruits they had gathered in their first missionary attempt, Jesus utters a sentence that is highly evocative: "I saw Satan fall from heaven like lightning." (Lk 10:18) With these words, the Lord affirms that the proclamation of the Kingdom of God is always a victory over the devil, but at the same time he also reveals that the building up of the Kingdom is continuously exposed to the attacks of the spirit of evil....it means that we prepare ourselves for the condition of struggle which characterizes the life of the Church in this final time of the history of salvation. (Pope John Paul II)[1]

---

1 Pope John Paul II, General Audience, August 13, 1986.

✟

1. What analogy best describes what happens in an exorcism?

The best image I have found to describe what happens in an exorcism is the image of a criminal prosecution which has as its goal the restoration of justice for a crime committed. All the elements of a trial are present in an exorcism by analogy: the "crime" is the demon's violation of God's law (sin and rebellion) and trespassing on God's temple (the human body). The indictment is the Church's investigation process, which concludes in a judgment that an actual possession requires the Church's action. The Church (i.e., the Church's spiritual jurisdiction and authority) is the court of prosecution, Jesus Christ is the Judge, the possessed person is the plaintiff asking for justice and the exorcist is the prosecutor. He has a jury (helpers and prayer partners) who assist in convicting the criminal. The "casting out" of the demon is the sentencing and imprisonment where God's and the victim's rights are fully vindicated. The reason for the judicial process is not only to expel the demon but to show his guilt publicly and re-establish the order of justice in Christ.

In this process, demons are always guilty, they can never plead ignorance or insanity, and their guilt can never be expiated; there is no Fifth Amendment or releases on technicalities in this court. Some striking language in the second exorcism prayer[2] bears witness to this judicial imagery:

> *For thou art guilty before the almighty God, Whose laws thou hast transgressed; thou art guilty before His Son, Jesus Christ Whom thou didst presume to tempt, Whom thou wast emboldened to nail*

---

[2] Again referring to the 1614 exorcism ritual; see the next footnote for specific reference.

to the Cross; thou art guilty before the human race, for through thy blandishments thou didst proffer it the poisoned cup of death.[3]

2. What other analogy describes exorcism well?

Exorcism is a very intense form of *spiritual healing*. This form of spiritual healing can be likened to surgery. When the diseased part is located, there is a surgical intervention to extract the spiritual "sickness" (i.e., the presence of a demon), so that it will not endanger the overall health of the person. When that is successfully accomplished, the priest then applies traditional healing remedies to restore equilibrium and to deal with the negative side-effects of the "sickness" on the person's body, soul and life.

The analogy of surgery, however, does not completely capture the reality of exorcism. A surgeon works *from the outside-in* to remove a diseased element. An exorcist works *from the inside-out* to expel an unclean spirit. He does this not with a surgical instrument but with a spiritual power. This is why we talk about the "expulsion" of a demon (from the inside-out) rather than the "removal" of a demon by an exorcism. This is also why it is customary to speak of the person as a "victim" whom the Church assists rather than a "patient" whom the Church treats. "Possession is not *cured*; rather, the possessed person is *freed*."[4]

3. What must a priest do to prepare the exorcee for an exorcism?

A priest's first responsibility is to see that the exorcee is spiritually prepared to participate in this action of the Church. He must assure that the person has faith in Jesus, or, if he is not a Christian, that the person accepts the Church's faith in Christ as the condition by which its ministers pray and act. (As mentioned

---

3 Weller, *Rituale*, pp.189-91.
4 Fortea, *Interview*, p. 94.

earlier,[5] an exorcism can actually be a mode of evangelization for those who do not know Jesus.) The exorcist must also assure that the person repents completely of all sin and goes to Confession (if Catholic or Orthodox), that he renounces any involvement in occult activities of the past, and forgives anyone who may have harmed him.

It is helpful that the person undertake some spiritual exercises such as holy reading or spiritual talks, practicing works of charity, daily prayer and going to daily Mass—if these are possible—prior to the exorcism. These help to prepare the soul of the person to willingly participate in the exorcism, but due to the nature of the affliction, they are always difficult. The priest will also maintain regular contact with the person during this time to build him up and assure him that Christ wants to liberate him from demonic influences. The greater the degree of personal cooperation in the preparation process, the greater will be the healing.

4. What is the role of prayer support in an exorcism? Must those who pray be present at the exorcism?

It is ideal to have a team of prayerful people in the physical place where the exorcism is being conducted, but that cannot always be arranged due to the difficulty of gathering and training the right people for such a ministry. Also, sometimes the victim does not want people to know of his affliction or is sensitive to other people being present in the actual service. Those concerns must always be respected.

Nonetheless, the priest must always try to gather as much prayer support for an exorcism as possible, even if the people are not physically present at the exorcism. It is common for an exor-

---

5 Cf. Chapter 3, Question 2.

cist to petition convents of contemplative nuns or church groups for prayer for exorcisms, always scrupulous to guard confidentiality. Undoubtedly the prayer of the Rosary during the time of exorcism itself is a powerful aid in liberation. The basic rule is that the more prayer there is before and during the exorcism, the more spiritual power there is for the expulsion of the demon(s). Exorcism is an act of faith, and prayer is its force multiplier.

5. What must a priest do to prepare his team of helpers for the exorcism?

Every exorcist needs a competent group of faithful people to help him in exorcism. He does not need many helpers, normally two to three people are sufficient for a team, but he should have a team of trained helpers to draw from if one or two are not available at any given time. It is especially helpful to choose strong men for this work since they may need to immobilize a person and endure a session that may last several hours, but anyone with vitality and basic good health will generally do.

The helpers must live morally pure lives and be in a state of grace at the time of the exorcism. If they are conscious of mortal sin or if they have not gone to Confession in some time, it is recommended that they do so before the exorcism. A priest should not use a non-baptized person or someone living in a state of sin as a helper in an exorcism because of that person's greater spiritual vulnerability at close quarters with demons.

Helpers are to fast and pray beforehand for the spiritual wellbeing of the exorcee and for the priest's and their own protection. They are to be prayerful and attentive during the course of the exorcism and follow the directives of the priest with precision and strict obedience at all times. They must not take individual initiative in anything whatsoever unless asked to do so by the exorcist. They must never speak to or attempt to exercise any power over the demon on their own. Above all, they must never, under any circumstances, ask the demon to come into them in order to free the individual from his oppression; this type of well-intentioned folly will lead only to the possession of two people instead of one.[6]

6. What personal preparations must the priest undertake for an exorcism?

Every exorcist must prepare himself in body, soul and spirit for the arduous task of an exorcism. The following are the elements of personal preparation of the priest for the ministry of exorcism:

<u>Mind</u>: the priest's mind is prepared for spiritual battle by study. He can memorize prayers, study the ritual, read Scripture and books, reports of other exorcisms, his own case notes, etc. that may help him understand the case and ply his trade more professionally. While an exorcism is not a battle of wits, which a human cannot hope to win against a demonic intelligence, the priest does, nonetheless, need to think on his feet in confronting such a foe. It is also helpful for the priest to take counsel with

---

[6] Those who saw the 1973 movie, *The Exorcist*, may remember that it ended with the inexperienced exorcist priest asking the demon to come out of the girl and into him. The movie portrayed this act as a victory for the Church since the girl was liberated in the process even though the priest jumped out the window, tumbled down the long Georgetown staircase and expired of a head injury there on the pavement! This, unfortunately is not only Hollywood exaggeration, it is an extremely dangerous message—perhaps intended?—by the makers of the movie to give people the impression that this type of technique "works" to remove demons. It is utter folly as it only creates two infested people and does not remove a demon from the first one. Remember, demons can only enter a person with an act of the individual's will.

other exorcists about a particular case if he is not sure how best to proceed.

Emotions: the priest's emotions are prepared for battle by fasting. Fasting withdraws the priest's emotions and imagination from the reach of the devil and makes him a more spiritual person. In the day before the exorcism he can do small penances such as giving up things he likes to eat, accepting harder tasks, being more charitable, etc. On the day of the exorcism, he must fast from food but do it with humility in ways that express his dependence upon God for success.[7]

Will: the priest's will is trained for warfare, above all, through faithfulness to duty. His fidelity to his many priestly duties prior to the exorcism is a reaffirmation of his humble obedience to God's Will. He most effectively fulfills God's Will when he does those things that he is supposed to do and attends with greater zeal to those others which he has previously neglected to do or which are more distasteful to him.

Body: he prepares his body for spiritual battle through health and rest. His body is the human instrument through which he carries on the warfare. The priest must have sufficient rest prior to and breaks during an exorcism because he is engaging in battle with a pure spirit, and he is the only one of the two combatants who suffers from the weakness of the flesh.[8] Rest is an essential element to his spiritual strength.

---

[7] In emphasizing the virtue of humility in the practice of fasting, I do not advocate that a priest abstains from all food on the day of the exorcism or the day previous. Fasting can be done according to the standard Lenten rules of the Church or in a creative way according to the priest's circumstances. My fast before an exorcism, for example, is to skip the meal previous to the exorcism on any given day. That way I maintain a spiritual discipline for the exorcism, but I do not encumber my need for energy in fulfilling my other many responsibilities.

[8] Cf. Mt 26:41

Spirit: the priest's spirit is prepared by intensity of prayer, the practice of virtue and spiritual direction. The priest must simply pray more and pray more *intensely* as he approaches an exorcism. He is advised to have a spiritual director who can hold him accountable to his priestly principles and integrity of life in the face of such close contact with demonic forces.

7. What if the person resists going to an exorcism?

This can be the most difficult situation an exorcist (or a family) faces, because one cannot force a person to undergo an exorcism, even if the person may really need one. Depending on the level of control a demon has over him, a truly possessed person may have a difficult time going to an exorcism or cooperating with those who want to bring him. At times, great patience and insistence is needed on the part of the helpers and family members in order to get the person to the place of exorcism. The first session will often be the hardest to get him to, but generally the subsequent sessions will see a greater cooperation from the individual since the grace of the exorcism works over time.

In a case of total obstinacy toward the exorcism, the priest must work with the family and look for a more opportune time to conduct the exorcism. When the priest makes a commitment to conduct an exorcism, however, he must demonstrate a heroic priestly zeal for the afflicted person's wellbeing, an attitude which reflects the zeal of the Good Shepherd who goes out in search of the lost sheep.[9]

8. How many exorcisms does it take to release a person from a demon?

It usually takes a long time to release a person from demonic possession. The number of exorcisms needed to liberate a per-

---
9 Cf. Mt 18:12-13

son from demonic influence is dependent upon several factors: the strength of the demon, the nature of the possession and the willingness of the person to cooperate with the Church in the expulsion.

If the demon is very strong, or if his deceptions are deeply intertwined with the personality, it might take many sessions to free the individual, even with his cooperation. It is not uncommon for a process of exorcisms to last for many months due to the difficulty of arranging schedules, places and helpers, among other factors. Also, there is rarely only one demon inside a possessed person, and so the process often has to be prolonged when new demons are uncovered that were not known to be there in the beginning.

When the process takes more time than the exorcist would like, the time delay is usually good for his humility, so that he does not confuse whose power actually expels demons; it is not his power, it is the Lord's. All exorcists would like to immediately cast demons out just like Jesus does in the gospels, but it does not usually work that way. Every exorcism is a healing process just as every possession is also a process.[10]

The experienced exorcist will know that there is no exorcism that works magically or is performed "in a hurry."[11] He will also be intimately aware that the deliberate, careful and discerning forward motion of an exorcism process is the exorcist's most devastating weapon against a demon. The exorcist sets the pace, which is an expression of his authority over the demon and the process. He must not falter but should generously persevere in the whole process until he sees the full liberation and healing of the individual he is helping. He must also have the humility to

---

10   M. Scott Peck, MD, *People of the Lie*, Simon and Schuster: New York, NY, 1983, p. 191.
11   Fortea, *Interview*, p. 102.

avoid taking on too many cases so that he can dedicate himself fully to the good of those he has promised to help.

9. What religious objects does a priest use during the course of the exorcism?

While the Church encourages the judicious use of sacramentals in the exorcism ritual, we must always keep in mind that the expulsion of a demon is due to the *faith* of the individual person and the authority of the Church, not to the use of religious objects. The skill of the exorcist, the faith of the helpers and the use of sacramentals add to the efficacy of the ritual, for sure, but are not the main reason why a demon is expelled. It is strong belief in Christ and His Power flowing through the Church that always has the decisive effect against a demon. The exorcist and helpers must always avoid any excesses with sacramentals or any use of religious objects that smacks of superstition.

Among the religious objects that may be employed in exorcism are holy water, exorcised salt, Scripture passages, relics, devotional prayers like that to St. Michael the Archangel, blessed oil, holy pictures, icons, and above all, the crucifix. The ritual says that the priest *ought to have a crucifix at hand or somewhere in sight. If relics of the saints are available, they are to be applied in a reverent way to the breast or the head of the person possessed (the relics must be properly and securely encased and covered). One will see to it that these sacred objects are not treated improperly or that no injury is done them by the evil spirit.*[12]

A priest is instructed that, when he finds anything, be it words or actions, that truly bother the demon, he is to use them frequently: *Let him inquire of the person possessed, following one or the other act of exorcism, what the latter experienced in his body or*

12　*The Rite of Exorcism*, I, n. 13, (Weller, p. 171).

soul while the exorcism was being performed, and to learn also what particular words in the form had a more intimidating effect upon the devil, so that hereafter these words may be employed with greater stress and frequency.[13]

10. Can a priest use the Eucharist to expel a demon?

The Church forbids this. The ritual states categorically that *one should not hold the holy Eucharist over the head of the person or in any way apply it to his body, owing to the danger of desecration.*[14] A priest may bless the person with the Eucharist from the altar in a Benediction service, but he may not employ the sacred species as a weapon in the conduct of an exorcism. If the exorcee is not Catholic, an exorcism can be an important moment to evangelize him about the Real Presence of Christ in the Eucharist and evoke Eucharistic faith in him to the extent possible. The devil certainly knows the infinite spiritual power of the Eucharist and fears it greatly, which is why most exorcisms are conducted in chapels or sacristies near the reserved Eucharist.

11. What happens if the person does not get help from one exorcist or wants to change for another?

Like any patient under treatment, the exorcee has a right to change doctors; however, this should only be done after a process of discernment. A particular priest may not be able to effectively help a person because of a personality conflict, lack of skill, lack of time, too great a distance between him and the exorcee, or other factors. What should be avoided at all costs is "shopping around" for a priest who suits the person's wishes. Another reason why an exorcee should not bounce from one exorcist to another is that *the demon* may want to destabilize the process with numerous exorcists and perhaps conflicting practices of exorcism.

---

13 *Ibid.*, n. 4, p. 169.
14 *Ibid.*, n. 13, p. 171.

It is in the demon's best interest to disrupt the exorcism process, and any break in the therapeutic relationship is potentially the manipulation of the demon. If a need to change from one priest to another is discerned, it should be decided by mutual consent of the exorcee and the exorcist and done very deliberately.

12. How long does an exorcism session last?

There are actually two questions here. The length of any given exorcism session is one matter; the length of the total process of exorcism is another. The latter was answered in Question 8 above.

With regard to the length of sessions, this depends on the judgment of the exorcist as to what is prudent at any given time. Some sessions last a short time and other sessions take many hours. The criterion for judging when to end an exorcism session is, first and foremost, the physical and mental state of the exorcee. Sometimes the demon progressively saps the energy of the person, and the exorcist cannot continue the healing without completely exhausting the person. There is no benefit for the exorcee in persevering too long in the arduous process. Nor must the priest overextend his own or his helpers' human capacities to the point of collapse. He must always make an on-site assessment about the physical and emotional resources of the person and the team in his determination of how long to let the session go. The golden mean applies: he must not quit too easily but he must not stretch human limits too far.

13. Are there ever any breaks in an exorcism?

Yes. There are no rules on this matter and the question of taking breaks is left up to the individual judgment of the exorcist. The exorcist must carefully gauge various factors in deciding when and if to take a break: the limits of the exorcee's strength, the fatigue factor for the helpers and his own stress level. However, he never takes a break at the demon's request—and demons do request it!

Common sense and good judgment is needed in deciding about breaks. Obviously, the priest does not want to stop for a break in the middle of a heightened reaction from the demon, nor must he take too many breaks from his prosecution of the demon, because any halt in the process is also a break for the demon. Sometimes a demon can only be expelled after a great deal of momentum has built up over the course of a session. An exorcist may let individual helpers get up and take breaks in turns while he continues with a session just to keep the pressure on the demon. It is also possible for him to take a break and leave his team praying for the person (especially the Rosary) to weaken the demon for when he returns.

14. Can't the demon re-gain his strength if the exorcisms are not all done at once?

When the Church "arrests" (binds) the demon in the exorcism process, the demon's natural strength is restricted, something akin to handcuffing a criminal and depriving him of his power to harm. The criminal may still be wicked, but the longer he is bound and rots in prison, the less evil he can do. If the Church applies its Christ-given authority correctly, eventually the Church will break the demon's strength and cast the demon out.

A demon may regain some measure of strength, however, if, during the intervals between exorcisms, an evil spiritual force intervenes, such as the renewal of the original curse by someone or the malfeasance of an external occult group who might be "praying" to strengthen a particular demon. This would be like the criminal in prison joining up with an already-existing prison gang or having harmful contraband smuggled into him by malefactors from the outside. That builds up the criminal's strength even though he is behind bars.

The experienced exorcist will make sure that the person completely repudiates any occult ties before entering into the exorcism, and then he will spiritually block any external occult power sources that try to interfere in the process during or between exorcism sessions. The priest will hold the exorcee accountable for staying clean of any occult influences in his life or around him: bad friends, drugs, New Age influences or items, occult internet sites, etc. Detachment from active sources of occult power will usually prevent the renewal of a demon's strength inside the victim.

15. How should a chapel or a room be arranged for an exorcism?

Sensationalized movies like *The Exorcist* or *The Exorcism of Emily Rose* create the impression that the devil is a potent aggressor in an exorcism, but we must be careful of the movie industry's depictions of the power of evil. While demons certainly may manifest wildly at times in the course of an exorcism, the demons are generally not free to move and plot against the exorcist in the course of the Church's ritual. The demon is actually the priest's captive in an exorcism and not the other way around.[15]

Accordingly, the priest orchestrates every aspect of the exorcism session in order to manifest the Church's authority over

---

15 For this reason I have never really been comfortable with the title and thesis of Malachi Martin's book, *Hostage to the Devil*. He makes the case that the priest, sacrificially, binds himself as a hostage to the evil spirit during the process of freeing an individual from the devil's power; but, while the heroic sacrifices that an exorcist makes are real, in actual fact, *the demon* is the one who is hostage to the priest/Church in an exorcism.

the demon. The priest chooses an appropriate place out of the way of onlookers or curiosity seekers (usually a remote chapel, sacristy or some other secluded setting). He chooses and trains his helpers who will assist at the exorcism, and he then arranges the setting of the room to give him a maximum strategic advantage over the demon who, because he is inside the body, has no other option but to accompany the exorcee to the place of battle. It is common to remove from close quarters hard objects and furniture as these may be used against the exorcist or helpers in a manifestation.

16. What is the position of the victim in an exorcism?

The exorcist has full freedom to determine the best conditions for doing an exorcism and what posture/position works best for a particular exorcee. The afflicted person usually sits in a chair while the exorcist stands to the side of the exorcee, close enough so that the exorcist's hand holding the crucifix may reach the exorcee's head without the exorcist having to bend over. Some exorcists stand behind the exorcee. If there are helpers, they are asked to sit closely by or positioned right next to the person in the event that there is need to stabilize the person during manifestations.

At times the exorcee is placed on a sofa or bed so that there is padding all around and so that he can be more easily subdued without hurting himself or others if the demon gets violent. Security of persons is important, especially when dealing with stronger demons, and for that reason, the exorcism ritual itself makes a specific command to the demon to not harm anyone or anything: *Neither shalt thou be emboldened to harm in any way this creature of God, nor the bystanders, nor any of their possessions.*[16]

---

16 Weller, *Rituale*, II, n. 2, p. 179.

The 2005 movie *The Exorcism of Emily Rose* showed the victim sitting up in a bed and the priest attempting to tie the girl's arms to bedposts with insubstantial shoe strings. A preternatural force operating through a fully possessed person is hardly going to be limited by a few shoe strings! If there is need for restraint, it is best to have professional restraints that are used in hospitals and/or strong men at the sides of the person to guard against any injury.

17. Are exorcisms always violent?

Not all exorcisms are violent, but most of them are rough and tumble to say the least. When an insolent and disobedient demon is "trapped" in a body and under the subjection of the Church, he usually reacts violently by attempting to flee or writhing in pain at the force that comes against it. Only the smarter and stronger demons can mask their pain to make the exorcist think that they are not really present. In times when there are no overt reactions of any demons to the exorcism ritual, the exorcist needs a strong spirit of discernment to make sure he does not short-circuit the process or get deceived by a hiding demon.

There is usually a burst of violent reaction from the demon at the beginning of an exorcism session when he first feels the sting of the Church's holiness, but he will progressively weaken as the session proceeds. The same gradual weakening effect happens progressively over the course of the whole exorcism process. An exorcism is a contest of spiritual forces that can result only in victor and vanquished—there are no partial winners or truces. When the demon's will is so broken that he cannot resist any more, that is when he is finally forced to leave.

18. Is a person always unconscious during an exorcism?

Not always, but it is most common that a person will blank out completely in an exorcism due to the demon's overpowering of his faculties. I liken his action to the art of ventriloquism, where a ventriloquist controls and speaks "through" the doll while at the same time maintaining his own separate identity. Another helpful image is the emergency broadcast system on television: a local authority can override the regular televised program to issue a severe weather warning or some other emergency message. The devil does the same in a possession. He overrides the ability of the person to control his own faculties and speaks and acts through the person. After an exorcism the person usually has no recollection of what happened, but that is because it was not him that was speaking and acting, it was the demonic mind and will.

19. Does the devil speak in a guttural voice in a possession?

Many people think that demons speak in guttural voices like in Hollywood horror movies. This rarely happens as such. Guttural speaking is a phenomenon that is usually limited to the most extreme cases of truly beast-like demons. The possessing demon speaks in the human voice of the victim with all his or her particularities of accent, vocabulary and terminology primarily because demons don't have vocal chords of their own and must use their victims' voices to communicate in human words. The distinguishing mark of the demon, however, is not the voice or language that he speaks but the *personality behind the voice*. An exorcist can usually tell that the "person" speaking is not the human victim, even though it may sound like his voice.

It is difficult at times to determine who is actually speaking, but when in doubt about the speaker, the exorcist must put the "person behind the voice" to the test. He may ask the person to recite the Hail Mary all the way through or to say the Name of Jesus devoutly. The demon will inevitably fail tests such as these.

20. Does an exorcee feel pain during an exorcism or does he feel the pain of the demon?

The *demon* certainly experiences the pain of the Church's attack—sometimes excruciatingly. I have heard many demons in the course of exorcisms say something like, "Stop, you're killing me" or "Oh, stop, I hate that!" or even the lament, "I'm dying." The demon's spiritual pain is very real; it is the pain of the damned which they experience whenever they come into contact with the sacred.

The question of whether a victim feels the pain of the demon is more complex. In *normal circumstances*, the victim does not feel the demon's pain directly, even though it might look like the person is suffering. What is showing on the person's face is the demon's pain, not the victim's. This is mostly the case with people who have become possessed or obsessed after childhood. Their emotions are more developed by the time the demon enters, and so the demon is less able to intertwine with or "download" his own agonizing emotions into the person's emotional life. However, since the warfare takes place inside a person's body, the victim may feel a natural sense of exhaustion or depression afterward.

In the case of childhood victimization, however, it is more likely that the victim will feel a whole range of demonic emotions and pain due to the fact that the demon entered the person in the formative stage of his emotional development. The demon is more intertwined with the inner life of his victim, who is more likely to experience himself as united with the demon—physically, emotionally and mentally. Demons can also exaggerate or intensify the natural woundedness of the victim, who undoubtedly experienced emotional trauma at the time of victimization.

The experienced exorcist will diligently command the demon to separate himself from the inner life of the victim and help the person to isolate and purify any recurring memories of the original trauma. He will also make sure to respect the person's limits in handling the stress that the exorcism brings and not overtax the person in prosecuting the demon. As mentioned earlier,[17] it is necessary for childhood victims of demons to have competent professional help for their emotional healing process, which can be seen as a necessary counterpart to the process of exorcism.

21. Can a demon jump from one person to another in an exorcism?

Except for true victimization by people practicing evil, demons can only enter a person with his permission. That is to say, demons can be sent in to other people through deliberate victimization, which is usually the result of some form of targeting of vulnerable people by others practicing the occult arts; but demons do not *jump* from one person to another, even in an exorcism. The exorcist must always instruct his team never, under any circumstances, to invite the devil to come out of a person and into himself because it never actually helps the original victim. It only creates a second victim due to the free, albeit misguided, invitation. There is no need to fear that demons can easily come into people without some form of invitation. They cannot be picked up like a contagious disease. If they were, no one would be free of their aggressions. We must always avoid the two extremes: that of believing that they we are invulnerable to them and that of attributing too much power to them.

---

17 See the Afterword to Chapter 4.

22. Does a demon act on his own or in concert with others?

Demons have individual missions, and in that sense, they can work individually to seduce and harm people. However, demons prefer to work in teams, "packs," or "gangs." They often tempt human beings with a coordinated barrage of temptations to weaken a person's resolve against sin. They operate in a kind of spiritual conspiracy against souls. Any one demon will have power to bring a sin about, but all of them working together will have greater power over an individual if he is not vigilant to the wiles of the world, the flesh and the devil.

If a demon gains successful entry into a body, he always tries to bring others in by influencing the person to engage in sinful activities or occult practices, which are doorways for *new* demons. When other demons enter, they act like a street gang and are more difficult to dislodge due to the protective power and combined resources of a group. A group of demons can also resist an exorcism longer than an individual demon can, for the same reason.

If there is only one demon inside of a person's body (which is rare), he can also coordinate his actions with other demons of his group who are "on the outside," so to speak, and their purpose is to increase the force of temptation to draw the person into sin or to seduce him into making an invitation for other demons to come in. Those outside can also harass the exorcist, the individual or anyone trying to help him be free of his demonic problems.

23. Can a demon hide from the exorcist to avoid being expelled?

In fact, it is rare when demons do *not* try to hide from the exorcist during an exorcism. Demons are creatures of darkness and do everything in their power to avoid the light that the prayer shines on them. A demon may "hide" in the same way that a vile insect will scurry under a cabinet when a light is turned on in a dark room. They recede to the interior places of control and woundedness where they try to remain in darkness for as long as they can. However, the nature of the Church's prayer is that it shines a penetrating spiritual light on all areas of darkness and woundedness of the person's inner life and exposes the demons over time.

Even in the case of stronger demons who may be able to resist the prayers of the exorcism for a longer time, I do not hold the opinions of some exorcists that demons can hide for hours and hours or over multiple sessions. If an exorcist is praying that long without seeing evidence of a demon's presence, there is usually something wrong with his method or his discernment. It is my experience that it is hard for demons to remain hidden from the power of prayer for more than half an hour to an hour, in normal circumstances.

The question of how many sessions it may take to *expel* a demon is a different question. The presence of the demon can be exposed early in an exorcism process, but the underlying causes of his power or control over the person may take time and many sessions to discover. As noted in questions 8 and 34 of this chapter, there are many reasons why *an exorcism process* may take a long time: a person may be giving the demon permission to stay, the demon may be attached to unhealed emotional woundedness, or the demons may be more difficult to root out due to their greater strength or the greater complexity of the case.

24. Do demons always talk in an exorcism?

Demons do not always talk in exorcisms for a couple of reasons. One is because they may be mute demons whose power to speak in human language is restricted for some reason. In this case it is difficult to get any information from them except through signs. Mute demons are usually weaker and are not the most difficult ones to cast out.

Another reason why demons may not talk is that they clam up like a disobedient child or a criminal under interrogation when they are confronted. The stronger ones can remain silent for a long time. The objective of the exorcist is to get them to reveal information that he can use to expel them, which, of course, they do not voluntarily give. The ritual requires him to ask certain questions in order to understand the nature of the possession and vulnerabilities of the demon, but getting that information can be quite a task at times.

At other times demons can use the opposite tactic: they can be "chatty" or give sly answers in order to distract the exorcist or derail the process into dead-end lines of questioning. Demons never cease to be deceivers, even when they are under the greatest restraint.

25. What language does the demon speak in an exorcism?

Angelic minds grasp the first principles of things and communicate with each other and with God in mental "concepts" rather than words.[18] However, if an angel or demon wishes to communicate a mental concept to a human being, he may communicate it to the human mind through what we would call *mental telepathy*, if the human mind is attuned to that kind of intuitive communicating. Speaking through the flesh is inherently frustrating to a demon, as it represents a severe reduction in his ability and facility to communicate. Theoretically, a demon may not have "learned" a particular human language; but once he turns his mind to understanding that language, he would grasp it

---

18 St. Thomas Aquinas, *Summa Theologica*, I.107.1 and 3.

intuitively and completely, better than the greatest poet laureate of that culture. Demons even use slang expressions and profanity very effectively!

A demon may speak in esoteric languages, as sometimes happens, but the demon usually answers in the language the exorcist uses to speak to him. There are times when the priest speaks one language and the demon responds in another, but this is rare. In one interesting case of exorcism, the demon spoke to me with the same accented English that was characteristic of the victim; however, the accent was somewhat thick and there were words that were hard for me to understand, so I commanded the demon to *spell* the word he was saying in order for me to understand the exact word—and he did.

26. Do the demons really yell out your sins to you in an exorcism?

Demons have no access to the purely spiritual parts of the human soul (mind and will), but they can "see" the unconfessed and unforgiven sins on a soul. So can angels, for that matter. Therefore, any person who participates in an exorcism, priest or helper, is vulnerable to having unconfessed or unrepented sins used against him by a demon in the course of the event. It is thus extremely important for anyone conscious of grave sin to make a sacramental confession before participating in an exorcism.

Since demons are also *intuitive* beings, it is possible for them to notice disordered *attachments* and propensities to sin in the soul, even if the sins have been confessed. These attachments and inclinations are in the sensitive faculty of the soul (i.e., imagination, emotions, passions, etc.) and will be much more readily accessible to the demonic understanding, as opposed to the spiritual faculties of mind and will, which are closed to them.

If one is in a state of grace, however, he need have no fear that the devil will dredge up his past sins. Since the sins of the past are blotted out by the virtue of Christ's redemption, the devil simply can't see those that are confessed. They are not there.

27. Can demons read a person's thoughts?

Neither angels nor demons can penetrate the mind of a person without his permission. The mind is a sacrosanct inner faculty of the soul that is closed to them. However, demonic intelligences are so acute and finely tuned to the weaknesses of human nature that they can often *predict* our thoughts. Fr. José Antonio Fortea, in his book, *Interview with an Exorcist*, expresses it best:

> Though demons can tempt us, they cannot read our thoughts. With their great intelligence, they can guess what we are thinking—but can never be absolutely certain. As spiritual beings, they are much more intelligent than we are, and as such, they can deduce things with greater accuracy and with fewer external signs than we can. But we always have to remember that demons are outside our souls; only God can truly read the soul.[19] This being said, if one directs his mind and will to a saint, an angel, or a demon, they can hear us. So it does not matter whether our prayer is verbal or merely mental. In certain cases of possession, I have observed that the demon obeys orders that have been given mentally.[20]

---

19 Fr. Fortea refers here to the impenetrable mind, will and conscience of man, which are the exclusive domain of God; however, spiritual beings such as demons can "see" and "intuit" the fleshly matter of the sensitive appetite, as noted in the previous question.
20 *Op. cit.*, p. 34. To supplement that insight, a colleague once told me a story that she walked into a mental hospital one day and passed by a one-way mirror where half a dozen or so women were waiting in a room. She noticed one woman who looked disturbed and said to herself, "My, she looks like she has a demon." Immediately, the woman, who could not see her from behind the mirror, jerked her head up and (her demon) said to my friend in piercing tones, "You're right, and a d***ed good one!" That

28. Should an exorcist ever mock or taunt a demon in an exorcism?

Never. When I first became involved in the ministry of exorcism, I used to engage in this type of assault on the demons thinking that it weakened them, but I've reevaluated that practice for several reasons:

First, taunting and mocking are species of the capital sins of Pride or Malice, the devil's sins. There is no way that any such expressions can assist an exorcist in fighting a prideful being: they are the weapons of the devil and can't be used for righteousness. Second, the example of the humble angels teaches us that this is wrong. Even the glorious St. Michael the Archangel was not one to taunt the devil. When he had to confront Satan, he asked the Lord to rebuke him rather than engage the devil in a personal assault. This incident is recounted in the Book of Jude which wisely cautions against "reviling angelic beings."[21] It is with the same angelic humility and trust in the power of God that the exorcist carries out his ministry against demons.

Finally, the demons themselves may even be emboldened by taunts. By this I mean that all proud beings, when stung or challenged by someone they consider their inferior, tend to strengthen their defensive reactions. Far from being intimidated by the mockery of an inferior human, their angelic pride kicks in and they fight harder. An exorcist may, however, remind the demon that he is inferior to God, that his ability to resist is limited and that the demon is even somehow serving God's plan by allowing God to manifest the authority of the Church. These truths will certainly weaken the strength of demonic pride.

---

seemingly "private" thought of my friend was picked up telepathically by the proud demon in control of his victim who wanted to make sure my friend knew it.
21 Cf. 1:8-9

29. Does a victim "see" the demon at any time?

The answer to this is clearly yes. It is not the case in all exorcisms or deliverances, but at break times or sometimes in the heat of battle, when the exorcist asks the victim to tell him what is happening "inside," there is usually a real clarity about the identity and activity of the demon. The exorcee has a different type of "sight" than seeing things with the eyes of the body; it is akin to a bad dream that a person can describe when he awakes. This "sight" is also due to the presence of the Light of Christ in an exorcism that exposes the demons for what they are.

30. Can a person experience a holy vision in the course of an exorcism?

Yes, this is not uncommon. It can be God's way of consoling an individual who has been subject to the vicious assaults of the devil. Such visions can give the person strength to persevere through the trials of the possession and exorcism.

In the famous case of Anneliese Michel[22] in Germany in 1976, the demons themselves complained that various persons were assisting her in the exorcism: the Blessed Virgin Mary, St. Joseph, Padre Pio, Theresa Neumann (the German stigmatist), a local holy woman who had died a few years earlier, St. Michael and Anneliese's guardian angel, her deceased infant sister, a deceased family friend, her deceased grandmother and others. Anneliese was apparently aware of all of them at one time or another during the course of the exorcisms, and the exorcist judged them to be authentic visions, not deceptions.

I know one person who experienced multiple visions of the Virgin Mary in different exorcisms, as well as an angelic choir and a vivid experience of the Passion of Christ while walking

---

22 Cf. Appendix H.

the sorrowful Way of the Cross. Two different victims I worked with "saw" a procession of people entering the church to stay with them during the Litany of the Saints at the beginning of the exorcism ritual, and these holy visions were tremendously consoling during their afflictions.

31. What is the role of angels in an exorcism?

Angels are the most underutilized spiritual forces in the world, but they are the exorcist's best friends. Indeed at the beginning of the exorcism ritual, in the Litany of Saints, we invoke the help of the three Archangels, Michael, Gabriel and Raphael, and then "all holy angels of God." An exorcist and his team need the invisible forces of good to fight and expel the entrenched forces of evil in this spiritual combat. Holy angels are the executors of God's Will.

The exorcist and the prayer team will frequently call on St. Michael and his host of exorcist angels, asking for assistance in various ways: binding the demons, forbidding interplay between the demons, separating the human from the demonic personalities, mental insight to know the tactics of the enemy, and the spiritual gift of angelic fervor to persevere in the arduous battle. Those familiar with the actual case of possession that led to the movie, *The Exorcist*, will know that it was St. Michael who eventually cast the demon out of the boy.

What is said of St. Michael can be said in general of all angels. They are available to the priest and his team to "enlighten, guide, strengthen and console" us in our exorcism work. They bring strength and consolation to the victim during his time of trial (St. Gabriel, the "strength of God" is chief of these) and are tremendous healers when we use them for that (St. Raphael, the "healing of God" is the chief of these). In short, there is nothing that the angels cannot and will not do for an exorcism team when asked, as long as it is in accord with God's Will. They are mighty servants of Our Lord and Our Lady and spiritual warriors by nature.

32. What are the "signs" by which an exorcist or a victim knows an evil spirit has departed?

The normal technique in an exorcism is for the exorcist to command a demon to reveal a sign of its departure. Without a tangible sign, it is difficult to tell whether the demon has left the body or not. The question he uses is simple: "By what sign will I know that you are definitively gone from this body?"[23] The priest must command him to answer truthfully because of the demon's deceptive nature, and the possessing demon will usually indicate some concrete sign or action of his departure. Once in an exorcism a demon said that the sign of his departure would be "when she wakes up." The victim, who had been totally unconscious of everything that had transpired in a long exorcism session,[24] at a certain point snapped awake, as if for the first time, and knew intuitively that the demon was gone.

Other signs may be expiration through the breath or mouth, making the Sign of the Cross, a convulsion, a noise, sight or sound, etc. It is also possible for the priest to "assign" a demon a particular sign, such as the "Hail Mary," if the demon refuses to give one. Even after the sign is given, however, one must verify that the demon is actually gone through careful monitoring and follow-up care of the victim.

---

[23] The 1614 exorcism ritual states it simply, *"I command thee, unclean spirit...thou shalt tell me by some sign or other thy name, and the day and hour of thy departure."* Cf. Weller, *Rituale*, p. 179.

[24] Please refer to the case-study of an exorcism described in the Afterword to this chapter.

33. Do all demons give signs when they depart?

No. The easiest signs of departure to discern are obviously the clear words and gestures, but if there is no overt sign of departure, sometimes common agreement among the exorcism team about their experiences can validate a demon's departure. They can all feel a tangible sense of relief, some "cloud" of oppression lifted from the room, a vivifying spirit of goodness return, etc. The effect of the departure of the demon is sometimes immediate. For example, once, after expulsion, a lady said to me, "Father, I feel as though I lost thirty pounds!" She also said that she could, for the first time, suddenly see everything around her in vivid color.

When all is said and done, however, it is the person himself who is the final judge of the departure of a demon. Even if there was no very distinct sign of a demon's departure, the person's feeling of relief and "enduring peace" is the surest sign of a demon's departure.

34. If the exorcism is performed correctly, why would a demon not leave?

There are only a few reasons why a demon would not leave the body of a possessed person through a properly-performed exorcism. First, there may be some legal reason holding it in (such as the person giving internal permission for it to stay); there may also be some strong occult force at play which gives the demon or the possession extra power; it may also be that the exorcist just has not given enough time for the process to reach its culmination and needs to persevere more. Usually, if the bishop's authority in a solemn exorcism seems not to be sufficient to expel a demon, it is probably because faith, prayer and/or perseverance are weak or lacking and need to be strengthened.

35. How does an exorcist know when all the demons are gone?

As mentioned above, the victim himself is the best judge of his own liberation from the evil spirits. The absence of symptoms of the demonic presence (short term) and the principle of "enduring peace" (long term) are the best ways for a victim to ascertain that he is free. There may also be a person with the charismatic "gift of discernment" who can render a judgment on the definitive liberation of the person. However, even where such a gift is present and put at the service of the Church, the gift must be put to the test, and the principle of "enduring peace" still applies as the final indicator of full deliverance.

36. What does it actually mean to "cast out" a demon?

In the exorcism, the priest, through the power of Christ and His Church, "breaks" the will of the demon and thus breaks the concentration of the demon's malevolence on that person or place. It would be like someone shattering the magnifying glass so it could not reflect the concentrated light of the sun burning its object. The shards of broken glass have no more power to magnify the rays of the sun and are easily swept up and thrown away. Or it may be likened to prying the vice grip of a very strong man's hand off an object that he is holding. When the devil's grip is broken off his victim, he can be ejected as long as the victim does not continue to allow him to be there by some internal permission or cooperation.

37. Where do demons go when they are cast out?

An exorcist should command demons to go to the Foot of the Cross or to go directly to Jesus. Some think that demons should be sent back to hell, but the priest does not have this authority! In the analogy of a criminal prosecution described in Question 1 above, the exorcist must realize that he is only the prosecutor, not the judge, and that implies a limit of his authority over a demon. His job is to *convict* the criminal and force him to stand before the Judge for his sentencing. It is not the job of the exorcist to send the criminal to prison, let alone decide what prison he will go to. Jesus the Judge is the supreme authority in that courtroom, and the successful prosecutor must trust that every demon's fate is in the hand of the Lord of Heaven and Earth.

38. Does the "Foot of the Cross" actually exist?

The "Foot of the Cross" is the *spiritual* place of our redemption which stands outside of time and space. Calvary is the place where Satan was vanquished. There is a Latin phrase which explains this well: *Crux stat dum volvitur mundum* (The Cross remains still while the world revolves [around it]). In a similar vein, in the Eastern Catholic traditions, the "Foot of the Cross" was code language for the *axis mundi* (the axis of the world) and was thought to be the center of the world, situated directly over hell.[25]

The priest symbolically stands at the Foot of the Cross each day when he offers the Holy Sacrifice of the Mass. As exorcist, he calls down the Precious Blood of Jesus from the Cross to liberate the victim from the malevolent will of the demon. "The Foot of the Cross" is that place where all humans may spiritually retreat to receive refreshment and grace; it is the ultimate Tribunal where Christ judges all demons because it was the place where Satan himself was judged.

39. What does the victim feel after a demon has left?

Most victims feel a combination of relief and exhaustion immediately after a successful exorcism, but not always. At times they

---

25 Rev. Jeffrey S. Grob, Mundelein Conference, 2007.

will have a renewed clarity of mind and soul, which is something akin to "waking up" from a long, dreary nightmare. Others may describe it as the feeling of a dirty cloud lifting off them or a heavy weight being taken off their body. These are all signs of liberation. The *Rite of Exorcism* contains several "post-deliverance" prayers of thanksgiving to God for being freed from the power of the demon. [26]

Depending upon how long the possession lasted, a victim may need professional help to assist in his longer-term healing. In some cases when a demon departs, the newly-freed victim is completely restored to health and experiences no negative side-effects at all. This is possible, but rare. In most cases, however, healing will happen through prayer and close contact with the sacraments, especially the Eucharist, as well as immersion into a supportive, prayerful family or community if possible. There is no substitute for an intense return to the grace of the sacraments, which is the best source of healing for a newly-freed victim of demonic possession. The exorcist has a responsibility to maintain contact with the person to assure that his healing progresses and that he stays out of future spiritual danger.

40. Is the exorcee persecuted before, during or after an exorcism?

All of these things are possible but should not be exaggerated. The exorcee often experiences an increase of persecutions and harassment prior to an exorcism, because the demon understands what is happening and wants to turn his victim away from going to the exorcism appointment. If there are oppressions, they usually are not powerful enough to hurt or stop him from remaining faithful to his commitment to the exorcism.

---

26 See Appendix B, Numbers 6-7, and Appendix D, Post-Liberation Prayers.

During the course of an exorcism, the demon can persecute the victim, but a good exorcist will bind the demon's power to harm the victim before, during and after the exorcism. The priest must anticipate some measure of oppression, inner and outer, and know that it sometimes "gets worse before it gets better." There is no substitute for a priest's kindness and ongoing encouragement to the victim during the whole course of the exorcism.

Finally, spirits of "retaliation" may afflict the person after an expulsion, and the priest must anticipate them and teach the person not to be fazed by them. At the end of each exorcism session, he should bind the power of any spirit of retaliation and spiritually seal the person, covering him with the Precious Blood of Jesus to protect him. These prayers are also expressions of the authority of Christ and generally work very effectively to inhibit any post-exorcism harassment.

41. Can a person be re-possessed?

While there is real danger of a demon leaving a person and returning with "seven demons worse than himself,"[27] it is slight. Fr. Fortea says that, as long as a person "lives in the grace of God, prays, and goes to Mass and regular confession (i.e., once a month or even more frequently), he has nothing to fear since he is protected; the evil cannot enter again."[28] It is only when the person falls back into a pattern of sin or seriously opens himself up to evil again that there will be problems.

I know the true story of a woman who was victimized by a family member practicing witchcraft but who was later freed through an exorcism. Some years after that, the woman got married, and, in a burst of imprudence, invited that same family member to the wedding. In that moment of emotional openness,

---
27 Mt 12:45
28 Fortea, *Interview*, p. 106

the wicked family member *renewed* the curse and sent another demon into her (or several). She was re-possessed and, soon after that, allegedly died from the new spiritual malady. There was no known natural cause of her death. The saving grace was that, in the course of the first possession, she learned to turn strictly to Jesus for help, and her last words at death were literally, "Father, into your hands I commend my spirit." This was a sign to all the family members that she died in grace. However, one can only wonder if she would be alive today had she not naively invited that occult family member to her wedding.

42. Does the devil retaliate against the priest if he does exorcisms? How about those who help him?

The devil is never pleased when a man of mere flesh and blood comes against him in warfare to take away his prized possession. Fr. Gabriele Amorth writes a pertinent passage on this matter: "I also want to refute a popular belief that, I do not know how, has managed to convince a good portion of the clergy: that is, the conviction that the devil retaliates against exorcists. My teacher, Father Candido, who exorcised full-time for thirty-six years, suffered some physical illnesses due partly to age, but not to the devil....I will continue to repeat this—and I beg you to believe me: the devil is already causing each one of us as much harm as he is allowed to do....a priest who is afraid of the devil's reprisal can be compared to a shepherd who is afraid of the wolf. It is a groundless fear."[29]

Demonic retaliations can potentially happen to the helpers of an exorcism as well, but if the priest blesses them and covers them, their loved ones and property, all their actions, projects and relationships with the Precious Blood of Jesus, they will be protected. I have never seen this type of prayer for protection fail.

---

29 Amorth, *An Exorcist Tells His Story*, p. 194.

Afterword to Chapter 6
Outline of an Exorcism[30]

Some years ago I was asked by a particular diocese to investigate the case of a woman who was asking for an exorcism. Hers was a very advanced state of possession when I met her, and this is the story of her exorcism. I used the 1614 *Rite of Exorcism* in its English translation to conduct the exorcism sessions.

History and Symptoms

Angie (not her real name) was a native of another country and had been suffering demonic problems since she was a teenager, due to the wickedness of certain family members who were steeped in the occult. According to her testimony, her aunt dedicated her to Satan at an early age, and her uncle promised the devil that he would deliver over the soul of his niece if only Satan would make him rich. It was as simple as that. When she was a teenager, she unsuspectingly gave them a series of personal items and pictures, which they used in satanic rituals to curse her and send demons into her. She was vulnerable to them because they were family members who, at that time, apparently she still had affection for. She did not know they were taking advantage of her innocence and performing satanic rituals to destroy her life.

When I met her, eighteen years later, she was in a constant state of internal suffering. She daily experienced visions of snakes, owls and wild animals, paranormal experiences of dead relatives and other creatures speaking to her and appearing to her, dreams of being buried alive, physical attacks and blockages, assaults by terrible lascivious images and sensations, evil presences punishing her for various things, emotional turmoil and an inability to

---

30 The name and details of the story have been modified to protect the identity and dignity of the person involved.

form any meaningful human relationships or keep a job. In addition to that, she was suffering horrible nightmares every single night and unable to sleep for more than a couple hours at a time. According to a credible psychiatric report, her intense emotional pain was not related to any identifiable psychosis or neurosis, and no amount of therapy or medicine helped her. She added to her problems by consulting with psychics several times over the course of the years.

Her real suffering can be seen in this paragraph that she wrote at the time of the initial evaluation:

Around July the "devil" came again, stronger this time. This situation is unbelievable. The devil (men and women) are visiting me almost every night, they buried me alive twice, dogs and other monsters are chasing me and arresting me. I lost my job and many more, and everybody walked away from my life again. I cannot describe what is going on right now with words. This may be what hell and death feel like. It is like they are reading me. They know my intentions, where I will go and what I will do the next day and they have the ability to stop it. The more I pray the stronger and horrifying their "reply" is. I am even hearing voices at this moment.

Signs of Possession

The major problem Angie had was the detestable presence of "someone" that was with her every day and harassed her internally and externally. "He" kept her awake, abused her, frightened her, and even physically attacked her. She felt that he was "assigned" to her and would not allow her to have a healthy relationship with a man. The spirit tried to isolate her and seemed intent on not allowing her to get married. Of this "someone" she said, "This thing has stolen my whole life," and "Every single decision I have made is somehow connected to him." She consulted many priests and even one bishop over the years, but no one effectively helped her. She experienced some temporary relief from prayer, but the demon was never expelled and the problems always came back; she was plunged back into the same chaos of life and brokenness that she had experienced for many years.

When I met her, she was practicing her Catholic faith regularly but attending a Protestant prayer/healing group that had prayed over her many times. Each time they prayed, there were serious manifestations, but they were never able to definitively free her from her problems. The Protestant pastor described her behavior in the prayer session as very stormy: writhing on the ground when touched by holy water, aversion to sacramentals, clouding of consciousness during the prayers, changing of the voice in tone and speed and speaking in a mocking voice to those who were trying to help her. On top of all this, Angie claimed that she did not remember anything about the sessions.

Exorcism process

The process of Angie's exorcism lasted one full year and spanned seven sessions. Due to its convenience, the sessions were conducted in the Protestant church where she was attending the prayer group. Each session included anywhere from two to six helpers, with a mixed team of Protestants and Catholics, but the rite was authorized by the local Catholic bishop, and I was the authorized exorcist. It was a full, solemn Catholic exorcism. During all seven sessions, Angie remembers nothing at all of the many hours spent on the exorcisms. Her only lucid moments were when we took breaks as well as one final experience of enlightenment in the seventh session described below.

Session one (February)

This session lasted nine hours, but this was because I was not experienced at that time and did not understand the need to restrict the length of sessions due to people's natural limitations. It was apparent from the beginning that there was some kind of serpent demon because, when I first placed the crucifix on her head, Angie slid out of the chair onto the floor like a snake. This demon was cast out. A second demon emerged calling himself "Legion" and said that he was 15 demons strong. This "coalition" of demons was not cast out in this session; but at the end of the whole exorcism process, we could account for all 15 demonic entities. In this coalition there were several of the other demons in her who called themselves with the names of the family members who were the victimizers. These were likely the possessing spirits of those family members that they sent into Angie by their curses and satanic acts.

Session two (mid-March)

This session lasted three and one quarter hours and focused on the uncle's demon and the spirits of the men who had participated in these rituals with him. The demon described them as "magicians." There were myriad curses and acts of victimization performed on Angie, all of which were described in detail by the demonic entity speaking through her under obedience. The exorcism prayers and a specific prayer of breaking undid the effects of all the satanic actions, and the exorcism cast out the possessing spirits of the group of magicians as one. The possessing spirit of the uncle[31] was stronger, and it did not leave. Nonetheless, Angie felt immense relief after the session. The demons said that their

---

31 This refers to the demonic spirit that possessed the uncle, not the human spirit of the uncle himself. As noted in Question 5 of Chapter 4, there is no credible Catholic theological tradition which asserts that human spirits possess other people, especially if the human being is still alive.

sign of departure would be her "waking up;" and true to form, when they left, she immediately snapped back to consciousness, not remembering a single detail of the three-plus-hour session.

Session three (late March)

This session lasted three hours and identified two other possessing spirits with family names—i.e., apparently two *other* family members had also victimized her by occult acts, but up to that point she was unaware that they were involved. These left after some prayer and commanding with the ritual. Then we dealt with another demon that described itself as a "black bird." Angie had complained, especially after the first exorcism, of dreams involving an ugly black bird banging at her window scaring her and trying to get in. In the initial interview she had spoken of some owl-like creature that haunted her. The name of the black bird demon confirmed this. When this demon was present, her face took on a bird-like appearance: the nose subtly narrowed like a beak, the eyes slanted and the mouth tightened and protruded somewhat. This demon said he would "fly out of the mouth" as his sign of departure, which seemed to happen when she opened her mouth stiffly and let out a gasp of wind. Then Angie woke up and was completely coherent again without the slightest memory of the whole session.

Interlude and Crisis Period

After the third session, Angie seemed exhausted by all the spiritual warfare for so many years and the stress of the sessions, and regretfully, she decided to short-circuit the process. It was obvious to the team that the remaining demons were attacking her faith and, despite the overwhelming "success" of the expulsions thus far, she was not convinced this process was really helping her. She wrote:

> *I am writing to inform you that I do not believe that the Lord really wants to heal or free me. For a reason unknown to me, he is letting me burn in hell.... Prayers and other supplications are not working because God doesn't want me to be happy. I accept my destiny and I will go on with that dark life until whatever is going on in the invisible world comes to an end or I leave this world. Fr. Tom, please annul any plan for exorcism and/or any other type of prayers you may have in mind. I lost faith in prayers and any other type of deliverance. You can't pray for someone who does not believe in prayers anymore. I will be free when God decides so and there is no need for me or anybody else to do anything about it. I guess what I am trying to tell you all here is that I AM GIVING UP. I AM DONE. THAT'S IT FOR ME. IT'S MORE THAN I CAN HANDLE. I tried though for almost 20 years. You can't say that I didn't try.*

All the members of the prayer team tried hard to convince her to continue, but she refused. Since no one can be forced to undergo an exorcism, we reluctantly suspended the process and just continued to intercede for her and maintain contact with her. The lesson learned was that an exorcism process requires a great deal of consistent effort and perseverance until the very end. There is an active, though unseen, force that works from the inside to undermine the process, and only with a firm decision by the person to continue until the final expulsion of all demons can the process come to a successful conclusion. A half-finished exorcism concedes the battlefield to the demon.

Session four (October)

After several months, due to a severe family crisis and much prayer, Angie decided to return to the exorcism process because she saw the need for it again. This was a great grace. The session, however, proved to be frustrating and inconclusive due to

Angie's ongoing distrust of the process and reluctance to cooperate interiorly with the exorcism.

One demonic presence manifested itself but would not leave despite more than three hours of labor. A member of the team sensed the presence of a demon that was very strong and protecting his territory. This demon would not speak except to claim that the exorcism prayers were not working. This was very discouraging for the team. All was not lost though. The prayer was helpful in weakening the demon, whom we believe left in the session on the next day.

Session five (the following day)

In this two and a half hour session, the power of prayer was evident. A member of the team who had a gift of spiritual sight said she saw an army of saints come into the church when we began the Litany of Saints; these stayed the whole time and, she claimed, even turned outward to fight off demons who wanted to prevent Angie's delivery. Also, the women of the group were inspired to pray over Angie's stomach, and when they did, she looked as if she were vomiting something, although nothing visible came out. There was no explicit sign of departure, but another member of the group "saw" the Precious Blood dripping down upon Angie and, according to the lady, demons were exiting Angie like white wisps which dissipated. We did not take this as an infallible sign that there was an expulsion, but we were encouraged by it. The spiritual force of the sacramental ritual can free the person of unseen influences which are not overtly battling with us. God's grace is never limited to the ministry of the priest alone. At least three members of the team heard the words, "It is finished," at the end.

Session six (mid-December)

This session lasted three hours and was the most discouraging of the six exorcisms up to this point. Just prior to this, Angie had three catastrophic incidents happen to her all in the space of a couple of weeks: the death of her sister, the exhaustion of her personal finances and the physical destruction of her apartment by water damage. These incidents not only filled her with grief but also seemed to play into a sense of foreboding that she had about not being able to ever be free of the oppression. She said she had "lost the will to survive." This was frightening to us. She came to the exorcism in a desperate state, feeling "numb" all over, listless, jobless, and hopeless. Yet, she manifested good will by simply continuing with the process.

It was also the most violent of all the sessions up to that point. Only with hindsight did we recognize that we had finally come to the last and strongest demon, and the demon was not going to leave without a fight. We did not expel the demon in this session, and it was a difficult session. In the course of our prayer there were at least three major attempts by Angie to run away and a few major fits of rage. At least two of those fits lasted for several minutes in literal wrestling with the woman to keep her down. The demon also tried to bite us through her and attempted to deceive us by using her voice to say that she wanted to stop and go home. In a lull while we were shifting and re-positioning ourselves, she jumped and violently tried to escape with flailing arms and screams. She was clearly under the influence of the demon and kept struggling for some time. In the end there was no expulsion, but the exorcism had at least brought her some peace in her difficult moments.

Seventh and last session (February, one year to the day after the first session)

Undoubtedly, this was the most grueling of all seven exorcism sessions. The exorcism lasted four hours and required the full strength of six people to hold Angie down from the violent actions of the final, possessing demon. This demon had the name of her uncle and, although he had come to the surface and spoke in earlier sessions, he had not left. We prayed and commanded for a good while, but it was difficult to interpret the demon's answers or actions. However, the prayer was working to weaken the demon for his ultimate expulsion.

Suddenly, at about the two hour mark, Angie had what can only be described as a "vision" in the course of the exorcism. We were not sure if it was from the Lord or from the demon so I rebuked the spirit of deception several times, and the vision continued for another fifteen to twenty minutes. Angie was actually "seeing," as if on a screen in her mind, a clear and shocking picture of all the evil that had been perpetrated on her and had pervaded her life for so many years. During the visions she was conscious and constantly expressed surprise with phrases like, "No one would believe this," "This is incredible," "Can't you guys see this?" and "People would think I'm crazy if they saw this," etc. In fact, she was seeing her life for the first time *as the Lord saw it*. She said that she now understood "what" exactly happened to cause all this and "how" it happened; she never understood these things so clearly before. She was, in effect, objectively viewing the story of her own victimization.

As the exorcism continued, the demon began to react with more violence: continuous attempts at biting us; writhing around, pushing back, jumping up and forward, swinging arms violently; a blood-curdling scream that was the most piercing of any of her exorcisms; kicking out violently and pulling the legs in; and twisting the arms to get out of the grip of the helpers. The strength of the demon physically threw one of the helpers over on his side a few times. The demon was grabbing and breaking the crucifix; grabbing and crushing the exorcism ritual book; vacillating between weak and strong moments and attempts to get out of our grip and bolt. There were also many insolent words from the demon such as his constantly yelling at me, "Shut up!" and taunting such as "You can't do anything" and "I am strong, I can take it," even in the midst of the worst pain that the ritual was causing him. He even called me "kiddy" and "child" numerous times, to which I always responded, "Yes, I am a child of God," to deflect his arrogance.

The final expulsion came when Angie herself made a valiant attempt to forgive her uncle in her heart and also to forgive God for permitting her to go through all this pain and sorrow. That was a crucial moment and sticking point in her faith life. The Satanists had attacked her very relationship with God, and the *spiritual abuse* was the worst damage of all. She also made an attempt to die to her "old life" and live a new life in Christ in a concrete act of faith. After the third or fourth repetition of this act of faith, Angie "snapped to" instantly and was surprised to see that she was on the floor. She remembered virtually nothing about the exorcism except her vision and the final act of faith that she had made consciously. The violence was over and her peace returned.

Chapter 7
Pastoral Considerations

Now, since the children are men of blood and flesh, Jesus likewise had a full share in ours, that by his death he might rob the devil, the prince of death, of his power, and free those who through fear of death had been slaves their whole life long. (Heb 2:14-15)

The Church has evidently never allowed men to shrug off their own responsibility by blaming their sins on the devil. It has not hesitated to speak out against such an evasion when it appears; with [John] Chrysostom it has said: "It is not the devil but men's own carelessness that is responsible for all their falls and for all the misfortunes they lament." In this area, Christian teaching with its energetic defense of man's liberty and dignity and its emphasis on the omnipotence and goodness of the Creator refuses to yield ground..... It has proscribed both superstition and magic; it has rejected every doctrinal capitulation to fatalism and every abdication of liberty in the face of violence. (Congregation for the Doctrine of the Faith, *Christian Faith and Demonology*, 1975)[1]

---

1 *Vatican Council II: Conciliar and Post-Conciliar Documents, New Revised Edition*, ed., Austin Flannery, OP, Costello Publishing Company, Inc., Northport, NY, 1992, p. 477.

✢

After describing the ministry of exorcism and its place in the life of the Church Militant, this chapter intends both to give priests some practical pastoral guidelines on how to conduct this ministry fruitfully and also to offer spiritual guidance to those who seek answers to demonic problems. Those priests who wish to embrace this ministry more fully need to be guided by the wisdom and the teaching of the Church if they are to be successful. They will also need the Church's protection since this ministry engages them in hand-to-hand combat with the forces of evil. Even though casting out demons and healing those who are spiritually afflicted has been less emphasized than many other tasks that priests must perform, it is nonetheless an extremely important pastoral ministry that has a continuous history throughout the life of the Church.

Cura animarum

The salvation of souls is the proper and predominant concern of the Roman Catholic priesthood and of each individual priest. This concern is summed up in the single phrase that the Church always gives to this work: *cura animarum*.[2] It is articulated well in Church documents like the *Catechism of the Catholic Church*, papal teachings[3] and the *Code of Canon Law*, the last canon of

---

2   The Latin word *cura*, "care, carefulness, attention, diligence," or "an attending, minding, healing, cure" (*Langenscheidt Shorter Latin Dictionary*, Hodder and Stoughton: London, 1966), is the root for the English word "curate" and the Spanish term "*cura*" and French "*curé*," all of which simply mean "parish priest," as opposed to religious order priest.

3   In recent decades the hierarchy has spoken out very forcefully and beautifully in re-affirming the gift and blessings of the priesthood and the intrinsic nature of it as an instrument for the salvation of souls: note especially Vatican II's document, *Presbyterorum Ordinis*, Pope Paul VI's *Sacerdotalis Caelibatus* in 1967, the 1992 Apostolic Exhortation, *Pastores Dabo Vobis*, of Pope John Paul II, among many others, as well as the recently-declared Year for Priests of Pope Benedict XVI.

which concludes: "having before one's eyes the salvation of souls, which is always the supreme law of the Church" (c. 1752). In fact, as we know, Pope Benedict recently established the "Year for Priests" and dedicated it to the patron saint of all priests, St. John Vianney, who was a model of pastoral zeal for the salvation of souls.

The *cura animarum* is not the concern only of the bishop in a diocese. It is the essential job description of every priest and, fortunately or unfortunately for us, there are many people with demonic problems that need attention from those who are the spiritual leaders of the Church. As I mentioned in the Introduction, our society is a breeding ground for serious demonic afflictions that are poised to reach epidemic proportions in the coming decades and which will undoubtedly be laid at the feet of priests. As good shepherds, we must be able to give proper guidance and assistance to those with truly spiritual problems.

In speaking about these subjects, the complaint I hear most is that, despite the thousands of priests that minister in any given area, state or region, there is rarely any priest who will pay attention to or help a person with demonic problems. I believe there are several basic reasons for this:

- Priests are already overworked and in high demand for every need of the faithful;

- Priests are not trained in seminary to deal with true demonic problems; and sometimes,

- Priests are either afraid of the demonic or of the high-intensity work that spiritual healing / deliverance seems to require; or

- Priests are fearful of involving themselves in such situations sometimes because their bishops or religious superiors are opposed to such work.

All these reasons may be mixed together in the complex reasoning of a priest to deny help to a person or refer that troubled person to a psychologist, but in most cases, a little information and training will equip priests for this ministry. Making the necessary information and resources available to priests is the motive for this book.

It must be emphasized that every priest is potentially an exorcist and deliverance minister, and the vast majority of cases that may ever be placed before him are not as complex as they seem on their face. There is no need for any priest to be afraid of the people who complain of spiritual problems. Most of their situations are rarely more difficult than any other pastoral challenge. They just *seem* more difficult because they carry the label "demonic" on the title of their story. When a priest generously tries to help people in the realm of spiritual healing, he will find that he can offer, simply by the gift of his priesthood, immense comfort to many who are deeply afflicted. In those times when he discovers that their problems are more complicated than originally understood, there always remains the option of referring them to professionals or exorcists with greater experience.

As an example of how relatively simple some cases can be, I cite the case of a first-year priest who referred a woman to me who was complaining of demonic problems for many years.[4] She had had several abortions and began to feel terribly oppressed

---

4 The name and identity are withheld and some details are omitted to protect the individual. The essence of the story is to communicate the relative facility of healing a good many cases of demonic problems.

by some spirit that had obviously entered her through abortion.[5] To further compound the problem, she visited an occult practitioner, seeking freedom; but this only made it worse. Finally, in desperation, she looked in the phone book for the nearest Catholic church that she could find, because she had seen on TV that Catholic priests cast demons out of people! She told the priest her story, and at the end of their meeting he prayed for her briefly, getting a very strong demonic reaction. He then called me and set up an appointment for both of us to pray with her a few days later. When we did, the demonic force manifested strongly for only about *thirty to forty seconds* and then left, never to return again. After that point she was completely liberated and only needed some emotional healing as a follow up. To think that she had suffered so many years for a "problem" that took less than 40 seconds to expel!

Would that all demonic obsessions could be expelled in such a short time! Nonetheless, this anecdote points out the fact that there are many people who suffer from demonic problems that have a relatively simple solution, if only the priests will dedicate, as this young priest did, a little time and attention to their needs, even within the context of a busy pastoral schedule. I would hasten to add that it is one of the greatest joys of the priestly life to see the victory of Christ in freeing someone who suffers so deeply from a demon's malice. In point of fact, the young priest, even without much experience of priesthood, would have been capable of doing the same simple prayer session to heal the lady if he had known how relatively simple it was. Since it was not a solemn (i.e. liturgical) exorcism, praying for her was simply a function of his priesthood. I included him in the prayer both so that he could follow up with her when I left and so that he

---

5 See my companion booklet, *Demonic Abortion*, for a fuller explanation of this phenomenon.

would know how to perform other simple deliverances in the future. Such prayer is fully within the competence of any priest for the assistance of suffering souls.

The bishop and the diocese certainly do have their proper responsibility in seeing to it that there is some priest available for exorcism ministry in the diocese. The diocese should provide training sessions both for priests interested in the ministry and also for discernment groups which could handle the screening of cases and many requests that come into the chancery office for spiritual help. Beyond formal exorcism, however, every priest is a spiritual healer and deliverer, and there is no substitute for individual priests on the front lines of the Church being willing to dedicate time to this ministry. In fact, if front line priests were managing people's demonic problems at the grass roots level, it is less likely that the diocese would get so many calls from people with problems that had become serious through lack of pastoral care.

The priestly role in helping people to discern the power of evil

It is helpful for the reader to think of a time when he experienced pain, whether physical or emotional, mild or sharp. One's overwhelming concern at a moment like that is undoubtedly the cessation of the pain! His second thought, if the pain is acute, is to find a professional who can help him to be permanently free of the pain. The same dynamic holds true when one is faced with hostile legal action, or a broken water pipe or a computer that has suddenly crashed, etc. In such cases, professional expertise is needed, and fast. So why should it be different for someone who suffers from the constant harassment of a demon?

This is really how afflicted people look at priests. Many share the opinion of the aforementioned non-Catholic lady who picked up the phone book and called a Catholic church because she heard on television that Catholic priests do this kind of thing; we are the "go-to" guys for demonic problems. And of course, demons don't just afflict Catholics! Catholics may be the first to think of calling a priests for such problems, but non-Catholics and persons of no faith at all often have need of the services of a "spiritual professional" who wears a Roman collar—and if they do not get our help, they will likely seek the services of those so-called "experts" who deal in tarot cards, psychic readings and esoteric "cleansings" of body and spirit, all of which will only enslave them further and lead to the possible damnation of their souls.

Although, as I mentioned above, the vast majority of spiritual problems are not complex, the priest is nonetheless seen as a resource to help people discern what exactly their problem may be and to find help for it. In Chapter 4 we took a brief look into the area of discernment,[6] but it is my intent here to emphasize the *pastoral need* for priests to be available to the faithful and others in giving them basic principles for sorting out demonic situations and problems that are rampant in our increasingly occult-infested world.

The priest also has a role in helping parents who are afraid that their kids may be dabbling in the occult or could be possessed or affected negatively by occult things. Parents need solid advice and resources from knowledgeable professionals to discern the dizzying array of unholy fascinations that their kids are drawn into. Everyone knows that drugs and heavy metal music are bad, but who knows what occult or evil influences lurk inside of seemingly "innocent entertainment" addictions like the Harry Potter series or video games like *Dungeons and Dragons*, *Runescape* and *Diablo*? There is an almost infinite variety of other

---

6 The accompanying booklet to this text, *Discernment Manual for Exorcists and Deliverance Ministers*, will give further insight into the techniques and issues related to discernment.

difficult-to-discern forces tantalizing our kids in their media-saturated culture, and priests are the spiritual professionals whom parents often turn to in order to get answers. We have to be prepared to help parents in their grave duty to protect their children and loved ones from spiritual evil.

Basic principles for giving spiritual help

Priests must provide spiritual help and advice to people based on principles derived from our faith and common sense. The few basic principles below can be of use to priests who are trying to help people fight the spiritual forces afflicting them or their loved ones. These principles are a basic primer of pastoral readiness for priests and provide a few points of practical advice for helping them remain faithful and fruitful in the hard work of spiritual warfare:

1. <u>Test all things</u>: St. John's first epistle says: "Beloved, Do not trust every spirit, but put the spirits to a test to see if they belong to God, because many false prophets have appeared in the world" (1 Jn 4:1). As a general rule this means that the priest must take no demonic problem at face value, no matter how sincerely the problem is described to him. This does not mean he discounts people's frank explanations of their problems. It just means that everything that a person believes, experiences and feels must be put to the test in order to understand it better in the light of God's grace.

2. <u>Get to the root of things</u>: Many people don't want to get to the root of their problems because to do so would cause them to have to make changes. People grow comfortable of even painful or dysfunctional lifestyles and are reluctant to change. If a person is not willing to get to the root of his problem and live a healthier life of faith, then there

is very little that the priest can do to help him. Some people seek to be dependent upon a spiritual healer. Others want a caretaker or rescuer that will give them a solution to their pain without any effort on their part. Still others want the priest just to wave a magic want and get rid of their problems, but priests are too busy to deal with people who don't really want to be healed. A very important consideration in any healing process is to find out if the person really desires to get to the root of the problem and is willing to make the effort to do so.

3. <u>Process of elimination</u>: The individual must not blame all of his problems on demons even if these seem to be caused by spiritual forces or past occult experiences. The human person is an incredible bundle of internal and external complexities, and human problems should not be over-spiritualized. As a general rule, natural causes should be investigated very carefully first, before it is presumed that a person's problems come from demons. This is not to say that we don't pray with people in the course of investigating their problems. It is rather to say that we go through a process of eliminating all natural explanations first before we blame a problem on demons. It is also quite possible that the situations are mixed, that is, that some cases include a combination of preternaturally and naturally caused phenomena. This makes proper discernment all the more imperative.

4. <u>Faith and prayer as the foundation of all healing</u>: a person without faith cannot be healed. There has to be some openness to a transcendent dimension of existence in order to deal with life's problems, especially problems that involve demons, and faith opens that door. If a person does not have explicit faith in Jesus, the faith of the Church suffices

as long as the person doesn't reject it. The person must also be taught how to pray and petition help from God in the process. As always, any deliverance from evil spirits needs the light and grace that prayer can provide, and without it, there is little hope of healing.

5. <u>There's "no free lunch"</u>: While a priest doesn't charge for his services, it is often good for him to let people know that his time is not free. He must set limits on what people can demand of him, keep very clear boundaries and give very clear timelines to show them that they must render an account of their healing process to God through him. A busy priest has no time to waste, and he is not in the business of forming co-dependent healing relationships, which help no one. It is also good for him to tell a person that he will take on a case for a determinate length of time or number of sessions, after which he will make a judgment as to whether he can help the person further or will need to refer him to someone else for help. These agreements up front give discipline to the whole healing relationship.

6. <u>The more concrete the better</u>: In deliverance and exorcism, we are trying to penetrate a mystery which has inherently deceptive and intelligent factors behind it. Demons defy diagnosis and shun the light. The more a priest is able to "name" the evil and bring to light what lies hidden, the better. The power of evil prefers abstraction and diversion, but by naming and exposing the demons and their behavior patterns, the mystery begins to be revealed in a way that was not clear at the beginning. The more concrete a priest is in his approach to deliverance, the better. The dynamics of a discernment process more often than not involve negative human behaviors or conditions of mind

that the person himself will be unaware of, but which may be the very reasons or conditions which keep demons from departing.

7. <u>Stay behind the shield of the Church</u>: The Church, as St. Paul says to Timothy, is "the pillar and bulwark of truth."[7] It is also a fortress of spiritual strength for those who enter battle at close quarters with evil spirits. Anyone seeking protection from the toxic ideas of today's modern media and influences will find refuge in the Church's doctrine. Anyone wanting protection from evil spirits will find it in the bosom of the Church's devotional and sacramental life and prayer. Either way, the Church is our protection, and the priest must never lay down his spiritual armor and adopt techniques for spiritual healing other than those approved by the Church. As mentioned before, it is dangerous for priests to act in the role of psychologist or mental health professional if we are not trained in these areas. We are spiritual healers and are most protected and effective remaining firmly in that role.

8. <u>There is no quick fix</u>: Priests must never promise people that their problems can be solved fairly quickly or easily. Even with a thorough inventory of problems and clear diagnosis of what is wrong, we can never be too categorical about the mystery of iniquity that we encounter in the life of a person. Again, people often naively look to the priest to be a fixer, a rescuer or a magician who can free them from pain by a simple formula or command. It is usually just not that easy! The priest must aggressively disabuse people of such naïve notions and work with them only if there is some indication that a person is taking responsi-

---

[7] 1 Tim 3:15

bility for his own healing. The priest who takes too much responsibility for the person's healing path is left with all the work—and all the blame when it fails, as it inevitably will if he becomes anyone's caretaker.

9. <u>Give sufficient time</u>: It hardly needs to be said that a busy priest must be very careful of the workload he takes on, especially as it pertains to vulnerable people who will inevitably want more and more attention from him. He must be very judicious in his discernment of which cases to take on and how long to remain serving people before referring them for help from others. However, when there is good will and cooperation with the healing efforts of the priest, it is very important that he give sufficient time to the people he agrees to help. A good priest who is particularly overloaded should try to enlist the help of a trusted and competent brother priest and/or other appropriate professional when he himself cannot provide support. A superficial approach to healing is always to the advantage of the evil ones, who do everything they can to derail the process and get people to believe that there is no hope for healing. The priest must be a good shepherd and allow sufficient time to take people through a healing process which is ultimately for the benefit of their immortal souls and worth the effort. It just can never be accomplished as quickly as one would like.

The state of grace and the Toehold-Foothold-Stronghold analogy

Priests must teach the faithful how to be fortified against the intrusions of the devil. It cannot be emphasized enough that the major fortification against the devil's work is living in a state of grace. The more one consciously lives and practices one's faith and avoids all sin, the more fortified he is against any weapon the devil may fashion against him. This is the simplest formula for spiritual protection, and it is possible for everyone.

Another major pearl of wisdom in this effort is what John LaBriola[8] calls the "Toehold-Foothold-Stronghold" analogy. That is, *the devil only operates with human permission* and will always work in a progressive fashion once he has an entrance point. The first "toehold" in our lives is sin. This toehold, if not addressed appropriately through sacramental Confession and conversion of heart, soon becomes a "foothold" due to the devil's aggressive action and desire to harm us. The demons constantly study our persons, habits and weaknesses, and if they find no repentance or reform of life they attempt to take more territory, i.e., permission to operate in our lives. When spiritual negligence has gone quite far, or if we are so unwise as to voluntarily participate in an occult act of some sort, they take more interior territory and penetrate further into our lives. At this stage, a demon may have built himself a "stronghold" of evil within our persons and can become a controller, causing increasing pain and sorrow and urging us on to greater evil and sin.

The obvious wisdom of this image is that the "strongman"[9] of the Gospel can never build his stronghold within a person unless he first has a toehold and then a foothold, in graduating increments of inner control. People who are fully possessed are rare for this very reason. It takes time and a regular pattern of ceding inner territory for a demon to achieve such a level of cooperation with the person that he can actually control his body and faculties. A demon is only able to advance incrementally to achieve that control, and even when he does, he can be repelled

---

[8] Author of *Onward Catholic Soldier: Spiritual Warfare According to Scripture, the Church and the Saints*, John Labriola, Huntington Beach: California, 2008.

[9] Cf. Mt 12:29

to some degree by a person's conversion, prayer or life of faith even if he is not able to be expelled entirely by these. In serious cases of obsession and possession, of course, a person needs the prayer of the Church in order to expel the demon, but acts of faith and authentic turning to God do restrain the "strongman" in his obsessive desire to obtain complete control.

This is also the reason why all exorcists will say that a sacramental Confession is a much more powerful spiritual force than an exorcism. Confession is a sacrament and exorcism is a sacramental. Exorcism is remedial; Confession is preventative *and* remedial. An ounce of prevention is worth a pound of cure, as the old proverb says. The Sacrament not only has sacramental graces that are given to those open to receiving them, but it is also a way to pull out the spiritual weeds in the soul of a person before the devil has had a chance to plant them deeply. Exorcism is reserved only for the most serious cases where demons have advanced to the level of stronghold, and a superior spiritual power is needed to expel them. Even in spiritual matters, it is better to nip a problem in the bud than to wait for years and have to pull out a fully-grown tree!

Teach them to close the doorways to the occult

Part of the ongoing effort to educate people about evil's deceits is to help them understand how evil enters a person's body (or life). Based upon the principle that evil can operate only where it is given permission and latitude to do so, there are just a few basic reasons why evil may enter into a person to do its work, and a few other reasons why it is restricted from doing so when it is opposed. The goal, of course, is to teach people how to prevent evil from ever gaining a serious foothold in their lives.

An analogy of blocking entrance to demons will set the stage. In Tolkein's epic trilogy, *The Lord of the Rings*,[10] the wizard Gandalf forcefully confronts the wickedest demonic being in the whole series—an infernal balrog that was awakened from the pit of hell in the Mines of Moria. To do so, he stands on a narrow bridge above a chasm to defend his friends who have fled to the other side away from the Balrog, and he pronounces authoritatively,[11] four distinct times, his prohibition of the demon's advance: "You cannot pass!" (In the popular movie version he yells only one time, "You *shall not* pass!") He then plants his wizard's staff on the bridge, shattering it so the demon cannot cross, and watches as the demon falls into the abyss. Gandalf himself eventually falls in his battle with the Balrog, giving his life to prevent the hideous creature from destroying his friends. Gandalf is thus an image of the Christian who whirls around and faces demons or any occult influence saying with full authority, "You cannot pass!" (i.e., into me or into the lives of my loved ones). Such a confrontation is real—and indeed necessary at times—in the life of every Christian. Christian authority is used not for selfish purposes but for the protection of the innocent and of loved ones.

The principle here is that stopping evil before it enters is much easier and less painful than getting it out once it comes in. Knowing evil's entry points and tactics helps in the warfare of keeping the devil out and even in getting him out once in. The exorcism ritual, for example, instructs the exorcist to command

---

10 J.R.R. Tolkien, *The Lord of the Rings* Trilogy, Part I: "The Fellowship of the Ring," Ballantine Books: New York, NY, 1965, pp. 428-430.

11 In his writing of this passage, Tolkien expresses, in a vivid way, the power of authoritative commands and their effect on evil things. For example, the first time Gandalf says, "You cannot pass!" Tolkien writes, "The orcs stood still and a dead silence fell." Then after another "You cannot pass!" command, Tolkien says, "The Balrog made no answer. The fire in it seemed to die…."

the demon to say how he entered because that information may provide clues as to how his power may be undone or neutralized. For instance, if a demon entered by a curse, the curse must be broken in order for the demon to be expelled.

The priest must constantly remind people that the best defense against the entrance of evil spirits is for a person to remain in a state of grace. The state of grace provides a veritable suit of spiritual armor, like St. Paul talks about in the sixth chapter of Ephesians. The state of grace technically can't be penetrated by spiritual evil unless, as the saying goes, the person "lets his guard down." According to our basic catechism, venial sin does not cause a person to lose the state of grace but mortal sin does. Sacramental Confession is a remedy for this type of sin and restores the state of grace so that a person will be deprived of his spiritual armor only until the next Confession. This spiritual protection is one of the many benefits of belonging to a church with a sacramental system that communicates God's very Life to us on a repeated basis.

There are just a few "doorways" to evil that the faithful need to be aware of and reminded about. These have been mentioned in earlier chapters but bear repeating for the sake of catechesis. The first doorway to evil is the *free invitation* that one makes for the devil to enter. This invitation may be expressed through terrible means such as satanic consecrations or even careless invitations that people make to demons asking them to possess them. It is frightening that this happens, but there it too much evidence of it to be denied. A human being's free will is the doorway by which he allows good or evil things to enter, and he bears the consequences of those invitations or permissions.

Milder forms of free invitation, yet nonetheless toxic, are occult games, objects and association with persons involved in the occult. How many men and women are being seduced by the New Age movement (and its contemporary offshoots), or satanic rock music/video games, or just simply in being careless and playing with spiritual fire in séances or visiting psychics! All of these things are doorways, and the person's embrace of them constitutes an act of the free will inviting something evil to enter. It does not matter, as many have said to me, that the person thought what he was doing was harmless: the deceiver wants susceptible people to think that he his harmless because otherwise no one would invite him in.

Victimization is the second way people can be infested by spiritual evil. An innocent individual (especially a child) may not have any intention of doing evil but can be victimized by the evil of others. For example, I helped in the case of a very emotionally wounded individual who was praying at an abortion clinic unaware that there were witches in the abortion clinic praying curses against her. She ended up infested with the evil because her woundedness made her open to it. I have also met many adults who were victims of abuse or wounding as children and, through the wounding, became infested with demons in their bodies. Practitioners of the occult, who are unfortunately not few, often take advantage of emotionally-vulnerable people and curse them or victimize them spiritually as a way of expressing their malice or their desire to control another. Oftentimes an exorcist must demand that a person receive therapy for healing inner woundedness at the same time he is receiving exorcism. The parallel processes will complement each other. He must make people aware that emotional healing of inner woundedness is also a protection to future victimization.

Finally, a *long history of unrepentant mortal sin* creates a doorway to evil that has to be closed in order for a person to be healed. Fr. John Corapi says convincingly that "sin is a letter of permission to the devil."[12] Sin is evil and has its root in the devil's rebellion against God. While all sins do not bring demons in to possess a person, a long history of unrepentant mortal sin certainly can. The seriousness of the spiritual evil that the person voluntarily embraces and the length of time that he embraces it constitute a literal and legal contract with the demons motivating the sin and can bring serious infestation over time. This is usually why it is frequently harder to exorcise or heal older people who have lived in serious violations of God's law for significant periods of their life. Conversion and moral integrity, however, are always necessary for all people and are pre-conditions for being delivered of spiritual evil.

The only other reason why a person may be infested with demons is that God, for some mysterious reason of His Divine Providence, allows the infestation. Fr. Gabriele Amorth, in his 1999 book, *An Exorcist Tells His Story*, gives indication that St. John Bosco, St. Gemma Galgani and other saints were possessed by demons for some period of time, with the general understanding that God allowed it for their sanctification. There is also the well-known case of the German girl, Anneliese Michel[13], spoken about earlier as the one whose story formed the basis of the movie *The Exorcism of Emily Rose*. Her spiritual director called her possession an "expiatory possession" due to the extraordinary grace that had been granted to her not only to suffer for the German people but also to be a high-profile witness to the reality of the devil in the modern world. It is my experience that all people who suffer from demonic possession or obsession are given an opportunity to see their suffering as a Way of the Cross

---

12 Fr. John A. Corapi, SOLT, *Immortal Combat* CD Series, #4: "The Role of the Sacramentals," Santa Cruz Media: Kalispell, MT, 2001.

13 See Chapter 6, Question 30, and Appendix H.

for their own sanctification and growth in faith. Whether they take advantage of the opportunity or not is another story.

With regard to demonic problems in general, we should not let people think that God wants them or allows them to be "victim souls" simply because they suffer some demonic affliction. Nor should we ever accept anyone making an "offering" of himself as a victim soul. This is a very dangerous way of thinking, because it presumes that God wishes a person to remain in a state of pain and sorrow—subject to the depredations of the devil—as a more or less permanent way of life or as a spirituality. The few cases of this in the Church's life are the rarest of phenomena, and people who think they are victim souls usually do so because of a lack of discernment or a tendency to over-spiritualize life's problems. In the exceptionally rare circumstances where God permits this, it has to be tested very carefully and fully by Church authorities in order to prove its authenticity; otherwise, we just cannot accept that people are chosen to be victim souls. The devil would like nothing more than to have unhealthy people interpreting his hateful actions as the will of God.

Parish-based initiatives and preaching

In preaching and teaching, it is imperative for priests to give true spiritual formation to their people. It is astounding how hungry the people are for basic spiritual insight that is common to us who have been through seminary training but is unfortunately lacking in people who live in a perverse secular culture. Regretfully, most Catholics have been fed a steady diet of nonsense or platitudes from the pulpit that rarely edify their minds or feed their deep interior hungers.

Spiritual men preach on spiritual topics. Spiritual leaders give formation to the faithful in spiritual growth and warfare. My own long experience of talking on these and other matters of

Church teaching bears this out: once I was giving an erudite pro-life talk to an audience with all the relevant statistics and effective quotes from the most current literature on the subject, and I received a polite applause when I finished. Then when I sat down an older, mature Catholic woman said to me, "Father, what we need from priests are not more statistics, but advice on spiritual warfare. Leave the statistics to the lay men and give us what we need to nurture our souls!" This point was well-taken. I can also say that the talks I have given on spiritual warfare, exorcism and deliverance are the most well-attended talks I have ever given with the most enthusiastic audiences, which are always followed by long, drawn-out question and answer periods that could go on far longer because of the need that people have for direction in these matters.

There are also many sermon topics that never fail to fortify the faith of God's people. The following is a partial list of what any priest may speak of on any given day from the pulpit or in seminar form: the reality of the devil and spiritual evil, types and modes of spiritual warfare, protection from spiritual evil, Catholic teaching on angels, how angels accompany us on the spiritual journey and how to develop a friendship with one's guardian angel, how to discern and resist temptation, stories of saints who fought with the evil one or overcame spiritual obstacles to holiness, how to practice and grow in virtue, the importance of living in a state of grace, the tactics of the devil and how to unmask his works and empty promises, the spiritual power of the sacraments for our protection and sanctification, modern occult phenomena and how to see them for what they are, etc. Relating these spiritual lessons to the prevailing culture is a way of giving people the ability to apply their faith to the concrete problems of life that they encounter on a daily basis. People look to priests for such knowledge and are often awash in a sea of moral relativism simply because they receive no guidance from the pulpit on fundamental points of spiritual warfare.

There is always a need to be creative in the way we present this information to our people. The primary form of communication with our people is through the daily and weekly preaching that is our bread and butter as pastors of souls. Then too we can offer seminars, adult education classes, days of recollection or retreats on these topics. No seminar or retreat on spiritual topics will be lacking in attendance, anywhere. There is no reason why priests cannot make the best possible literature available to people in pamphlet, book or electronic form from the many credible organizations that offer it to the faithful. Also, we can provide, as time permits, spiritual direction to church leaders and religious formation to the young so that the messages will get into the hands of those who most need it and who will likely propagate it with zeal. Finally, there is absolutely no substitute for devotional prayer and a fervent sacramental life to help people stay free from the devil "and all his works and all his empty promises." Spiritual leadership of God's people is not only a duty of the priest to give but is a right of the faithful to receive.

Spiritual resources for busy people

Among the many questions I get when I give talks about exorcism and deliverance is, "Where can I get more information about x-y-z?" People raising families and busy at their work need resources that are quick and reliable and give us teachings that are in accord with our faith. So the list below is a resource list for priests to become familiar with and make available to their parishioners or any other interested persons. More resources are available in the Bibliography at the back of this book.

Best resources on spiritual warfare

- John Labriola, *Onward Catholic Soldier: Spiritual Warfare According to Scripture, the Church and the Saints*, Huntington Beach: California, 2008.

- Michael H. Brown, *Prayer of the Warrior*, Faith Publishing Co.: Milford, OH, 1993.

- Fr. John A. Corapi, SOLT, *Immortal Combat* CD/DVD Series, Santa Cruz Media, Inc., PO Box 9440, Kalispell, MT 59904; Phone: 1-888-800-7084; Website: www.fathercorapi.com.

- Dom Lorenzo Scupoli, *The Spiritual Combat and a Treatise on Peace of Soul*, TAN Books and Publishers: Rockford, IL, 1990.

Best websites for spiritual warfare and healing resources

- St. Michael's Call: www.saint-mike.org

- Christian Healing Ministries: www.christianhealingmin.org

Best overall teachers on spiritual warfare and deliverance from a Catholic perspective

- Fr. Michael Scanlan, T.O.R. and Randall Cirner, *Deliverance From Evil Spirits: A Weapon for Spiritual Warfare*, St. Anthony Messenger Press: Cincinnati, OH, 1980.

- The Intercessors of the Lamb, 4014 North Post Road, P.O. Box 12988, Omaha, Nebraska, 68112; Phone: 402-455-5262; Website: http://www.bellwetheromaha.org.

- Fr. John H. Hampsch, CMF, Claretian Teaching Ministry, 20610 Manhattan Place Suite 120, Torrance, CA, 90501-1863; Phone: 310-782-6408; Website: www.claretiantapeministry.org.

- Neal Lozano, *Resisting the Devil: A Catholic Perspective on Deliverance*, Our Sunday Visitor, Inc.: Huntington, IN, 2009.

Best resources for deliverance and healing

- Neal Lozano, *Unbound: A Practical Guide to Deliverance from Evil Spirits*, Chosen Books: Grand Rapids, MI, 2003.

- Francis MacNutt, *Deliverance from Evil Spirits: A Practical Manual*, Chosen Books: Grand Rapids, MI, 1995.

- _____, *Healing*, Ave Maria Press: Notre Dame, IN, 2006.

- Fr. Michael Scanlan, T.O.R. and Randall Cirner, *Deliverance From Evil Spirits: A Weapon for Spiritual Warfare*, St. Anthony Messenger Press: Cincinnati, OH, 1980.

Best resources for healing the family tree

- Fr. John H. Hampsch, CMF, *Healing Your Family Tree: A God-designed Solution For Difficult Problems*, Queenship Publishing Company: Goleta, CA, 1989.

- Kenneth McAll, *A Guide to Healing the Family Tree*, Queenship Publishing Company: Goleta, CA, 1996.

Best resources on the angels

- Fr. Jean Danielou, SJ, *The Angels and Their Mission According to the Fathers of the Church*, Christian Classics from Ave Maria Press: Notre Dame, IN, n.d.

- Peter Kreeft, *Angels (and Demons): What Do We Really Know About Them?* Ignatius Press: San Francisco, CA, 1995.

- The website of the religious order: Opus Sanctorum Angelorum, www.opusangelorum.org.

Best resources on the art of discernment

- Susan P. Brinkmann, OCDS, *Learn to Discern: Is it Christian or New Age* (A Women of Grace Study Series), Simon Peter Press, Inc.: Oldsmar, FL, 2008.

- Fr. Thomas J. Euteneuer, *Discernment Manual for Exorcists and Deliverance Ministers*, Human Life International: Front Royal, VA, 2010.

- Fr. Timothy M. Gallagher, OMV, *The Discernment of Spirits*, The Crossroad Publishing Company, New York, NY, 2005.

- Fr. Thomas H. Green, S.J., *Weeds Among The Wheat, Discernment: Where Prayer and Action Meet*, Ave Maria Press, Notre Dame, IN, 1986.

- Fr. Benedict Groeschel, CFR, *A Still, Small Voice: A Practical Guide on Reported Revelations*, Ignatius Press: San Francisco, CA, 1993.

Each and every one of these resources is a font of information and wisdom and for the most part can be fully and explicitly endorsed without exception. The only non-Catholic resources listed above (Christian Healing Ministries, Lozano and the book by McAll) are reliable sources of information and have very little that would be objectionable to Catholic sensitivities. However, this is not to be taken as a full endorsement of everything that appears in any of these resources or on the above-listed websites, which are changing constantly. It just constitutes a "short list" of some of the most reliable materials and resource sites for the average person of faith interested in the subjects of spiritual warfare, spiritual protection, healing and discernment.

For further resources on healing, deliverance and exorcism please consult the Bibliography at the back of the book.

Appendix A
General Rules Concerning Exorcism
(Part I of the 1614 *Rite of Exorcism*[1])

1. A priest — one who is expressly and particularly authorized by the Ordinary — when he intends to perform an exorcism over persons tormented by the devil, must be properly distinguished for his piety, prudence, and integrity of life. He should fulfill this devout undertaking in all constancy and humility, being utterly immune to any striving for human aggrandizement, and relying, not on his own, but on the divine power. Moreover, he ought to be of mature years, and revered not alone for his office but for his moral qualities.

2. In order to exercise his ministry rightly, he should resort to a great deal more study of the matter (which has to be passed over here for the sake of brevity), by examining approved authors and cases from experience; on the other hand, let him carefully observe the few more important points enumerated here.

3. Especially, he should not believe too readily that a person is possessed by an evil spirit; but he ought to ascertain the signs by which a person possessed can be distinguished from one who is suffering from some illness, especially one of a psychological nature.[2] Signs of possession may be the following: ability to speak with some facility in a strange tongue or to understand

---

[1] Rev. Philip T. Weller, STD, Trans. *The Roman Ritual, Vol. II, Christian Burial, Exorcisms, Reserved Blessings, Etc.*, The Bruce Publishing Co., Milwaukee, WI, 1964. pp. 169-175.

[2] From the emended text of the 1952 edition.

it when spoken by another; the faculty of divulging future and hidden events; display of powers which are beyond the subject's age and natural condition; and various other indications which, when taken together as a whole, build up the evidence.

4. In order to understand these matters better, let him inquire of the person possessed, following one or the other act of exorcism, what the latter experienced in his body or soul while the exorcism was being performed, and to learn also what particular words in the form had a more intimidating effect upon the devil, so that hereafter these words may be employed with greater stress and frequency.

5. He will be on his guard against the arts and subterfuges which the evil spirits are wont to use in deceiving the exorcist. For oftentimes they give deceptive answers and make it difficult to understand them, so that the exorcist might tire and give up, or so it might appear that the afflicted one is in no wise possessed by the devil.

6. Once in a while, after they are already recognized, they conceal themselves and leave the body practically free from every molestation, so that the victim believes himself completely delivered. Yet the exorcist may not desist until he sees the signs of deliverance.

7. At times, moreover, the evil spirits place whatever obstacles they can in the way, so that the patient may not submit to exorcism, or they try to convince him that his affliction is a natural one. Meanwhile, during the exorcism they cause him to fall asleep, and dangle some illusion before him, while they seclude themselves, so that the afflicted one appears to be freed.

8. Some reveal a crime which has been committed and the perpetrators thereof, as well as the means of putting an end to it. Yet the afflicted person must beware of having recourse on this

account to sorcerers or necromancers or to any parties except the ministers of the Church, or of making use of any superstitious or forbidden practice.

9. Sometimes the devil will leave the possessed person in peace and even allow him to receive the holy Eucharist, to make it appear that he has departed. In fact, the arts and frauds of the evil one for deceiving a man are innumerable. For this reason the exorcist must be on his guard not to fall into this trap.

10. Therefore, he will be mindful of the words of our Lord (Mt 17.20), to the effect that there is a certain type of evil spirit who cannot be driven out except by prayer and fasting. Therefore, let him avail himself of these two means above all for imploring the divine assistance in expelling demons, after the example of the holy fathers; and not only himself, but let him induce others, as far as possible, to do the same.

11. If it can be done conveniently the possessed person should be led to church or to some other sacred and worthy place, where the exorcism will be held, away from the crowd. But if the person is ill, or for any valid reason, the exorcism may take place in a private home.

12. The subject, if in good mental and physical health, should be exhorted to implore God's help, to fast, and to fortify himself by frequent reception of penance and holy communion, at the discretion of the priest. And in the course of the exorcism he should be fully recollected, with his intention fixed on God, whom he should entreat with firm faith and in all humility. And if he is all the more grievously tormented, he ought to bear this patiently, never doubting the divine assistance.

13. He ought to have a crucifix at hand or somewhere in sight. If relics of the saints are available, they are to be applied in a reverent

way to the breast or the head of the person possessed (the relics must be properly and securely encased and covered). One will see to it that these sacred objects are not treated improperly or that no injury is done them by the evil spirit. However, one should not hold the holy Eucharist over the head of the person or in any way apply it to his body, owing to the danger of desecration.

14. The exorcist must not digress into senseless prattle nor ask superfluous questions or such as are prompted by curiosity, particularly if they pertain to future and hidden matters, all of which have nothing to do with his office. Instead, he will bid the unclean spirit keep silence and answer only when asked. Neither ought he to give any credence to the devil if the latter maintains that he is the spirit of some saint or of a deceased party, or even claims to be a good angel.

15. But necessary questions are, for example: the number and name of the spirits inhabiting the patient, the time when they entered into him, the cause thereof, and the like. As for all jesting, laughing, and nonsense on the part of the evil spirit — the exorcist should prevent it or contemn it, and he will exhort the bystanders (whose number must be very limited) to pay no attention to such goings on; neither are they to put any question to the subject. Rather they should intercede for him to God in all humility and urgency.

16. Let the priest pronounce the exorcism in a commanding and authoritative voice, and at the same time with great confidence, humility, and fervor; and when he sees that the spirit is sorely vexed, then he oppresses and threatens all the more. If he notices that the person afflicted is experiencing a disturbance in some part of his body or an acute pain or a swelling appears in some part, he traces the sign of the cross over that place and sprinkles it with holy water, which he must have at hand for this purpose.

17. He will pay attention as to what words in particular cause the evil spirits to tremble, repeating them the more frequently. And when he comes to a threatening expression, he recurs to it again and again, always increasing the punishment. If he perceives that he is making progress, let him persist for two, three, four hours, and longer if he can, until victory is attained.

18. The exorcist should guard against giving or recommending any medicine to the patient, but should leave this care to physicians.

19. While performing the exorcism over a woman, he ought always to have assisting him several women of good repute, who will hold on to the person when she is harassed by the evil spirit. These assistants ought if possible to be close relatives of the subject, and for the sake of decency the exorcist will avoid saying or doing anything which might prove an occasion of evil thoughts to himself or to the others.

20. During the exorcism he shall preferably employ words from Holy Writ, rather than forms of his own or of someone else. He shall, moreover, command the devil to tell whether he is detained in that body by necromancy, by evil signs or amulets; and if the one possessed has taken the latter by mouth, he should be made to vomit them; if he has them concealed on his person, he should expose them; and when discovered they must be burned. Moreover, the person should be exhorted to reveal all his temptations to the exorcist.

Finally, after the possessed one has been freed, let him be admonished to guard himself carefully against falling into sin, so as to afford no opportunity to the evil spirit of returning, lest the last state of that man become worse than the former.

Appendix B

Ritus Exorcizandi Obsessos A Daemonio[1]
(Part II of the 1614 *Rite of Exorcism*)

1. Sacerdos ab Ordinario delegatus, rite confessus, aut saltem corde peccata sua detestans, peracto, si commode fieri possit, Sanctissimo Missae sacrificio, divinoque auxilio piis precibus implorato, superpelliceo et stola violacea indutus, et coram se habens obsessum ligatum, si sit periculum, eum, se, et astantes communiat signo crucis, et aspergat aqua benedicta, et genibus flexis, aliis respondentibus, dicat Litanias ordinarias usque ad Preces exclusive. Postea dicat:

Ant. Ne reminiscaris, Domine, delicta nostra, vel parentum nostrorum: neque vindictam sumas de peccatis nostris.	Ant. Remember not, O Lord, our crimes, nor the offenses of our parents. Nor take vengeance for for our sins.
Pater Noster secreto usque ad	Our Father, secretly until:
V. Et ne nos inducas in tentationem.	V. And lead us not into temptation.
R. Sed libera nos a malo.	R. But deliver us from evil.

Psalmus 53

DEUS, in nomine tuo salvum me fac: * et in virtute tua judica me.	Save me, O God, by thy name, and judge me in thy strength.

---

1 Translation by Jason Spadafore. Used with permission.

Deus, exaudi orationem meam: * auribus percipe verba oris mei.	O God, hear my prayer: give ear to the words of my mouth.
Quoniam alieni insurrexerunt adversum me, et fortes quaesierunt animam meam: * et non proposuerunt Deum ante conspectum suum.	For strangers have risen up against me; and the mighty have sought after my soul: and they have not set God before their eyes.
Ecce enim Deus adjuvat me: * et Dominus susceptor est animae meae.	For behold God is my helper: and the Lord is the protector of my soul.
Averte mala inimicis meis: * et in veritate tua disperde illos.	Turn back the evils upon my enemies; and cut them off in thy truth.
Voluntarie sacrificabo tibi, * et confitebor nomini tuo, quoniam bonum est:	I will freely sacrifice to thee, and will give praise, O God, to thy name: because it is good:
Quoniam ex omni tribulatione eripuisti me: * et super inimicos meos despexit oculus meus.	For thou hast delivered me out of all trouble: and my eye hath looked down upon my enemies.
Gloria Patri.	Glory be to the Father.
Sicut erat.	As it was in the beginning.

V. Salvum (-am) fac servum tuum (ancillam tuam).

R. Deus meus, sperantem in te.

V. Esto ei, Domine, turris fortitudinis.

R. A facie inimici.

V. Nihil proficiat inimicus in eo (ea).

V. Save Thy servant.

R. For his/her hope, O my God, is in Thee.

V. Be a tower of strength for him/her, O Lord.

R. Against the face of the enemy.

V. Let the enemy do nothing unto him/her.

R. Et filius iniquitatis non apponat nocere ei.

V. Mitte ei, Domine, auxilium de sancto.

R. Et de Sion tuere eum (eam).

V. Domine, exaudi orationem meam.

R. Et clamor meus ad te veniat.

V. Dominus vobiscum.

R. Et cum spiritu tuo.

R. And let not the son of iniquity come to harm him/her.

V. Send him/her aid, O Lord, from Thy holy place.

R. And from Sion watch over him/her.

V. Lord, hear my prayer.

R. And let my cry come to Thee.

V. The Lord be with you.

R. And with thy spirit.

Oratio

Oremus.

DEUS, cui proprium est miseri semper et parcere: suscipe deprecationem nostram; ut hunc famulum tuum, quem (hanc famulam tuam, quam) delictorum catena constringit, miseratio tuae pietatis clementer absolvat. DOMINE sancte, Pater omnipotens, aeterne Deus, Pater Domini nostri Jesu Christi, qui illum refugam tyrannum et apostatum gehennae ignibus deputasti, quique Unigenitum tuum in hunc mundum misisti, ut illum rugientem contereret: velociter attende, accelera, ut eripias hominem ad imaginem

Let us pray.

God, whose nature is ever merciful and forgiving, accept our prayer that this servant of yours, bound by the fetters of sin, may be pardoned by your loving kindness. Holy Lord, almighty Father, everlasting God and Father of our Lord Jesus Christ, who once and for all consigned that fallen and apostate tyrant to the flames of hell, who sent your only-begotten Son into the world to crush that roaring lion; hasten to our call for help and snatch from ruination and from the clutches of the noonday devil

et similitudinem tuam creatum, a ruina, et daemonio meridiano. Da, Domine, terrorem tuum super bestiam, quae exterminat vineam tuam. Da fiduciam servis tuis contra nequissimum draconem pugnare fortissime, ne contemnat sperantes in te, et ne dicat, sicut in Pharaone, qui jam dixit: Deum non novi, nec Israel dimitto. Urgeat illum dextera tua potens discedere a famulo tuo N. (a famula tua N.), ✠ ne diutius praesumat captivum tenere, quem tu ad imaginem tuam facere dignatus es, et in Filio tuo redemisti: Qui tecum vivit et regnat in unitate Spiritus Sancti Deus, per omnia saecula saeculorum.

R. Amen.

this human being made in your image and likeness. Strike terror, Lord, into the beast now laying waste your vineyard. Fill your servants with courage to fight manfully against that reprobate dragon, lest he despise those who put their trust in you, and say with Pharaoh of old: "I know not God, nor will I set Israel free." Let your mighty hand cast him out of your servant, N., + so he may no longer hold captive this person whom it pleased you to make in your image, and to redeem through your Son; who lives and reigns with you, in the unity of the Holy Ghost, God, forever and ever.

R. Amen.

2. Deinde praecipiat daemoni hunc in modum:

PRAECIPIO tibi, quicumque es, spiritus immunde, et omnibus sociis tuis hunc Dei famulum (hanc Dei famulam) obsidentibus: ut per mysteria incarnationis, passionis, resurrectionis, et ascensionis Domini nostri Jesu Christi, per missionem Spiritus Sancti, et per adventum ejusdem

I command you, unclean spirit, whoever you are, along with all your allies now attacking this servant of God, by the mysteries of the incarnation, passion, resurrection, and ascension of our Lord Jesus Christ, by the descent of the Holy Spirit, by the coming of our Lord for judgment, that you tell me by

Domini ad judicium, dicas mihi nomen tuum, diem, et horam exitus tui, cum aliquo signo: et ut mihi Dei ministro licet indigno, prorsus in omnibus obedias: neque hanc creaturam Dei, vel circumstantes, aut eorum bona ullo modo offendas.	some sign your name, and the day and hour of your departure. I command you, moreover, to obey me to the letter, I who am a minister of God despite my unworthiness; nor shall you be emboldened to harm in any way this creature of God, or the bystanders, or any of their possessions.

3. Deinde legantur super obsessum haec Evangelia, vel saltem unum.

Lectio sancti Evangelii secundum Joannem (Joan. 1, 1-14)	A reading of the Holy Gospel according to John (John 1, 1-14)

Haec dicens, signat se et obsessum in fronte, ore et pectore.

IN PRINCIPIO erat Verbum, et Verbum erat apud Deum, et Deus erat Verbum. Hoc erat in principio apud Deum. Omnia per ipsum facta sunt: et sine ipso factum est nihil, quod factum est: in ipso vita erat, et vita erat lux hominum: et lux in tenebris lucet, et tenebrae eam non conprehenderunt. Fuit homo missus a Deo, cui nomen erat Johannes. Hic venit in testimonium, ut testimonium perhiberet de lumine, ut omnes crederent per illum.	In the beginning was the Word: and the Word was with God: and the Word was God. The same was in the beginning with God. All things were made by Him: and without Him was made nothing that was made. In Him was life: and the life was the light of men. And the light shineth in darkness: and the darkness did not comprehend it. There was a man sent from God, whose name was John. This man came for a witness, to give testimony of the light,

Non erat ille lux, sed ut testimonium perhiberet de lumine. Erat lux vera, quae illuminat omnem hominem venientem in hunc mundum. In mundo erat, et mundus per ipsum factus est, et mundus eum non cognovit. In propria venit, et sui eum non receperunt. Quotquot autem receperunt eum, dedit eis potestatem filios Dei fieri, his, qui credunt in nomine ejus: qui non ex sanguinibus, neque ex voluntate carnis, neque ex voluntate viri, sed ex Deo nati sunt (hic genuflectitur). Et Verbum caro factum est, et habitavit in nobis: et vidimus gloriam ejus, gloriam quasi unigeniti a patre, plenum gratiae et veritatis.

R. Deo gratias.

that all men might believe through Him. He was not the light, but was to give testimony of the light. That was the true light, which enlighteneth every man that cometh into this world. He was in the world: and the world was made by Him: and the world knew Him not. He came unto His own: and his own received Him not. But as many as received Him, he gave them power to be made the sons of God, to them that believe in His name. Who are born, not of blood, nor of the will of the flesh, nor of the will of man, but of God. And the Word was made flesh and dwelt among us (and we saw His glory, the glory as it were of the only begotten of the Father), full of grace and truth.

R. Thanks be to God.

Lectio sancti Evangelii secundum Marcum (Marc. 16, 15-18)

IN ILLO tempore: Dixit Jesus discipulis suis: Euntes in mundum universum, praedicate Evangelium omni creaturae. Qui crediderit, et baptizatus fuerit,

A reading of the holy Gospel according to St. Mark (Mark 16.15-18)

At that time Jesus said to His disciples: "Go into the whole world and preach the Gospel to all creation. He that believes and is baptized will be saved;

salvus erit: qui vero non crediderit, condemnabitur. Signa autem eos, qui crediderint, haec sequentur: In nomine meo daemonia ejicient: linguis loquentur novis: serpentes tollent: et si mortiferum quid biberint, non eis nocebit: super aegros manus imponent, et bene habebunt.

he that does not believe will be condemned. And in the way of proofs of their claims, the following will accompany those who believe: in my name they will drive out demons; they will speak in new tongues; they will take up serpents in their hands, and if they drink something deadly, it will not hurt them; they will lay their hands on the sick, and these will recover."

Lectio sancti Evangelii secundum Lucam (Luc. 10, 17-20)

A reading of the holy Gospel according to St. Luke (Luke 10.17-20)

IN ILLO tempore: Reversi sunt autem septuaginta duo cum gaudio, dicentes ad Jesum: Domine, etiam daemonia subiciuntur nobis in nomine tuo. Et ait illis: videbam Satanan sicut fulgur de caelo cadentem. Ecce dedi vobis potestatem calcandi supra serpentes, et scorpiones, et super omnem virtutem inimici: et nihil vobis nocebit. Verumtamen in hoc nolite, gaudere quia spiritus vobis subjuciuntur: gaudete autem, quod nomina vestra scripta sunt in caelis.

At that time the seventy-two returned in high spirits. "Master," they said, "even the demons are subject to us because we use your name!" "Yes," He said to them, "I was watching Satan fall like lightning that flashes from heaven. But mind: it is I that have given you the power to tread upon serpents and scorpions, and break the dominion of the enemy everywhere; nothing at all can injure you. Just the same, do not rejoice in the fact that the spirits are subject to you, but rejoice in the fact that your names are written in heaven."

Appendix B

Lectio sancti Evangelii secundum Lucam (Luc. 11, 14-22)

A reading of the holy Gospel according to St. Luke (Luke 11, 14-22)

IN ILLO tempore: Erat Jesus ejiciens daemonium, et illud erat mutum. Et cum ejecisset daemonium, locutus est mutus, et admiratae sunt turbae. Quidam autem ex eis dixerunt: In Beelzebub principe daemoniorum ejicit daemonia. Et alii tentantes, signum de caelo quaerebant ab eo. Ipse autem ut vidit cogitationes eorum, dixit eis: Omne regnum in seipsum divisum desolabitur, et domus supra domum cadet. Si autem et satanas in seipsumdivisus est, quomodo stabit regnum ejus? quia dicitis, in Beelzebub me ejicere daemonia. Si autem ego in Beelzebub ejicio daemonia, filii vestri in quo ejiciunt? Ideo ipsi judices vestri erunt. Porro si in digito Dei ejicio daemonia: profecto pervenit in vos regnum Dei. Cum fortis armatus custodit atrium suum, in pace sunt ea, quae possidet. Si autem fortior eo superveniens vicerit eum, universa arma

At that time, Jesus was driving out a demon, and this particular demon was dumb. The demon was driven out, the dumb man spoke, and the crowds were enraptured. But some among the people remarked: "He is a tool of Beelzebul, and that is how he drives out demons!" Another group, intending to test Him, demanded of Him a proof of His claims, to be shown in the sky. He knew their inmost thoughts. "Any kingdom torn by civil strife," He said to them, "is laid in ruins; and house tumbles upon house. So, too, if Satan is in revolt against himself, how can his kingdom last, since you say that I drive out demons as a tool of Beelzebul. And furthermore: if I drive out demons as a tool of Beelzebul, whose tools are your pupils when they do the driving out? Therefore, judged by them, you must stand condemned. But, if, on the contrary, I drive out demons by the finger of God,

ejus auferet, in quibus confidebat, et spolia ejus distribuet. | then, evidently the Kingdom of God has by this time made its way to you. As long as a mighty lord in full armor guards his premises, he is in peaceful possession of his property; but should one mightier than he attack and overcome him, he will strip him of his armor, on which he had relied, and distribute the spoils taken from him."

V. Domine, exaudi orationem meam.

R. Et clamor meus ad te veniat.

V. Dominus vobiscum.

R. Et cum spiritu tuo.

V. Lord, hear my prayer.

R. And let my cry come to Thee.

V. The Lord be with you.

R. And with thy spirit.

Oratio

Oremus.

OMNIPOTENS Domine, Verbum Dei Patris, Christe Jesu, Deus et Dominus universae creaturae; qui sanctis Apostolis tuis dedisti potestatem calcandi super serpentes et scorpiones: qui inter cetera mirabilium tuorum praecepta dignatus es dicere: Daemones effugate: cujus virtute motus tamquam fulgur de caelo satanas cecidit: tuum sanctum nomen cum timore et tremore suppliciter deprecor, ut indignissimo mihi servo tuo, data

Let us pray.

Almighty Lord, Word of God the Father, Jesus Christ, God and Lord of all creation; who gave to your holy Apostles the power to trample underfoot serpents and scorpions; who along with the other mandates to work miracles was pleased to grant them the authority to say: "Depart, you devils!" and by whose might Satan was made to fall from heaven like lightning; I humbly call on your holy name in fear and trembling, asking that you grant me,

venia omnium delictorum meorum, constantem fidem, et potestatem donare digneris, ut hunc crudelem daemonem, brachii tui sancti munitus potentia, fidenter et securus aggrediar: per te, Jesu Christe, Domine Deus noster, qui venturus es judicare vivos et mortuos, et saeculum per ignem.

R. Amen.

your unworthy servant, pardon for all my sins, steadfast faith, and the power--supported by your mighty arm--to confront with confidence and resolution this cruel demon. I ask this through you, Jesus Christ, our Lord and God, who are coming to judge both the living and the dead and the world by fire.

R. Amen.

4. Deinde muniat se et obsessum signo crucis, imponat extremam partem stolae collo ejus, et, dextera manu sua capiti ejus imposita, constanter et magna cum fide dicat ea quae sequuntur:

V. Ecce Crucem Domini, fugite, partes adversae.

R. Vicit leo de tribu Juda, radix David.

V. Domine, exaudi orationem meam.

R. Et clamor meus ad te veniat.

V. Dominus vobiscum.

R. Et cum spiritu tuo.

V. Behold the Cross of the Lord! Begone, ye adverse powers!

R. The lion of the tribe of Judah hath conquered, the rod of David!

V. Lord, hear my prayer.

R. And let my cry come to Thee.

V. The Lord be with you.

R. And with thy spirit.

Oratio

Oremus.

DEUS, et Pater Domini nostri Jesu Christi, invoco nomen

Let us pray.

God and Father of our Lord Jesus Christ, I appeal to your

sanctum tuum, et clementiam tuam supplex exposco: ut adversus hunc, et omnem immundum spiritum, qui vexat hoc plasma tuum, mihi auxilium praestare digneris. Per eumdem Dominum. R. Amen.

holy name, humbly begging your kindness, that you graciously grant me help against this and every unclean spirit now tormenting this creature of yours; through Christ our Lord. R. Amen.

Exorcismus Primus[2]

EXORCIZO te, immundissime spiritus, omnis incursio adversarii, omne phantasma, omnis legio, in nomine Domini nostri Jesu ✠ Christi eradicare, et effugare ab hoc plasmate Dei. ✠ Ipse tibi imperat, qui te de supernis caelorum in inferiora terrae demergi praecepit. Ipse tibi imperat, qui mari, ventis, et tempestatibus imperavit. Audi ergo, et time, satana, inimice fidei, hostis generis humani, mortis adductor, vitae raptor, justitiae declinator, malorum radix, fomes vitiorum, seductor hominum, proditor gentium, incitator invidiae, origo avaritiae, causa discordiae, excitator dolorum: quid stas, et resistis, cum scias, Christum

I cast you out, unclean spirit, along with every satanic power of the enemy, every spectre from hell, and all your fell companions; in the name of our Lord Jesus + Christ! Begone! And stay far from this creature of God. + For it is He who commands you, He who flung you headlong from the heights of heaven into the depths of hell. It is He who commands you, He who once stilled the sea and the wind and the storm. Hearken, therefore, and tremble in fear, Satan, you enemy of the faith, you foe of the human race, you begetter of death, you robber of life, you corrupter of justice, you root of all evil and vice, seducer of

---

[2] I have chosen to use the words "primus," "secundus" and "tertius" instead of the standard Roman numerals, I, II, and III to designate the three exorcisms. This will help to avoid confusion with my labeling of Parts I, II, and III of the exorcism ritual itself.

Dominum vias tuas perdere? Illum metue, qui in Isaac immolatus est, in Joseph venumdatus, in agno occisus, in homine crucifixus, deinde inferni triumphator fuit. Sequentes cruces fiant in fronte obsessi. Recede ergo in nomine Pa ✠ tris, et Fi ✠ lii, et Spiritus ✠ Sancti: da locum Spiritui Sancto, per hoc signum sanctae ✠ Crucis Jesu Christi Domini nostri: Qui cum Patre et Spiritu Sancto vivit et regnat Deus, per omnia saecula saeculorum. R. Amen.

men, betrayer of the nations, instigator of envy, font of avarice, cause of discord, author of pain and sorrow. Why, then, do you stand and resist, knowing as you must that Christ the Lord brings your plans to nothing? Fear Him, who in Isaac was offered in sacrifice, in Joseph sold into bondage, slain as the paschal lamb, crucified as man, yet triumphed over the powers of hell. (The three Signs of the Cross which follow are traced on the brow of the possessed person.) Begone, then, in the name of the Father, ✠ and of the Son, ✠ and of the Holy ✠ Spirit. Give place to the Holy Spirit by this sign of the Holy ✠ Cross of our Lord Jesus Christ, who lives and reigns with the Father and the Holy Spirit, God, forever and ever. R. Amen.

V. Domine, exaudi orationem meam.	V. Lord, hear my prayer.
R. Et clamor meus ad te veniat.	R. And let my cry come to Thee.
V. Dominus vobiscum.	V. The Lord be with you.
R. Et cum spiritu tuo.	R. And with thy spirit.

Oratio

Oremus.

DEUS, conditor et defensor

Let us pray.

God, Creator and defender of

generis humani, qui hominem ad imaginem tuam formasti: respice super hunc famulum tuum N., qui (hanc famulam tuam N., quae) dolis immundi spiritus appetitur, quem vetus adversarius, antiquus hostis terrae, formidinis horrore circumvolat, et sensum mentis humanae stupore defigit, terrore conturbat, et metu trepidi timoris exagitat. Repelle, Domine, virtutem diaboli, fallacesque ejus insidias amove: procul impius tentator aufugiat: sit nominis tui signo ✠ (in fronte) famulus tuus munitus (famula tua munita) et in animo tutus (-a) et corpore. Tres cruces sequentes fiant in pectore daemoniaci. Tu pectoris ✠ hujus interna custodias. Tu viscera ✠ regas. Tu ✠ cor confirmes. In anima adversatricis potestatis tentamenta evanescant. Da, Domine, ad hanc invocationem sanctissimi nominis tui gratiam, ut, qui hucusque terrebat, territus aufugiat, et victus abscedat, tibique possit hic famulus tuus (haec famula tua) et corde firmatus (-a) et mente sincerus (-a),

the human race, who made man in your own image, look down in pity on this your servant, N., now in the toils of the unclean spirit, now caught up in the fearsome threats of man's ancient enemy, sworn foe of our race, who befuddles and stupefies the human mind, throws it into terror, overwhelms it with fear and panic. Repel, O Lord, the devil's power, break asunder his snares and traps, put the unholy tempter to flight. By the sign + (on the brow) of your name, let your servant be protected in mind and body. (The three Crosses which follow are traced on the breast of the possessed person.) Keep watch over the inmost recesses of his (her) + heart; rule over his (her) + emotions; strengthen his (her) + will. Let vanish from his (her) soul the temptings of the mighty adversary. Graciously grant, O Lord, as we call on your holy name, that the evil spirit, who hitherto terrorized over us, may himself retreat in terror and defeat, so that this servant of yours may sincerely and steadfastly render

debitum praebere famulatum. Per Dominum.

R. Amen.

Exorcismus Secundus

ADJURO te, serpens antique, per judicem vivorum et mortuorum, per factorem tuum, per factorem mundi, per eum, qui habet potestatem mittende te in gehennam, ut ab hoc famulo Dei, N., qui (ab hac famula Dei N., quae) ad Ecclesiae sinum recurrit, cum metu, et exercitu furoris tui festinus discedas. Adjuro te iterum ✠ (in fronte) non mea infirmitate, sed virtute Spiritus Sancti, ut exeas ab hoc famulo Dei N., quem (ab hac famula Dei N., quam) omnipotens Deus ad imaginem suam fecit. Cede igitur, cede non mihi, sed ministro Christi. Illius enim te urget potestas, qui te Cruci suae subjugavit. Illius brachium contremisce, qui devictis gemitibus inferni, animas ad lucem perduxit. Sit tibi teror corpus hominis ✠ (in pectore), sit tibi formido imago Dei ✠ (in fronte). Non resistas, nec

you the service which is your due; through Christ our Lord.

R. Amen.

I adjure you, ancient serpent, by the Judge of the living and the dead, by your Creator, by the Creator of the whole universe, by Him who has the power to consign you to hell, to depart forthwith in fear, along with your savage minions, from this servant of God, N., who seeks refuge in the fold of the Church. I adjure you again, + (on the brow) not by my weakness but by the might of the Holy Spirit, to depart from this servant of God, N., whom almighty God has made in His image. Yield, therefore, yield not to my own person but to the minister of Christ. For it is the power of Christ that compels you, who brought you low by His Cross. Tremble before that mighty arm that broke asunder the dark prison walls and led souls forth to light. May the trembling that afflicts this human

moreris discedere ab homine isto, quoniam complacuit Christo in homine habitare. Et ne contemnendum putes, dum me peccatorem nimis esse cognoscis. Imperat tibi Deus. ✠ Imperat tibi majestas Christi. ✠ Imperat tibi Deus Pater, ✠ imperat tibi Deus Filius, ✠ imperat tibi Deus Spiritus Sanctus. ✠ Imperat tibi sacramentum crucis. ✠ Imperat tibi fides sanctorum Apostolorum Petri et Pauli, et ceterorum sanctorum. ✠ Imperat tibi Martyrum sanguis. ✠ Imperat tibi continentia Confessorum. ✠ Imperat tibi pia Sanctorum et Sanctarum omnium intercessio. ✠ Imperat tibi christianae fidei mysteriorum virtus. ✠

Exi ergo, transgressor. Exi, seductor, plene omni dolo et fallacia, virtutis inimice, innocentium persecutor. Da locum, dirissime, da locum, impiissime, da locum Christo, in quo nihil invenisti de operibus tuis: qui te spoliavit, qui regnum tuum destruxit, qui te victum ligavit, et vasa tua diripuit: qui te projecit in tenebras

frame, + (on the breast) the fear that afflicts this image (on the brow) of God, descend on you. Make no resistance nor delay in departing from this man, for it has pleased Christ to dwell in man. Do not think of despising my command because you know me to be a great sinner. It is God + Himself who commands you; the majestic Christ + who commands you. God the Father + commands you; God the Son + commands you; God the Holy + Ghost commands you. The mystery of the Cross commands + you. The faith of the holy Apostles Peter and Paul and of all the saints commands + you. The blood of the Martyrs commands + you. The continence of the Confessors commands + you. The devout prayers of all holy men and women command + you. The saving mysteries of our Christian faith command + you.

Depart, then, transgressor. Depart, seducer, full of lies and cunning, foe of virtue, persecutor of the innocent. Give place, abominable creature,

exteriores, ubi tibi cum ministris tuis erit praeparatus interitus. Sed quid truculente reniteris? quid temerarie detractas? Reus es omnipotenti Deo, cujus statuta transgressus es. Reus es Filio ejus Jesu Christo Domino nostro, quem tentare ausus es, et crucifigere praesumpsisti. Reus es humano generi, cui tuis persuasionibus mortis venenum propinasti.

Adjuro ergo te, draco nequissime, in nomine Agni ✠ immaculati, qui ambulavit super aspidem et basiliscum, qui conculcavit leonem et draconem, ut discedas ab hoc homine ✠ (fiat signum crucis in fronte), discedas ab Ecclesia Dei ✠ (fiat signum crucis super circumstantes): contremisce, et effuge, invocato nomine Domini illius, quem inferi tremunt: cui Virtutes caelorum, et Potestates, et Dominationes subjectae sunt: quem Cherubim et Seraphim indefessis vocibus laudant, dicentes: Sanctus, sanctus, sanctus Dominus Deus Sabaoth. Imperat tibi Verbum ✠ caro factum. Imperat tibi

give way, you monster, give way to Christ, in whom you found none of your works. For He has already stripped you of your powers and laid waste your kingdom, bound you prisoner and plundered your weapons. He has cast you forth into the outer darkness, where everlasting ruin awaits you and your abettors. To what purpose do you insolently resist? To what purpose do you brazenly refuse? For you are guilty before almighty God, whose laws you have transgressed. You are guilty before His Son, our Lord Jesus Christ, whom you presumed to tempt, whom you dared to nail to the Cross. You are guilty before the whole human race, to whom you proffered by your enticements the poisoned cup of death.

Therefore, I adjure you, profligate dragon, in the name of the spotless + Lamb, who has trodden down the asp and the basilisk, and overcome the lion and the dragon, to depart from this man (woman) + (on the brow), to depart from the

natus ex Virgine. Imperat tibi Jesus ✠ Nazarenus, qui te, cum discipulos ejus contemneres, elisum atque prostratum exire praecepit ab homine: quo praesente, cum te ab hominem separasset, nec porcorum gregem ingredi presumebas. Recede ergo nunc adjuratus in nomine ejus ✠ ab homine, quem ipse plasmavit. Durum est tibi velle resistere. ✠ Durum est tibi contra stimulum calcitrare. ✠ Quia quanto tardius exis, tanto magis tibi supplicium crescit, quia non homines contemnis, sed illum, qui dominatur vivorum et mortuorum, qui venturus est judicare vivos et mortuos, et saeculum per ignem. R. Amen.

Church of God + (signing the bystanders). Tremble and flee, as we call on the name of the Lord, before whom the denizens of hell cower, to whom the heavenly Virtues and Powers and Dominations are subject, whom the Cherubim and Seraphim praise with unending cries as they sing: Holy, holy, holy, Lord God of Sabaoth. The Word made flesh + commands you; the Virgin's Son + commands you; Jesus + of Nazareth commands you, who once, when you despised His disciples, forced you to flee in shameful defeat from a man; and when He had cast you out you did not even dare, except by His leave, to enter into a herd of swine. And now as I adjure you in His + name, begone from this man (woman) who is His creature. It is futile to resist His + will. It is hard for you to kick against the + goad. The longer you delay, the heavier your punishment shall be; for it is not men you are contemning, but rather Him who rules the living and the dead, who is coming to judge both the living and the dead and the world by fire. R. Amen.

V. Domine, exaudi orationem meam.

R. Et clamor meus ad te veniat.

V. Lord, hear my prayer.

R. And let my cry come to Thee.

V. Dominus vobiscum.	V. The Lord be with you.
R. Et cum spiritu tuo.	R. And with thy spirit.

Oratio

Oremus.	Let us pray.
DEUS caeli, Deus terrae, Deus Angelorum, Deus Archangelorum, Deus Prophetarum, Deus Apostolorum, Deus Martyrum, Deus Virginum, Deus, qui potestatem habes donare vitam post mortem, requiem post laborem: quia non est alius Deus praeter te, nec esse poterit verus, nisi tu, Creator caeli et terrae, qui verus Rex es, et cujus regni non erit finis; humiliter majestati gloriae tuae supplico, ut hunc famulum tuum (hanc famulam tuam) de immundis spiritibus liberare digneris. Per Christum Dominum nostrum. R. Amen.	God of heaven and earth, God of the Angels and Archangels, God of the Prophets and Apostles, God of the Martyrs and Virgins, God who have power to bestow life after death and rest after toil; for there is no other God than you, nor can there be another true God beside you, the Creator of heaven and earth, who are truly a King, whose Kingdom is without end; I humbly entreat your glorious majesty to deliver this servant of yours from the unclean spirits; through Christ our Lord. R. Amen.

Exorcismus Tertius

ADJURO ergo te, omnis immundissime spiritus, omne phantasma, omnis incursio satanae, in nomine Jesu Christi ✠ Nazareni, qui post lavacrum Joannis in desertum ductus est,	Therefore, I adjure you every unclean spirit, every spectre from hell, every satanic power, in the Name of Jesus Christ of Nazareth, who was led into the desert after His

et te in tuis sedibus vicit: ut, quem ille de limo terrae ad honorem gloriae suae formavit, tu desinas impugnare: et in homine miserabili non humanam fragilitatem, sed imaginem omnipotentis Dei contremiscas. Cede ergo Deo ✠ qui te, et malitiam tuam in Pharaone, et in exercitu ejus per Moysen servum suum in abyssum demersit. Cede Deo ✠ qui te per fidelissimum servum suum David de rege Saule spiritualibus canticis pulsum fugavit. Cede Deo ✠ qui te in Juda Iscariote proditore damnavit. Ille enim te divinis ✠ verberibus tangit, in cujus conspectu cum tuis legionibus tremens et clamans dixisti: Quid nobis et tibi, Jesu, Fili Dei altissimi? Venisti huc ante tempus torquere nos? Ille te perpetuis flammis urget, qui in fine temporum dicturus est impiis: Discedite a me, maledicti, in ignem aeternum, qui paratus est diabolo et angelis ejus. Tibi enim, impie, et angelis tuis vermes erunt, qui numquam morientur. Tibi, et angelis tuis inexstinguibile praeparatur incendium: quia

baptism by John to vanquish you in your citadel, to cease your assaults against the creature whom He has formed from the slime of the earth for His own honor and glory; to quail before wretched man, seeing in him the image of almighty God, rather than his state of human frailty. Yield then to God, + who by His servant, Moses, cast you and your malice, in the person of Pharaoh and his army, into the depths of the sea. Yield to God, + who, by the singing of holy canticles on the part of David, His faithful servant, banished you from the heart of King Saul. Yield to God, + who condemned you in the person of Judas Iscariot, the traitor. For He now flails you with His divine scourges, + He in whose sight you and your legions once cried out: "What have we to do with you, Jesus, Son of the Most High God? Have you come to torture us before the time?" Now He is driving you back into the everlasting fire, He who at the end of time will say to the wicked: "Depart from me, you

tu es princeps maledicti homicidii, tu autor incestus, tu sacrilegorum capit, to actionum pessimarum magister, tu haereticorum doctor, tu totius obscoenitatis inventor.

Exi ergo, ✠ impie, exi, ✠ scelerate, exi cum omnia fallacia tua: quia hominem templum suum esse voluit Deus. Sed quid diutius moraris hic? Da honorem Deo Patri ✠ omnipotenti, cui omne genu flectitur. Da locum Domino Jesu ✠ Christo, qui pro homine sanguinem suum sacratissimum fudit. Da locum Spiritui ✠ Sancto, qui per beatum Apostolum suum Petrum te manifeste stravit in Simone mago; qui fallaciam tuam in Anania et Saphira condemnavit; qui te in Herode rege in honorem Deo non dante percussit; qui te in mago Elyma per Apostolum suum Paulum caecitatis caligine perdidit, et per eumdem de Pythonissa verbo imperans exire praecepit. Discede ergo nunc, ✠ discede, ✠ seductor. Tibi eremus sedes est. Tibi habitatio serpens est: humiliare, et prosternere. Jam

accursed, into the everlasting fire which has been prepared for the devil and his angels." For you, O evil one, and for your followers there will be worms that never die. An unquenchable fire stands ready for you and for your minions, you prince of accursed murderers, father of lechery, instigator of sacrileges, model of vileness, promoter of heresies, inventor of every obscenity.

Depart, then, + impious one, depart, + accursed one, depart with all your deceits, for God has willed that man should be His temple. Why do you still linger here? Give honor to God the Father + almighty, before whom every knee must bow. Give place to the Lord Jesus + Christ, who shed His most Precious Blood for man. Give place to the Holy + Spirit, who by His blessed Apostle Peter openly struck you down in the person of Simon Magus; who cursed your lies in Annas and Saphira; who smote you in King Herod because he had not given honor to God; who

non est differendi tempus. Ecce enim dominator Dominus proximat cito, et ignis ardebit ante ipsum, et praecedet, et inflammabit in circuitu inimicos ejus. Si enim hominem fefelleris, Deum non poteris irridere. Ille te ejicit, cujus oculis nihil occultum est. Ille te expellit, cujus virtuti universa subjecta sunt. Ille te excludit, qui tibi, et angelis tuis praeparavit aeternam gehennam; de cujus ore exibit gladius acutus: qui venturus est judicare vivos et mortuos, et saeculum per ignem. R. Amen.

by His Apostle Paul afflicted you with the night of blindness in the magician Elyma, and by the mouth of the same Apostle bade you to go out of Pythonissa, the soothsayer. Begone, + now! Begone, + seducer! Your place is in solitude; your abode is in the nest of serpents; get down and crawl with them. This matter brooks no delay; for see, the Lord, the ruler comes quickly, kindling fire before Him, and it will run on ahead of Him and encompass His enemies in flames. You might delude man, but God you cannot mock. It is He who casts you out, from whose sight nothing is hidden. It is He who repels you, to whose might all things are subject. It is He who expels you, He who has prepared everlasting hellfire for you and your angels, from whose mouth shall come a sharp sword, who is coming to judge both the living and the dead and the world by fire. R. Amen.

5. Praedicta omnia, quatenus opus sit, repeti possunt, donec obsessus sit omnino liberatus.

6. Jubavit praeterea plurimum super obsessum saepe repetere Pater Noster, Ave Maria et Credo, atque haec, quae infra notantur, devote dicere.

7. Canticum Magnificat, ut supra; in fine Gloria Patri. Canticum Benedictus, ut supra, in fine Gloria Patri.

Oratio post Liberationem

ORAMUS te, Deus omnipotens, ut spiritus iniquitatis amplius non habeat potestatem in hoc famulo tuo N. (hac famula tua N.), sed ut fugiat, et non revertatur: ingrediatur in eum (eam), Domine, te jubente, bonitas et pax Domini nostri Jesu Christi, per quem redempti sumus, et ab omni malo non timeamus, quia Dominus nobiscum est: Qui tecum vivit et regnat in unitate Spiritus Sancti Deus, per omnia saecula saeculorum. R. Amen.

Almighty God, we beg you to keep the evil spirit from further molesting this servant of yours, and to keep him far away, never to return. At your command, O Lord, may the goodness and peace of our Lord Jesus Christ, our Redeemer, take possession of this man (woman). May we no longer fear any evil since the Lord is with us; who lives and reigns with you, in the unity of the Holy Spirit, God, forever and ever. R. Amen.

Appendix C
Exorcism Against Satan and the Fallen Angels[1]
(Part III of the 1614 *Rite of Exorcism*, also known as the Exorcism of Pope Leo XIII)

The following exorcism can be used by bishops, as well as by priests who have this authorization from their Ordinary.

In the name of the Father, and of the Son, and of the Holy Ghost. Amen.

Prayer to St. Michael the Archangel

O most illustrious Prince of the heavenly hosts, holy Michael the Archangel, from thy heavenly throne defend us in the battle against the princes and powers, against the rulers of this world's darkness. Come to the assistance of humankind, whom God has created in His own image and likeness, and whom He has purchased at a great price from Satan's tyranny. Thee the holy Church does venerate as her patron and guardian. To thee the Lord has entrusted the service of leading the souls of the redeemed into heavenly blessedness. Intercede for us to the God of peace, that He would crush Satan under our feet, lest he any longer have power to hold men captive and do harm to the Church. Present our prayers at the throne of the Most High, so that he

---

[1] Weller, *Rituale*, pp. 223-229; Weller's edition appends a translator's note that says, "Whereas the preceding rite of exorcism is designated for a particular person, the form given here is meant especially to be employed to expel the devil's sway over a locality (parish, city, etc.)."

may all the more speedily favor us with His mercy. Lay hold of the dragon, the ancient serpent, no other than the demon, Satan, and cast him bound into the abyss, so that he may no longer seduce mankind.

Exorcism

In the Name of Jesus Christ, our Lord and God, with confidence in the intercession of the Virgin Mary, Mother of God, of blessed Michael the Archangel, of the holy Apostles Peter and Paul, and all the saints, and with assurance in the sacred power of our ministry, we steadfastly proceed with the task of expelling the molestations of the devil's frauds.

Psalm 67

God need only bestir Himself, then His enemies are scattered, and those who hate Him flee from His presence. As smoke is driven away, so do they vanish; as wax is melted before the fire, so do sinners perish before God.

> V. Behold the Cross of the Lord, begone, ye hostile powers!
>
> R. *The Lion of Judah's tribe hath conquered, He Who is the rod of Jesse.*
>
> V. Let Thy mercy, O Lord, be upon us.
>
> R. *Even as we have trusted in Thee.*

We cast thee out, every unclean spirit, every devilish power, every assault of the infernal adversary, every legion, every diabolical group and sect, by the name and power of our Lord Jesus ✝ Christ, and command thee to fly far from the Church of God and from all who are made to the image of God and redeemed by the Precious Blood of the Divine Lamb. ✝ Presume never again, thou cunning serpent, to deceive the human race, to persecute the Church of God, nor to strike the chosen of God and sift them as wheat. ✝ For the Most High God commands thee, ✝ He to Whom thou didst hitherto in thy great pride presume thyself equal; He Who desireth that all men might be saved, and come to the knowledge of truth. God the Father ✝ commandeth thee! God the Son ✝ commandeth thee! God the Holy Spirit ✝ commandeth thee! The majesty of Christ commands thee, the Eternal Word of God made flesh, ✝ Who for the salvation of our race, lost through thine envy, humbles Himself and was made obedient even unto death; Who built His Church upon a solid rock, and proclaimed that the gates of hell should never prevail against her, and that He would remain with her all days, even to the end of the world! The sacred mystery of the Cross ✝ commands thee, as well as the power of all mysteries of the Christian faith! ✝ The most excellent Virgin Mary, Mother of God ✝ commands thee, who in her lowliness crushed thy proud head from the first moment of her Immaculate Conception! The faith of the holy Apostles Peter and Paul and the other Apostles ✝ commands thee! The blood of the Martyrs commands thee, as well as the pious intercession ✝ of holy men and women!

Therefore, accursed dragon and every diabolical legion, we adjure thee by the living ✝ God, by the true ✝ God, by the holy ✝ God, by the God Who so loved the world that He gave His Sole-Begotten Son, that whosoever believeth in Him shall not perish, but shall have life everlasting – cease thy deception of men and thy giving them to drink of the poison of eternal damnation; desist from harming the Church and fettering her freedom! Get thee gone, Satan, founder and master of all falsity, enemy of mankind! Give place to Christ in Whom thou didst find none of they works; give place to the One, Holy, Catholic, and Apostolic Church which Christ Himself bought with His Blood! Be thou brought low under God's mighty hand; tremble and flee as we call upon the holy and awesome Name of Jesus, before Whom hell trembles, and to Whom the Virtues, Powers, and Dominations are subject; Whom the Cherubim and Seraphim praise with unfailing voices, saying: Holy, holy, holy, the Lord God of Hosts!

> V. O Lord, hear my prayer.
>
> R. *And let my cry come unto Thee.*
>
> V. The Lord be with you.
>
> R. *And with Thy spirit.*

Let us pray.

Prayer

O God of heaven and God of earth, God of the Angels and God of the Archangels, God of the Patriarchs and God of the Prophets, God of the Apostles and God of Martyrs, God of Confessors and God of Virgins! O God, Who hast the power to bestow life after death and rest after toil; for there is no other God beside Thee, nor could there be a true God apart from Thee, the Creator of all things visible and invisible, of Whose Kingdom there shall be no end. Hence we humbly appeal to Thy sublime Majesty, that Thou wouldst graciously vouchsafe to deliver us by Thy might from every power of the accursed spirits, from their bondage and from their deception, and to preserve us from all harm. Through Christ our Lord. R. *Amen.*

> V. From the snares of the devil.
>
> R. *Deliver us, O Lord.*
>
> V. That Thou wouldst assist Thy Church to serve Thee in all security and freedom.
>
> R. *We beseech Thee, hear us.*

V. That Thou wouldst vouchsafe to humble the enemies of holy Church.

R. *We beseech Thee, hear us.*

The surroundings are sprinkled with holy water.

Appendix D
"The New *Rite of Exorcism:* A Potent Weapon Is Weakened"[1]

The Catholic Church has a gift that no other church, Christian or otherwise, can even imagine having—namely, a written exorcism ritual. This little book that makes the devil shake in his boots! As one who uses the ritual, I know how much of a *tour de force* it is against the power of evil. That being said, the exorcism ritual is not what it was in its glory days.

The Title Sets the Stage

Although the Second Vatican Council authorized the revision of all liturgical books, it is hard to believe that the Council envisioned the radicalized changes made to such an important weapon of the Church militant as the 1614 *Rite of Exorcism*. Its 1999 revision is called *De Exorcismis et Supplicationibus Quibusdam* ("On Exorcisms and other Supplications"). Even the change in title signals the change in focus: the 1614 ritual is about freeing those obsessed by demons; the 1999 revision is about prayers and supplications. I am sure the devil is happy to have the focus diverted from breaking his power to pious prayers.

---

1 Rev. Thomas J. Euteneuer, published in the *New Oxford Review*, April 2010 edition for the "Libera Nos a Malo" series on exorcism. Used with permission.

I do not say this for effect. I say it because it is true. It appears as if someone actually took a knife to the old ritual and then, when all the pieces were cut up and lying in a pile, discarded some and cobbled the rest together in a new order and called it a "revision." It is no surprise, as Fr. Gabriele Amorth noted in his 1999 book *An Exorcist Tells His Story*, that the revision was conducted without the input of a single practicing exorcist.

Before proceeding to some specifics, it is important to mention something fundamental to the discussion of any liturgical document: liturgical texts are the Church's texts, and as bad as their revisions may be, they still have spiritual power because they are the official prayers of the Church. Objectively speaking, they exercise a spiritual power that no individual has.

Another aspect to be respected about this particular ritual is that its "official" language is Latin. As a sacred liturgical language, Latin is odious to demons. When a priest uses this language, even when it is poorly pronounced, he is using the mother tongue of the Church and not his own personal language or a language used for secular purposes. He does not have to speak Latin fluently because he is not there to engage in a conversation with the demon. He only has to *read* the prayers and have intense faith in the Church's words.

The new ritual was the last of the liturgical rites to be "revised" after the Second Vatican Council, and it displays some serious deficits while adding only a few minor advantages to the pastoral practice of exorcism. First and foremost is the sad reality that the revisionists transformed what had been a truly economical, spiritually focused ritual into a cumbersome liturgical ceremony. The continuous rubrical references to the "celebration" of exorcism exasperate the exorcist who expects the ritual to be a potent weapon against evil. I ask you: who "celebrates" an exorcism? Liturgical revisionists perhaps; but not exorcists, I guarantee you. An exorcism is a war, not a celebration. The only celebration we could possibly speak of in an exorcism is when the demon is expelled and goes to the Foot of the Cross by the power of the Church. That is cause for celebration! The war that precedes it is hardly a picnic.

Because the revision is more a pious liturgy than an instrument of warfare, it is overloaded with all kinds of truly extraneous and distracting elements, most of which simply have to be skipped over by exorcists in order for the ritual to be used effectively. While the Litany of Saints and Gospel reading are transported from the 1614 original, the other added elements border on annoying. What need, for example, does an exorcism have for an opening greeting to the "assembly"? If there is an "assembly" attending an exorcism, the exorcist is doing something wrong! What place does a homily or a rite to bless holy water have in the course of an exorcism? The exorcist should already have holy water at his side as a weapon. Likewise, what need have we for general intercessions in an exorcism? Intense prayer, yes; petitions for social needs, political leaders and good weather, no.

Moreover, many of the deprecatory prayers (appeals to God) prior to the imperative prayers (commanding the demon proper) are excessively long and distracting. The purpose of the deprecatory prayers is *to ask God's assistance in the warfare against demons*, and the 1614 ritual recognized that shorter deprecatory prayers are more suited to the pastoral nature of the rite that is being performed because the possessed often become fully overtaken by the demons as soon as the ritual prayers begin. The priest often has to shorten or abandon the prayers in order to start commanding the demon once it becomes active. When you are getting mugged by a criminal, you don't want the cop on the street corner reading the instruction manual on how to make an arrest.

Nor should an exorcist persist in long appeals to God when his charge is in a fully possessed state.

In short, the revised ritual prescribes too much ceremony for the priest to complete before going to war. He is expected to pray the secret prayer, bless water (and salt), do an aspersion, pray the Litany, recite Psalm 90, read a Gospel passage, impose hands, conduct a profession of faith or renew the person's baptismal promises (as if the person were even conscious at that point), recite the Lord's Prayer, brandish the Cross and breathe on the possessed person (known as "exsufflation"). All these elements give the devil a veritable *vacation* before his punishment comes.

In addition to these distractions, other annoyances include the weakening of some of the language and the gratuitous removal of the many signings of the cross. For example, Exorcism #2 of the old ritual included 23 signings of the cross, which have been reduced to just three in the equivalent exorcism of the new ritual. Concerning language changes, one simply has to wonder why certain potent terms were re-worked. For example, the term *satánica potestas* ("every Satanic power") was replaced with *omnis tenebrarum potestas* ("every power of darkness"). Did the revisionists think exorcists are afraid of the term "Satanic"? Afraid of offending the devil maybe? Other such language changes throughout take the punch out of the text.

There is a need for order, harmony and solidity in every structure, and the "architecture" of the exorcism ritual is no different. The core strength of the original ritual was its series of three exorcisms. These were an organic progression of prayers, each one building upon the preceding prayer and intensifying the warfare against the fiend as the prayers continued. The imagery and language were almost entirely biblical and increased in aggressiveness from the first to the last. The text took quite literally a millennium to fashion, being sewn carefully together from many earlier texts that had been tested through pastoral use over the centuries.

In contrast, the new ritual gives the impression of a hodgepodge of prayers that someone tampered with just for the sake of making changes. Most elements of this ritual did not need to be changed *at all*. The organic triple exorcism sequence was totally dismantled; only one re-worked exorcism was retained as the "major exorcism," while the other two were relegated to optional and either whittled down or rewritten. The passage commanding the demon to obey the Church was mysteriously eliminated, and the powerful St. Michael Prayer was displaced from its superior position in the 1614 ritual to the *last place* in the new ritual, which must have pleased Michael's arch-nemesis, Satan, to no end.

We have much to thank Pope Benedict for, not the least of which was the fight to retain permission to use the 1614 ritual when the inadequate 1999 revision came out. He was not the only one who knew that the loss of this gift would weaken the Church's warfare against the power of evil in this world and ultimately her ability to save souls—the devil certainly knew it too. Since the issuance of Benedict's *motu proprio* on the Tridentine Latin Mass, it is generally accepted that the more powerful 1614 ritual can be used freely by those priests who have delegation to perform exorcisms. I, for one, welcome the chance to use the Church's own "nuclear option" when it comes to fighting mankind's most powerful enemy.

Appendix E
Commentary on the 1985 Letter of the Congregation for the Doctrine of the Faith: *On the Current Norms Governing Exorcism*[1]

<u>NOTE</u>: *The text of the Vatican document appears below in* regular print *followed by commentary in italics.*

For several years, in certain areas of the Church, assemblies formed to pray for liberation from the influence of demons (though they do not perform exorcisms as such) have been increasing in number. These assemblies are often led by members of the laity, even when there is a priest present.

<u>COMMENTARY</u>: *This short letter addressed to Roman Catholic bishops of the world is listed on the Vatican website as a "disciplinary document" under the Congregation for the Doctrine of the Faith section. As such, it is important to keep in mind that this document does not intend to clarify any doctrine or theology regarding the* Rite of Exorcism. *This brief disciplinary instruction in 1985 was followed by the revised* Rite of Exorcism *in 1999 and the* Instruction on Prayers for Healing *in 2000, which were broader* canonical and liturgical *clarifications on the subject of the proper norms for using exorcism prayers.*

---

1 CONGREGATIO PRO DOCTRINA FIDEI, Epistula *Inde Ab Aliquot Annis*, (*Epistula Ordinariis locorum missa: in mentem normae vigentes de exorcismis revocantur*), 29 septembris 1985, AAS 77 (1985), pp. 1169-1170.

On the Current Norms Governing Exorcism begins by declaring the primary focus of its concern; namely, the "assemblies" that gather to pray for deliverance from evil spirits and that are "often led by members of the laity." The document is about the discipline of prayer groups, and does not specifically speak about how individual priests may conduct exorcisms and deliverances. It specifically limits its commentary to lay-led prayer assemblies in which demons are addressed.

Since the Congregation for the Doctrine of the Faith has been asked what is the proper attitude towards these activities, this Dicastery deems it necessary to make known to all Ordinaries the response which follows:

1. Canon 1172 of the Code of Canon Law declares that no one may licitly perform exorcisms on those who are obsessed,[2] unless he has obtained particular and express permission from the local ordinary (section 1), and it decrees that this permission is to be granted by the Ordinary only to priests who are outstanding in piety, knowledge, prudence, and integrity of life (section 2). Bishops are therefore strongly urged to enforce the observance of these prescriptions.

<u>COMMENTARY</u>: *The Congregation pronounces on the "proper attitude" of bishops toward these activities. The letter first and foremost reiterates the clear rules of canon 1172 of the* Code of Canon Law *that states that only priests who are properly delegated by their bishops may perform exorcisms. A lay person, even a consecrated religious, may not, under any circumstances, perform an exorcism. Here, again, it is not emitting an interpretation of canon law but simply reiterating the law which was promulgated two years earlier in the*

---

[2] In Church documents, the normal term used to refer to possessed individuals is the term, "obsessus," or "vexatus" (the latter being used exclusively in the new ritual); these words would refer to what I have described in this book as "seriously obsessed" and "possessed" persons.

revised Code of Canon Law. *The "proper attitude" of bishops in such situations is thus to draw clear lines of demarcation in two areas: distinguishing the role of the ministerial priesthood from the lay faithful in the matter of exorcism and, by extension, distinguishing solemnly authorized (i.e., public) exorcism from other forms of prayer.*

With rare candor, the document "strongly urges" the bishops to "enforce" these "prescriptions" (i.e., canon law and the public/private, clergy/laity distinctions.)

2. It follows also from these same prescriptions that Christ's faithful may not employ the formula of exorcism against Satan and the fallen angels which is excerpted from that formula made official by order of the Supreme Pontiff Leo XIII, and certainly may not use the entire text of that exorcism. Let all bishops take care to admonish the faithful about this matter whenever such instruction is required.

<u>COMMENTARY</u>: *Here again, the directive is restrictive of "Christ's faithful," i.e., the laity. It restricts in fairly clear terms ("may not employ") the use of Part III of the 1614 exorcism ritual, which was promulgated during the reign of Pope Leo XIII and added officially to the 1925 revision of the* Rite of Exorcism.[3] *It is called "Exorcism Against Satan and the Fallen Angels" and has, from its inclusion in the ritual, been considered an exorcism over places, not persons. The context indicates that the restriction relates to the use of this prayer during prayer in "assemblies," but it is silent on whether this prayer can be used privately. A strict interpretation would prohibit all uses of this prayer whatsoever by the laity, but since the Leo XIII prayer has entered into the devotional life of the Church (one can even find it on the internet!), I do not believe that this is intended. A more reasonable interpretation would seem to maintain the public/private distinction above and allow this prayer to be prayed*

---

3 Cf. Appendix C.

in private by the laity. Lacking more precise directives from church authorities about the private recitation of this prayer, I believe we can fall back on a basic hermeneutic of church law, namely, that what is not prohibited is allowed.

While there is no overt restriction put upon priests regarding the private recitation of the Exorcism of Pope Leo XIII, the 1614 ritual contains a rubric indicating that priests must have the express authorization of their bishops to pray this prayer (understood to mean "in public"). Seemingly then, what is not prohibited (private recitation) is allowed, unless and until the proper Church authority offers some further clarification.

Finally, the paragraph prohibits use of the full exorcism ritual by the laity.

3. Finally, for the same reasons, Bishops are asked to guard lest those who lack the required power attempt to lead assemblies in which prayers are employed to obtain liberation from demons, and in the course of which the demons are directly disturbed and an attempt is made to determine their identity. This applies even to cases which, although they do not involve true diabolical possession, nevertheless are seen in some way to manifest diabolical influence.[4]

---

[4] Neal Lozano makes a helpful clarification in his new book, *Resisting the Devil: A Catholic Perspective on Deliverance*, Our Sunday Visitor, Inc.: Huntington, IN, 2009: "Father Francis Martin clarified the cardinal's [Ratzinger's] letter in a talk at Mundelein Seminary, and later through personal correspondence. He stated that it is clear that the restrictions in point three of Cardinal Ratzinger's letter are to be applied to public assemblies. He also wrote, 'When asked by Fr. Rufus Pereira concerning the third paragraph of [the] Statement of the Congregation of the Doctrine of the Faith, September 19, 1984 [actually 1985], the then- Prefect of the Congregation, Cardinal Joseph Ratzinger, replied that the restriction applied to public assemblies.' While Cardinal Ratzinger (now Pope Benedict XVI) clearly restricts exorcisms and prayers for exorcism to authorized clergy, there is nothing here that prohibits the laity from using the imperative. 'Exorcisms' refers to the Rite of Exorcism—a sacramental, not the imperative command." (p. 148)

COMMENTARY: Three key items are discussed in this critical paragraph: 1. The need for "required power;" 2. The stirring up of demons and attempting to identify them; and 3. The application of these principles to cases that do not reach the level of full possession.

As such, the term "required power" is an ambiguous phrase but, in this context, it seems to mean permission from the bishop to perform an exorcism. It is hard to see what else it could mean here. The term "power" is used in church documents to mean some ecclesiastical power that is either inherent in an office itself or delegated to another, but the only prayer in question here that requires "power" is exorcism. The assemblies referred to are those "in which prayers are employed to obtain liberation from demons." In church language, then, this "required power... to obtain liberation from demons" can only mean the permission to exorcise, and the laity do not have it. This phrase then is hardly more than a reiteration of what was said in paragraphs 1 and 2.

The specification about avoiding stirring up demons and trying to identify them is helpful. The letter asks the bishops to "guard" against this practice by untrained people in public assemblies since the direct confrontation of demons (i.e., using imperative commands) is the proper purview of those who are trained and supervised by the Church. In a solemn exorcism a priest must command the demon to reveal its name and other bits of information helpful for expulsion, but he does so in a controlled environment where the authority of the Church is able to be applied properly. The CDF wishes to avoid provoking such demonic manifestations in open prayer assemblies, but it does not seem to restrict private *deliverance prayer groups that seek to help people who are not fully possessed. Neal Lozano offers some further guidance on this point:*

> In his third point, Ratzinger specifically forbids the organizing of meetings "during which, for the purpose

of deliverance, such prayers are used to directly invoke demons and where their identity is sought." When the people of God gather, Jesus Christ should be the center; invoking demons or provoking them to manifest in public assemblies is not the way the Church should gather.

These restrictions placed on public assemblies and ministries do not apply to the private ministry unless the local bishop, for pastoral reasons, places restrictions on such activity. Although the word of command that is used in deliverance ministry can bear resemblance to the commands used by a priest in a public exorcism, they are not the same because the context is different.

However, although the Church has not restricted the imperative command to clergy, it remains true that there is a need for sound pastoral guidance and teaching for both deliverance ministry and the work of the exorcist. (pp. 148-149)

Finally, the document makes little distinction between cases of "true diabolical possession" and those that "in some way manifest diabolical influence." This distinction is usually only made clear when the prayer takes place, but the document does not intend to provide discernment into these cases. It only advises that serious demonic problems, whenever and however they are brought to light, ought to be dealt with by authorized and trained persons, whether duly-appointed exorcists or prayer teams with ecclesiastical supervision.

Of course, the enunciation of these norms should not stop the faithful of Christ from praying, as Jesus taught us, that they may be freed from evil (cf. Mt 6:13). Moreover, Pastors should take this opportunity to remember what the tradition of the

Church teaches about the function properly assigned to the intercession of the Most Blessed Virgin Mary, the Apostles and the Saints, even in the spiritual battle of Christians against the evil spirits.

COMMENTARY: Far from prohibiting the faithful from praying for deliverance from evil, the CDF cites the last petition of the Our Father as the proper mode for untrained lay people ("the faithful of Christ") to pray for liberation from demonic oppression. In technical terms, the untrained lay faithful are to pray strictly "deprecative," i.e., petitioning, prayers for liberation but not enter into any form of aggressive prayers against demons or dialogue with them. Entering into conflict with demons is the proper role of priests and those specialized lay prayer groups with trained deliverance ministers that have some sort of supervision by the Church.

May I take this occasion to convey my great feelings of esteem for you, remaining your servant in the Lord,

Joseph Card. Ratzinger, Prefect

Appendix F

Instruction on Prayers for Healing, September 14, 2000

Congregation for the Doctrine of the Faith

Disciplinary Norms

Art. 1 – It is licit for every member of the faithful to pray to God for healing. When this is organized in a church or other sacred place, it is appropriate that such prayers be led by an ordained minister.

Art. 2 – Prayers for healing are considered to be liturgical if they are part of the liturgical books approved by the Church's competent authority; otherwise, they are non-liturgical.

Art. 3 – § 1. Liturgical prayers for healing are celebrated according to the rite prescribed in the *Ordo benedictionis infirmorum* of the *Rituale Romanum* (28) and with the proper sacred vestments indicated therein.

> § 2. In conformity with what is stated in the *Praenotanda*, V., *De aptationibus quae Conferentiae Episcoporum competunt* (29) of the same *Rituale Romanum*, Conferences of Bishops may introduce those adaptations to the Rite of Blessings of the Sick which are held to be pastorally useful or possibly necessary, after prior review by the Apostolic See.

Art. 4 – § 1. The Diocesan Bishop has the right to issue norms for his particular Church regarding liturgical services of healing, following can. 838 § 4.

§ 2. Those who prepare liturgical services of healing must follow these norms in the celebration of such services.

§ 3. Permission to hold such services must be explicitly given, even if they are organized by Bishops or Cardinals, or include such as participants. Given a just and proportionate reason, the Diocesan Bishop has the right to forbid even the participation of an individual Bishop.

Art. 5 – § 1. Non-liturgical prayers for healing are distinct from liturgical celebrations, as gatherings for prayer or for reading of the Word of God; these also fall under the vigilance of the local Ordinary in accordance with can. 839 § 2.

§ 2. Confusion between such free non-liturgical prayer meetings and liturgical celebrations properly so-called is to be carefully avoided.

§ 3. Anything resembling hysteria, artificiality, theatricality or sensationalism, above all on the part of those who are in charge of such gatherings, must not take place.

Art. 6 – The use of means of communication (in particular, television) in connection with prayers for healing, falls under the vigilance of the Diocesan Bishop in conformity with can. 823 and the norms established by the Congregation for the Doctrine of the Faith in the *Instruction* of March 30, 1992. (30)

Art. 7 – § 1. Without prejudice to what is established above in art. 3 or to the celebrations for the sick provided in the Church's liturgical books, prayers for healing – whether liturgical or non-liturgical – must not be introduced into the celebration of the Holy Mass, the sacraments, or the Liturgy of the Hours.

§ 2. In the celebrations referred to in § 1, one may include special prayer intentions for the healing of the sick in the general intercessions or prayers of the faithful, when this is permitted.

Art. 8 – § 1. The ministry of exorcism must be exercised in strict dependence on the Diocesan Bishop, and in keeping with the norm of can. 1172, the Letter of the Congregation for the Doctrine of the Faith of September 29, 1985, (31) and the *Rituale Romanum*. (32)

> § 2. The prayers of exorcism contained in the *Rituale Romanum* must remain separate from healing services, whether liturgical or non-liturgical.
>
> § 3. It is absolutely forbidden to insert such prayers of exorcism into the celebration of the Holy Mass, the sacraments, or the Liturgy of the Hours.

Art. 9 – Those who direct healing services, whether liturgical or non-liturgical, are to strive to maintain a climate of peaceful devotion in the assembly and to exercise the necessary prudence if healings should take place among those present; when the celebration is over, any testimony can be collected with honesty and accuracy, and submitted to the proper ecclesiastical authority.

Art. 10 – Authoritative intervention by the Diocesan Bishop is proper and necessary when abuses are verified in liturgical or non-liturgical healing services, or when there is obvious scandal among the community of the faithful, or when there is a serious lack of observance of liturgical or disciplinary norms.

<u>Endnotes</u>

(28) *Rituale Romanum, De Benedictionibus*, 39.
(29) And those equivalent to him in law by virtue of canon 381, § 2.

(30) Cf. CONGREGATION FOR THE DOCTRINE OF THE FAITH, *Instruction on Some Aspects of the Use of the Instruments of Social Communication in Promoting the Doctrine of the Faith:* Libreria Editrice Vaticana (1992).

(31) Cf. CONGREGATION FOR THE DOCTRINE OF THE FAITH, Epistula *Inde Ab Aliquot Annis*, Ordinariis locorum missa: in mentem normae vigentes de exorcismis revocantur: AAS 77(1985), 1169-1170.

(32) *Rituale Romanum*, Ex Decreto Sacrosancti Oecumenici Concilii Vaticani II instauratum, Auctoritate Ioannis Paulii II promulgatum, *De Exorcismis et Supplicationibus Quibusdam,* Editio typica, Typis Polyglottis Vaticanis, MIM, *Praenotanda*, 13-19.

Appendix G
Pope John Paul II's Catechesis on the Fallen Angels

From the General Audience of August 13, 1986[1]

The fall of the rebellious angels

1. Continuing the theme of the previous catecheses, which were dedicated to the article of the faith that concerns the angels, God's creatures, we shall begin today to explore *the mystery of the freedom* which some of them have turned against God and his plan of salvation for mankind.

As the evangelist Luke testifies, when the disciples returned to the Master full of joy at the fruits they had gathered in their first missionary attempt, Jesus utters a sentence that is highly evocative: "I saw Satan fall from heaven like lightning" (Lk 10:18). With these words, the Lord affirms that the proclamation of the Kingdom of God is always a victory over the devil, but at the same time he also reveals that the building up of the Kingdom is continuously exposed to the attacks of the spirit of evil. When we consider this, as we propose to do with today's catechesis, it means that *we prepare ourselves for the condition of struggle* which characterizes the life of the Church in this final time of the history of salvation (as the Book of Revelation asserts: cf. 12:7). Besides this, it will permit us to clarify *the true faith of the Church* against those who pervert it by exaggerating the importance of the devil, or by denying or minimizing his malevolent power.

---

1 All italics and biblical references in the original.

The preceding catecheses on the angels have prepared us to understand the truth which Sacred Scripture has revealed and which the Tradition of the Church has handed on about Satan, that is, the fallen angel, the wicked spirit, who is also called the devil or demon.

2. This "fall," which has the character of rejection of God with the consequent state of "damnation," consists in the free choice of those created spirits who have radically and irrevocably *rejected God and His Kingdom* usurping His sovereign rights and attempting to subvert the economy of salvation and the very order of the entire creation. We find a reflection of this attitude in the words addressed by the tempter to our first parents: "You will become like God" or "like gods" (cf. Gen 3:5). Thus the evil spirit tries to transplant into man the attitude of rivalry, insubordination and opposition to God, which has, as it were, become the motivation of all his existence.

3. In the Old Testament, the narrative of the fall of man as related in the Book of Genesis, contains a reference to an attitude of antagonism which Satan wishes to communicate to man in order to lead him to sin (Gen 3:5). In the Book of Job too, we read that Satan seeks to generate rebellion in the person who is suffering (cf. Job 1:11; 2:5-7). In the Book of Wisdom (cf. Wis 2:24), Satan is presented as the artisan of death, which has entered man's history along with sin.

4. In the Fourth Lateran Council (1215), the Church teaches that the devil (or Satan) and the other demons *"were created good by God but have become evil by their own will."* In fact, we read in the Letter of St. Jude: "... the angels who did not keep their dignity, but left their own dwelling, are kept by the Lord in eternal chains in the darkness, for the judgment of the great day" (Jude 6). Similarly, in the *Second Letter of St. Peter*, we hear of "angels

who have sinned" and whom God "did not spare, but... cast in the gloomy abysses of hell, reserving them for the judgment" (2 Pet 2:4). It is clear that if God "does not forgive" the sin of the angels, this is because they remain in their sin, because they are eternally *"in the chains" of the choice that they made at the beginning*, rejecting God, against the truth of the supreme and definitive Good that is God Himself. It is in this sense that St. John writes that *"the devil has been a sinner from the beginning..."* (Jn 3:8). And he has been a *murderer* "from the beginning", and "has not persevered in the truth, because *there is no truth in him*" (Jn 8:44).

Satan: cosmic liar and murderer

5. These texts help us to understand the nature and the dimension of the sin of Satan, which consists in the denial of the truth about God, as He is known by the light of the intellect and revelation as infinite Good, *subsistent Love and Holiness*. The sin was all the greater, in that the spiritual perfection and the epistemological acuteness of the angelic intellect, with His freedom and closeness to God, were greater. When, by an act of his own free will, he *rejected the truth* that he knew about God, Satan became the cosmic "liar and the father of lies" (Jn 8:44). For this reason, he lives in radical and irreversible denial of God, and *seeks to impose* on creation - on the other beings created in the image of God, and in particular on people - his own tragic "lie about the good" that is God. In the Book of Genesis, we find a precise description of this lie and falsification of the truth about God, which Satan (under the form of a serpent) tries to transmit to the first representatives of the human race: God is jealous of His own prerogatives and therefore wants to impose limitations on man (cf. Gen 3:5); Satan invites the man to free himself from the impositions of this yoke by making himself "like God."

6. In this condition of existential falsehood, Satan - according to St. John - also becomes a "murderer", that is *one who destroys the supernatural life* which God had made to dwell from the beginning in Him and in the creatures made "in the likeness of God": the other pure spirits and men; Satan *wishes to destroy life lived in accordance with the truth*, life in the fullness of good, the supernatural *life of grace and love*. The author of the Book of Wisdom writes: ". . .death has entered the world through the envy of the devil, and those who belong to him experience it" (Wis 2:24). And Jesus Christ warns in the Gospel: *"... fear rather him who has the power to destroy both soul and body in Gehenna"* (Mt 10:28).

7. As the result of the sin of our first parents, this fallen angel has acquired *dominion over man to a certain extent.* This is the doctrine that has been constantly professed and proclaimed by the Church, and which the *Council of Trent* confirmed in its treatise on original sin (cf. DS 1511): it finds a dramatic expression *in the liturgy of baptism*, when the catechumen is asked to renounce the devil and all his empty promises.

In Sacred Scripture, we find various indications of this influence on man and on the dispositions of his spirit (and of his body). In the Bible, Satan is called *"the prince of the world"* (cf Jn 12:31; 14:30; 16:11), and even "the god of this world" (2 Cor 4:4). We find *many* other names that describe his nefarious relationship with man: "Beelzebul" or "Belial," "unclean spirit," "tempter," "evil one" and even "Antichrist" (1 Jn 4:3). He is compared to a "lion" (1 Pet 5:8), to a "dragon" (in Revelation) and to a "serpent" (Gen 3). Very frequently, he is designated by the name "devil"— from the Greek *diaballein* (hence *diabolos*)—which means: to "cause destruction, to divide, to calumniate, to deceive." In truth, all this takes place from the beginning through the working of the evil spirit who is presented by Sacred Scripture as *a person*, while it is declared that *he is not alone*: "there are many of us," the devils cry out to Jesus in the region of the Gerasenes (Mk 5:9); and Jesus, speaking of the future judgment, speaks of "the devil and his angels" (cf. Mt 25:41).

8. According to Sacred Scripture, and especially the New Testament, the dominion and the influence of Satan and of the other evil spirits embraces *all the world*. We may think of Christ's parable about the field (the world), about the good seed and the bad seed that the devil sows in the midst of the wheat, seeking to snatch away from hearts the good that has been "sown"in them (cf. Mt 13:38-39). We may think of the numerous exhortations to vigilance (cf. Mt 26:41; 1 Pet 5:8), to prayer and fasting (cf. Mt 17:21). We may think of the strong statement made by the Lord: "This kind of demon cannot be cast out by any other means than prayer" (Mk 9:29). The action of Satan consists primarily in tempting men to evil, by influencing their imaginations and higher faculties, to turn them away from the law of God. Satan *even tempts Jesus* (cf. Lk 4:3-13), in the extreme attempt to thwart what is demanded by the economy of salvation, as this has been pre-ordained by God.

It is possible that in certain cases the evil spirit goes so far as to exercise his influence not only on material things, but even *on man's body* so that one can speak of "diabolical possession" (cf. Mk 5:2-9). It is not always easy to discern the preternatural factor operative in these cases, and the Church does not lightly support the tendency to attribute many things to the direct action of the devil; but in principle it cannot be denied that Satan can go to this extreme manifestation of his superiority, in his will to harm and lead to evil.

9. To conclude, we must add that the impressive words of the Apostle John, "The whole world lies under the power of the evil one" (1 Jn 5:19), allude also to the presence of Satan in the his-

tory of humanity, a presence which becomes all the more acute when man and society depart from God. The influence of the evil spirit can *conceal itself* in a more profound and effective way: it is in his "interests" to make himself unknown. Satan has the skill in the world to induce people to deny his existence in the name of rationalism and of every other system of thought which seeks all possible means to avoid recognizing his activity. This, however, *does not signify the elimination of man's free will and responsibility*, and even less the frustration of the saving action of Christ. It is, rather, a case of conflict between the dark powers of evil and the powers of redemption. The words that Jesus addressed to Peter at the beginning of the Passion are eloquent in this context: "... Simon, behold, Satan has sought to sift you like wheat: but I have prayed for you, that your faith may not fail" (Lk 22:31).

This helps us understand how Jesus, in the prayer that he taught us, the "Our Father", that is, the prayer of the Kingdom of God, terminates almost brusquely, unlike so many other prayers of his era, by reminding us of our condition as people *exposed to the snares of evil and of the evil one*. The Christian, appealing to the Father with the Spirit of Jesus and invoking His Kingdom, cries with the power of faith, "Let us not succumb to temptation, free us from evil, from the evil one. O Lord, let us not fall into the infidelity to which we are seduced by the one who has been unfaithful from the beginning."

Appendix H
The Redemptive Suffering of Anneliese Michel

A 23-year-old Bavarian girl named Anneliese Michel who was possessed by six powerful demons and was given a series of exorcisms in 1975-76 may serve as an example for those who suffer from demonic problems and cannot immediately be freed of their afflictions. Her story was popularized in 2005 by the movie called *The Exorcism of Emily Rose*. The research of the case, by Felicitas Goodman,[1] was the main inspiration for the movie and is the source of the three quotes that will be cited later in this Appendix.

This young woman was demonically afflicted from the earliest time in her life, but it was not apparent that her problems were related to demons until she was in her teens. She had many health problems and social problems growing up and, despite her regular practice of the Catholic faith, had increasing attacks of a spiritual nature that were interpreted as psychiatric or other health problems for many years. She went to numerous doctors, psychiatrists and counselors and took medication to control the attacks, but the medication had little or no effect on the demonic nature of her problems. Goodman says that she probably became demonically-infested by being cursed by a witch in her village when she was a young child. Once the unclean spirits entered, they exercised increasing control over her life to the point that in her late teens and early twenties her life became almost unmanageable. She was not able to eat, have normal friendships, live a

---

1 Felicitas D. Goodman, *The Exorcism of Anneliese Michel*, Resource Publications: Eugene, OR, 2005.

healthy family life, etc. due to the regular, almost daily demonic attacks which paralyzed her body, soul and spirit. It is incredible to know that during the height of the attacks she finished high school successfully and was attempting to finish her college thesis when she eventually died through causes related to the possession.

Anneliese is the model of one who suffers heroically under such demonic oppression. She suffered not only from the demons, but also from the Church leaders who delayed an inexcusable length of time (literally years) before providing her the appropriate pastoral care for one in such extreme distress. By all accounts hers was one of the worst cases of demonic possession known in modern times and universally belittled and mocked by the secular establishment when the details of the matter became known. While the local bishop did eventually offer the services of two generous exorcists to assist her, the "official" Church ultimately refused to stand by the exorcists and the parents in court afterwards when they were accused of causing her death by neglect.

Anneliese's voluntary acceptance of her sufferings "as a sacrificial victim for Germany, for the youth of the country, for the priests" (her own words) was in no way understood or appreciated by those who saw her plight. Yet, her spiritual maturity was extraordinary for one so young, and her gracious acceptance of the Cross shows that there is no action of the devil that cannot be transformed into grace by God's mighty power.

Three quotes from her spiritual diary and other commentaries about her life give insight into the purity of her soul during the worst years of demonic possession:

She suffered with deep humility and faith in Christ: Once, in conversation with her spiritual director, Anneliese told him "about the abject terror that had pervaded her the week prior to the conversation and how it made her think of the Savior's shudders of death on the Mount of Olives—that is how that must have been, only much worse...."[2]

She suffered in perfect union with Christ: "At about eight in the evening [of Holy Thursday], Anneliese went across the street to the Unsere Liebe Frau church to pray. As she told Peter [her boyfriend] the next day, she had barely knelt down when a crushing fear descended on her that escalated into mortal terror. At that same time she felt that a thousand weights were pressing her down into the bench. She broke into such a heavy sweat that very soon her clothes were drenched. The veins stood out grossly on her hands and, looking at them, she was afraid that they might burst and she would start sweating blood. 'The death agony of the Lord,' she thought. 'I am experiencing the death agony of the Savior.' She continued praying all the while feeling the pain of the stigmata....On the way home she told him what had happened on Thursday, and that she now had an idea of what Jesus suffered during the last days of his life."[3]

She suffered with perfect charity towards her neighbor: Her spiritual director commented after her death that "evil can never be victorious. Nor did Anneliese die as a result of the exorcism. She died because she chose to. She offered herself as a sacrificial victim for Germany, for the youth of the country, for the priests. God accepted that. So good triumphed over evil, as it should; it was she who won in the end."[4]

---

2 *Ibid.*, p. 149.
3 *Ibid.*, pp. 160-62.
4 *Ibid.*, pp. 178-79.

Needless to say, a real possession is a destructive and desolate experience for the possessed individual, and in the end, Anneliese succumbed and died just after her 23rd birthday. Some have argued that the exorcism process itself was the cause of her death. However, an actual death due directly to the proper application of a Church exorcism has to extremely rare in history; and in this case, her spiritual director was clear that her death was not from the exorcism. Some speculate that a combination of misdiagnosed medications and her inability to eat anything during most of her ordeal led to her demise. Ultimately she died, according to her spiritual director, in *a deliberate gift of self* for her people. He called her experience an "expiatory possession," that is, a suffering for the sins of others. She did not choose it; it was chosen for her, but she accepted it and turned it into a redemptive experience of God's grace. It is evident that God permitted her death in this dramatic way just as He permitted the death of His only-begotten Son for the eternal salvation of others and as a witness to the reality of evil in a faithless age.

If we look only at her death at a young age or the tragic circumstances of her possession, we will not see the meaning of her life or the heroism of her suffering. We have to see her agony, and its fruits, with the eyes of faith in a remarkable "coincidence" that happened soon after her death. Namely, less than two years after Anneliese died in a gift of self for the German Church and clergy, a young priest by the name of Joseph Ratzinger was named Archbishop of Munich, the very region where Anneliese lived, suffered and died.

And we all know the rest of the story.

Appendix I
Other Scripture Passages Related to Deliverance

Now, since the children are men of blood and flesh, Jesus likewise had a full share in ours, that by his death he might rob the devil, the prince of death, of his power, and free those who through fear of death had been slaves their whole life long. (Heb 2:14-15)

Now have salvation and power come, the reign of our God and the authority of his Anointed One. For the accuser of our brothers is cast out who night and day accused them before our God. They defeated him by the blood of the Lamb and by the word of their testimony; love for life did not deter them from death. So rejoice you heavens, and you that dwell therein! (Rev 12:10-12)

Stay sober and alert. Your opponent the devil is prowling like a roaring lion looking for someone to devour. Resist him, solid in your faith, realizing that the brotherhood of believers is undergoing the same sufferings throughout the world. (1 Pt 5:8-9)

He named twelve as His companions whom He would send to preach the good news; they were likewise to have authority to expel demons. (Mk 3:14)

Signs like these will accompany those who have professed their faith: they will use my name to expel demons, they will speak entirely new languages, they will be able to handle serpents, they will be able to drink deadly poison without harm, and the sick upon whom they lay their hands will recover. (Mk 16:17-18)

> Let the faithful rejoice in their glory,

> Shout for joy and take their rest.
> Let the praise of God be on their lips
> And a two-edged sword in their hand,
> To deal out vengeance to the nations
> And punishment on all the peoples;
> To bind their kings in chains
> And their nobles in fetters of iron;
> To carry out the sentence pre-ordained;
> This honor is for all his faithful.
> (Psalm 149:5-9)[1]

When a strong man fully armed guards his courtyard, his possessions go undisturbed. But when someone stronger than he comes and overpowers him, such a one carries off the arms on which he was relying and divides the spoils. (Lk 11:21-22)

Then I saw an angel come down from heaven, holding the key to the abyss and a huge chain in his hand. He seized the dragon, the ancient serpent, who is the devil or Satan, and chained him up for a thousand years. The angel hurled him into the abyss, which he closed and sealed over him. He did this so that the dragon might not lead the nations astray until the thousand years are over....[Then] the devil who led them astray was hurled into the pool of burning sulfur, where the beast and the false prophet had also been thrown. There they will be tortured day and night, forever and ever. (Rev 20:1-3, 10)

---

[1] *The Grail Psalter*, The Grail Society, England, 1963.

Bibliography

Church Documents:

Catechism of the Catholic Church, Libreria Editrice Vaticana: Città del Vaticano, 1994; nn. 1673 (on exorcism), 2116-2117 (on occult phenomena) and 2851 (on the devil).

Code of Canon Law, English/Latin edition, Canon Law Society of America, Washington, DC, 1983; c. 1172.

Compendium: Catechism of the Catholic Church, Libreria Editrice Vaticana: Città del Vaticano, 2006.

Congregation for the Doctrine of the Faith, *Christian Faith and Demonology*, 1975. (See *Vatican Council II: Conciliar and Post-Conciliar Documents, New Revised Edition*, ed., Austin Flannery, OP, Costello Publishing Company, Inc., Northport, NY, 1992.)

Congregation for the Doctrine of the Faith, *On the Current Norms Governing Exorcism* (*Inde Ab Aliquot Annis*), 1985.

Congregation for the Doctrine of the Faith, *Letter to the Bishops of the Catholic Church on some aspects of Christian meditation.* 1989.

Congregation for the Doctrine of the Faith, *Instruction on Prayers for Healing*, 2000.

The Pontifical Council for Culture and The Pontifical Council for Interreligious Dialogue, *Jesus Christ, The Bearer of the Water of Life: A Christian reflection on the "New Age,"* 2003.

Rituale Romanum, Ex Decreto Sacrosancti Oecumenici Concilii Vaticani II instauratum, Auctoritate Ioannis Paulii II promulgatum, *De Exorcismis et Supplicationibus Quibusdam, Editio typica*, Typis Polyglottis Vaticanis, MIM.

United States Conference of Catholic Bishops, Committee on Doctrine, *Guidelines For Evaluating Reiki as an Alternative Therapy*, March 25th, 2009

Rev. Philip T. Weller, STD, Trans. *The Roman Ritual, Vol. I: The Sacraments and Processions,* Copyright 1950; *Vol. II, Christian Burial, Exorcisms, Reserved Blessings, Etc.*, Copyright 1964; *Vol. III: The Blessings,* The Bruce Publishing Co., Milwaukee, WI, 1946.

Individual Authors:

Mortimer Adler, *The Angels and Us*, MacMillan Publishing Co., Inc.: New York, NY, 1982.

Thomas B. Allen, *Possessed: The True Story of An Exorcism*, iUniverse.com, Inc.: New York, 2000.

Gabriele Amorth, *An Exorcist Tells His Story*, Ignatius Press: San Francisco, CA, 1999.

_____, *An Exorcist: More Stories*, Ignatius Press: San Francisco, CA, 2002.

St. Thomas Aquinas, *On Evil*, Notre Dame University Press: Notre Dame, IN, 1995.

_____, *Summa Theologica*, Christian Classics: Westminster, MD, 1948.

Edgardo Arrellano, *Urgency of Deliverance Prayer and Healing Ministry* (Books 1 and 2), Two Hearts Media Organization: Dover, DE, 2005.

Jordan Aumann, O.P., *Spiritual Theology*, Sheed and Ward: London, 1980. Particularly Chapter 14, "Discernment of Spirits."

Corrado Balducci, *The Devil: "Alive and Active in Our World,"* Alba House: New York, NY, 1990.

Nick Baglio: *The Rite: The Making of A Modern Exorcist*, Doubleday: New York, NY, 2009.

Johnnette S. Benkovic, *The New Age Counterfeit*, Queenship Publishing: Goleta, CA, 1993.

Joseph Brennan, *The Kingdom of Darkness*, Acadian House: Lafayette, LA, 1989.

Susan P. Brinkmann, OCDS, *Learn to Discern: Is it Christian or New Age* (A Women of Grace Study Series), Simon Peter Press, Inc.: Oldsmar, FL, 2008.

Gerald Daniel Brittle, *The Demonologist: The Extraordinary Career of Ed and Lorraine Warren*, iUniverse, Inc., Lincoln, NE, 2002.

Tonino Cantelmi and Christina Cacace, *Il Libro Nero del Satanismo: Abusi, Rituali e Crimini*, San Paolo: Torino, Italy, 2007.

Nicolas Corte, *Who is the Devil?* Hawthorn Books: New York, 1958.

Leon Cristiani, *Evidence of Satan in the Modern World*, TAN Books and Publishers, Inc.: Rockford, IL, 1974.

Joan Carroll Cruz, *Angels and Devils*, TAN Books and Publishers, Inc.: Rockford, IL, 1999.

Constance Cumbey, *The Hidden Dangers of the Rainbow: The New Age Movement and Our Coming Age of Barbarism*, Huntington House, Inc.: Lafayette, IN, 1983.

Michael W. Cuneo, *American Exorcism: Expelling Demons in the Land of Plenty*, Doubleday: New York, 2001.

Jean Danielou, SJ, *The Angels and Their Mission According to the Fathers of the Church*, Christian Classics from Ave Maria Press: Notre Dame, IN, n.d.

Jeremy Davies, *Exorcism: Understanding Exorcism in Scripture and Practice*, The Incorporated Catholic Truth Society: London, England, 2008.

Pellegrino Ernetti, OSB, *La Catechesi di Satana*, Edizioni Segno:Udine, Italy, 1992.

Thomas J. Euteneuer, "The 1999 Revision of the Rite of Exorcism: The Devil Is In The Details," *Latin Mass Magazine*, Advent/Christmas, 2006.

_____, "Libera Nos A Malo," 6-part series for *New Oxford Review*, November 2009 to June 2010 issues.

José Antonio Fortea, *Interview With An Exorcist: An Insider's Look at the Devil, Demonic Possession, and the Path to Deliverance,* Ascension Press: Westchester, PA, 2006.

Robert J. Fox, *The World and Work of the Holy Angels*, Fatima Family Apostolate: Alexandria, SD, 2001.

Franciscan Friars of Marytown, *A Notebook on the Devil and Exorcism*, Franciscan Marytown Press: Kenosha, WI, 1974.

Timothy M. Gallagher, OMV, *The Discernment of Spirits*, The Crossroad Publishing Company, New York, NY, 2005.

Theodore Geiger, *Begone Satan* and *Mary Crushes The Serpent: Thirty Years' Experiences of An Exorcist Told In His Own Words*, St. John's Abbey: Collegeville, MN, n.d.

John Patrick Gillese, *Begone, Satan!* Our Sunday Visitor, Inc.: Huntington, IN, 1974.

Felicitas D. Goodman, *The Exorcism of Anneliese Michel*, Resource Publications: Eugene, OR, 2005.

Thomas H. Green, S.J., *Weeds Among The Wheat, Discernment: Where Prayer and Action Meet*, Ave Maria Press, Notre Dame, IN, 1986.

Jeffrey S. Grob, *A Major Revision of the Discipline on Exorcism: A Comparative Study of the Liturgical Laws in the 1614 and 1998 Rites of Exorcism,* Archdiocese of Chicago: unpublished doctoral thesis, 2006.

Benedict Groeschel, CFR, *A Still, Small Voice: A Practical Guide on Reported Revelations*, Ignatius Press: San Francisco, CA, 1993.

John H. Hampsch, CMF, *Healing Your Family Tree: A God-designed Solution For Difficult Problems*, Queenship Publishing Company: Goleta, CA, 1989.

John A. Hardon, S.J., *Meditations on the Angels*, Eternal Life: Bardstown, KY, 2006.

_____, *Catholic Catechism on the Angels*, Eternal Life: Bardstown, KY, 2000.

Georges Huber, *My Angel Will Go Before You*, Four Courts Press: Dublin, Ireland, 2006.

Istituto Sacerdos et al., *Esorcismo e Preghiera di Liberazione*, Edizioni Art: Roma, 2005.

David M. Keily and Christina McKenna, *The Dark Sacrament: True Stories of Modern Day Demon Possession and Exorcism*, Harper One: New York, NY, 2007.

Joseph Keininger, ORC, *The Discernment of Spirits in Our Times* (booklet), Opus Sanctorum Apostolorum: Detroit, MI, 2006.

Peter Kreeft, *Angels (and Demons): What Do We Really Know About Them?* Ignatius Press: San Francisco, CA, 1995.

Lawrence LeBlanc and José Antonio Fortea, *Anneliese Michel: The True Story of a Case of Demonic Possession*, unpublished manuscript, 2007.

Neal Lozano, *Resisting the Devil: A Catholic Perspective on Deliverance*, Our Sunday Visitor, Inc.: Huntington, IN, 2009.

_____, *Unbound: A Practical Guide to Deliverance from Evil Spirits*, Chosen Books: Grand Rapids, MI, 2003.

John Loren and Mark Sanford, *Deliverance and Inner Healing*, Chosen Books: Grand Rapids, MI, 2008.

Francis MacNutt, *Deliverance from Evil Spirits: A Practical Manual*, Chosen Books: Grand Rapids, MI, 1995.

_____, *Healing*, Ave Maria Press: Notre Dame, IN, 2006.

Malachi Martin, *Hostage to the Devil: The Possession and Exorcism of Five Americans*, HarperSanFrancisco, ed.: San Francisco, CA, 1992.

Kenneth McAll, *A Guide to Healing the Family Tree*, Queenship Publishing Company: Goleta, CA, 1996.

Terry Ann Modica, *Overcoming the Power of the Occult*, Queenship Publishing: Goleta, CA, 1996.

N.a., *St. Michael and the Angels*, TAN Books and Publishers: Rockford, IL, 1993.

Nanni, Gabriele, *Il Dito di Dio e Il Potere Di Satana: L'esorcismo*, Cittá Del Vaticano: Librería Editrice Vaticana, 2004.

Christopher Neil-Smith, *The Exorcist and the Possessed: The Truth About Exorcism*, James Pike Ltd., St. Ives, Cornwall (England), 1974.

Basil Nortz, O.R.C., *Deliver Us From Evil*, Order of Canons Regular of the Holy Cross: Detroit, MI, 2000.

Mitch Pacwa, S.J., *Catholics and the New Age*, Servant Publications: Ann Arbor, MI, 1992.

M. Scott Peck, MD, *Glimpses of the Devil: A Psychiatrist's Personal Accounts of Possession, Exorcism, and Redemption*, Simon and Schuster: New York, NY, 2005.

_____, *People of the Lie*, Simon and Schuster: New York, NY, 1983.

Derek Prince, *Blessing or Curse: You Can Choose*, Chosen Books: Grand Rapids, MI, 1990.

Pseudo-Dionysius: The Complete Works, The Classics of Western Spirituality, tr. Colm Luibheid, Paulist Press: New York, 1987.

Chad Ripperger, F.S.S.P., *Introduction to the Science of Mental Health, Vol. 2: Sacred and Other Spiritual Causes*, Chapter 10: Demonic Influences, 2003.

Adolf Rodewyk, *Possessed by Satan: The Church's Teaching on the Devil, Possession, and Exorcism*, Doubleday: New York, 1975.

John Salza, *Masonry Unmasked: An Insider Reveals the Secrets of the Lodge*, Our Sunday Visitor, Inc.: Huntington, IN, 2006.

Michael Scanlan, T.O.R. and Randall Cirner, *Deliverance From Evil Spirits: A Weapon for Spiritual Warfare*, St. Anthony Messenger Press: Cincinnati, OH, 1980.

Dom Lorenzo Scupoli, *The Spiritual Combat and a Treatise on Peace of Soul*, TAN Books and Publishers: Rockford, IL, 1990.

Jeffrey J. Steffon, *Satanism: Is it Real?* Servant Publications: Ann Arbor, MI, 1992.

Dominic Szymanski, O.M.C., *The Truth About the Devil*, Marytown, IL, n.d.

Herbert Thurston, S.J., *Ghosts and Poltergeists*, Henry Regnery Company: Chicago, IL, 1954.

Gerald Vann, *The Devil and How to Resist Him*, Sophia Institute Press: Manchester, NH, 1957.

Tracy Wilkinson, *The Vatican's Exorcists: Driving Out the Devil in the 21st Century*, Warner Books: New York, NY, 2007.

Electronic or video resources:

John A. Corapi, SOLT, Audio CD Series, *Immortal Combat (1. The Reality of This Spiritual Combat, 2. Healing and Deliverance, 3. Humility: the Spiritual Nuclear Weapon, 4. The Role of the Sacramentals, 5. The Role of the Sacraments, 6. Our Allies: Angels, Saints and Souls in Purgatory, 7. The Power of the Cross of Christ, 8. Questions and Answers)*, Santa Cruz Media: Kalispell, MT, 2001.

Devil Worship: The Rise of Satanism (documentary), Jeremiah Films, Inc., 1989.

The Exorcist (movie), 1974.

The Exorcism of Emily Rose (movie), 2005.

Interview With an Exorcist: José Antonio Fortea Cucurull (video documentary), St. Joseph Communications, 2005.

In the Grip of Evil: An In-Depth Look At Exorcism and The Terrifyingly True Story Behind The Film The Exorcist (video documentary), Henninger Media Development, 1997.

John H. Hampsch, C.M.F., Audio Cassette Series, *Spiritual Warfare*, Claretian Tape Ministry, Los Angeles, CA, n.d.

_____, Audio CD, *How to "Raze" Hell*, Claretian Tape Ministry, Los Angeles, CA, n.d.

Malachi Martin: Audio Cassette Series, *The Eternal War* ("God's Rule Overturned, " "The Priesthood in Crisis," "The Keys of the Kingdom"), *The Tempter's Hour* ("Windswept House," "Pact with Darkness," "The Emmaus Factor"), *The Kingdom of Darkness* (2 tape series) and *Crossing the Desert* ("After the Cold War," "The Hidden Dynamic," "Our Invisible Guides").

Michael Schmitz, Audio CD, *The Evil One: His Existence, His Being and His Snares*, www.mptrinity.com, 2007.

Emiliano Tardif, (video documentary) *El Ocultismo: Conversaciones con el Padre Emiliano Tardif,* Centro Latinoamericano por la Unidad, Miami, FL, 2000.

Index

absorption, 118
addictions, 103, 121, 149, 204
Adler, Mortimer, 27, 284
adolescents and dabbling, 119, 204
Alcuin, 79
Amorth, Fr. Gabriele, 11, 23-24, 34, 37-38, 64, 69, 72, 187, 215, 256, 284
angels, xxi-xxiv, xxix, xxxv, 2, 8, 13, 19-20, 22-23, 25-28, 30-36, 39, 43, 47, 60, 80, 91, 101, 104, 107, 118, 140, 175-180, 217, 221, 226, 245, 247-248, 250, 253, 262, 271-275, 282, 284-288, 290
  Also see "archangels," and "fallen angels"
  angelic armies, 47
  angelic hierarchy, 20, 25, 34
  angelic natures, 35
  choirs, 179
  destroying angel, 8
  difference between angels and archangels, 25
  gender of angels, xxxv, 28
  guardian angel, 39, 107, 118, 179, 217
  holy angels, 23, 26, 32, 60, 180, 286
  lower angels, 26, 34
  nine choirs, 25
  preternatural beings, 28, 169, 275
  supernatural beings, 27
Anointing of the Sick, 9, 131, 133, 138, 151
Apostles, 11-12, 29, 56, 62, 126, 130, 137, 236, 242, 245, 247-248, 251-253, 266, 275
  Also see "St. John," "St. Luke," "St. Mark," "St. Matthew," "St. Paul," and "St. Peter"
archangels, xxxv, 2, 25-26, 32, 47, 79-80, 163, 178, 180, 245, 250-251, 253
  Also see "St. Gabriel," "St. Michael," and "St. Raphael"
Asmodeus, 24, 28
Athanasian Creed, 80
authority, xxviii-xxxi, 2-3, 5-6, 8-10, 12, 25-26, 32, 44-48, 51, 53, 56-58, 61-63, 75, 81, 90, 93, 95, 99, 106-107, 127, 129, 134-138, 142-144, 146, 155, 162-163, 166-167, 170, 178, 182-184, 186, 212, 236, 263-264, 267, 269, 281
authority of the Catholic Church, xxix, xxxi, 3, 44-46, 56-58, 99, 138, 143, 163, 167, 178, 263-264
  chancery, 92-96, 203
  diocesan officials, 92
  local Ordinary, 60-62, 70, 261, 268
authorization, xxxii, 57, 61, 71, 74, 77, 92, 128, 138, 250, 263
axis mundi, 184
  Also see "Foot of the Cross"
Beelzebub (Beelzebul), 10, 22-24,

235, 274
Bible, 17, 20, 22, 28, 49, 109, 274
  Also see "Scripture, Sacred"
  Acts of the Apostles, 12, 29, 130
  Book of Jude, 178, 272
  Book of Revelation, 2, 13, 27, 29, 47, 54, 271, 274
  Book of Tobit, 28
  Book of Wisdom, 5, 40, 272, 274
  Exodus, 7-8
  New Testament, 20, 24, 26, 29, 39, 126, 131, 275
  Old Testament, xxvi, 5-6, 8, 28, 272
  Vulgate Bible, 20
blasphemy, 10, 15, 22
Blessed Giovanni Calabria, 37
Buddhists, 13
Calvary, 13-14, 48, 184
Canon Law, xxxiv, 60-61, 63, 67, 69-70, 72, 75-76, 86, 91, 138, 199, 261-262, 283
  1917 *Code of Canon Law*, 69
  1983 *Code of Canon Law*, 60, 63, 69-70, 75, 91, 138
Catechism of the Catholic Church, xxi-xxii, xxix, 19, 57, 68, 131, 199, 213, 283, 287
Catechumenate, 63, 74
Catholic Church, xxi-xxii, xxxiv, 12, 19, 57, 61-62, 68, 77-78, 89, 91, 131, 138, 184, 199, 202-203, 255, 283
  Also see "Eastern Catholic Church," and "Vatican"
  authority of the Catholic Church, xxix, xxxi, 3, 44-46, 56-58, 99, 138, 143, 163, 167, 178, 263-264
  Church's power, 10, 21
  Council of Trent, 274
  Magisterium, xxii-xxiii, xxxiii, 70, 92
Charismatic Renewal, 131
Christian churches, 12
Christian Faith and Demonology, xxii-xxiii, 71, 198, 283
Church Militant, xxiii, xxvi, xxix-xxx, xxxvii, 47, 199, 255
  spiritual combat, 48, 137, 180, 219, 289
Church of Satan, 49-50
The Cloud of Unknowing, 128
command, 1, 6, 15, 47, 56, 68-69, 84, 95, 131, 133, 137, 139, 141-143, 145, 151, 168, 172, 181, 183, 208, 212, 227, 231-232, 238, 242, 244, 249, 251-252, 263-265
commanding demons, 136
  commands of binding, 143
  commands of loosing, 142-143
  imperative (i.e., commanding) prayers, 145
  rebukes, 144
Congregation for the Doctrine of the Faith, xxii, 43, 71, 73, 91, 126, 131, 134, 139, 198, 260-261, 267-270, 283
  Also see "*Christian Faith and Demonology*," "*Declaration on Masonic Associations*," "*Instruction on Prayers for Healing*," "*On the Current Norms Governing Exorcism*," and "*Inde Ab Aliquot Annis*"
Corapi, Fr. John, xxi, 34, 214-215, 219, 289
Cornelius, 1, 62
courage, xxiv, 65, 98, 140, 231
Cross, xxiii, 5, 8, 56, 60, 128, 132, 142, 145, 155-156, 179-181, 183-184, 212, 215, 226, 237, 239,

241-243, 251-252, 257-258, 278, 288, 290
  Also see "Foot of the Cross," and "Sign of the Cross"
cura animarum, 98, 117, 199-200
damned souls, 104-106
  haunting, 105-106
Danielou, Jean, 25-26, 221, 285
Dante, 26, 31
  Also see "*The Divine Comedy*"
Dante's *Inferno*, 31
David and Goliath, 2
Davies, Fr. Jeremy, xxxii, 5, 51, 69, 112
Declaration on Masonic Associations, 91
deliverance, xxi, xxiii, xxxiii-xxxiv, 7-9, 11-12, 14-15, 45, 50, 64, 66, 70-71, 74-76, 78, 80, 83, 87-88, 98, 101-103, 112-114, 116, 119-120, 126-129, 131-136, 138-140, 142, 145-149, 151-152, 179, 183, 193, 200-201, 203-204, 207, 217-222, 224, 261, 263-266, 281, 284, 286-289
  Church generally forbids lay people from commanding demons, 136
  Church's concept of deliverance, 127
  commitment to discernment, 147
  deliverance from evil, 9, 71, 101, 127-128, 133-134, 136, 148, 207, 219-220, 261, 266, 287-289
  deliverance ministers, 12, 98, 113, 116, 132, 134-135, 204, 221, 266
  emotional sickness, 132
  enduring peace as sign of liberation, 85, 152, 182-183
  examples of deliverance prayers and commands, 139
  faith-filled common sense, 148
  faith healing, 132
  insufflatio, 150
  oversight of ecclesiastical authority, 146
  pastoral approach to deliverance ministry, 135
demon(s), xxi-xxiii, xxx-xxxii, xxxiv-xxxv, 2-4, 6-8, 10-16, 18, 21-24, 26-54, 57-58, 60, 62-65, 69, 71, 77-88, 90, 98-104, 106-108, 112-114, 117-123, 127-130, 133, 135-137, 139-141, 143-145, 147, 150-152, 154-156, 158-159, 161-188, 190-197, 199, 202-204, 206-208, 210-215, 221, 225, 234-237, 251, 255-257, 259-261, 263-266, 272, 274-275, 277-278, 281, 285, 287
  Also see "fallen angels," and "repentance - impossibility of for demons"
  allowed by God to roam the world, 48
  ancestral spirits, 103
  apostate angels, xxix, 27, 31-32
  Book of Jude, 178, 272
  demonic personalities, 30-31, 180
  demons cannot read thoughts, 177
  demons of lesser strength, 127
  demons of sin, 101
  demons of trauma, 101-102
  demons operate in packs, 173
  demons speak in exorcisms, 114, 170
  demons with biblical names, 24
  difference between demons and devils, 26

difference between demons and ghosts, 103
disguised as "angel of the light," 30
driving out demons, 6-7, 235, 289
fall like lightning from heaven, 3, 154, 236, 271
female fertility deities, 28
generational spirits, 101-102
Gerasene demoniac, 50-51
ghosts, 7, 103-105, 289
higher demons, 34
incubus, 28
inverted hierarchy, 32
Legion, xxv, 1, 4, 21-22, 48, 51-53, 191, 251-252
the most important demons, 23
occult demons, 101, 142
one-way commanding, binding and rebuking of demons, 139
poltergeists, 104, 289
psychology of demons, 50
retaliation against victims, 186
retaliation of demons, 31, 186-187
sucubus, 28
unclean spirits, xxxii, 1, 4, 14-15, 21-22, 26, 69, 88, 102, 108, 119, 121, 126, 137, 139, 141, 144, 156, 181, 226, 231, 238, 240, 245, 251, 274, 277
"wandering" souls, 104
wicked feminine creatures, 28
demonic activity, xxxiv, 11, 33-34, 55, 94, 100
Also see "infestation," "obsession," "oppression," "possession," and "temptation"
demonic manifestations, 11, 29, 65, 106, 113-114, 150, 167-168, 190, 264, 275
intertwined, 120, 162, 171
spiritual sickness, 58, 132, 156
violence, xxviii, 4, 6-7, 50, 52, 144-145, 150, 168-169, 195-198
devil, xxii-xxiii, xxv-xxvi, xxviii-xxxi, xxxiii-xxxv, 1-6, 8-10, 12-14, 17-20, 22, 24, 26-30, 33, 36-42, 45-49, 51, 54-55, 58-60, 63-65, 69, 71-72, 79-80, 83-84, 88-91, 101, 106, 108, 113, 115-116, 122, 124-126, 128-130, 132, 140, 145, 147, 154, 160, 164, 167, 170, 172-173, 177-179, 183, 187-189, 198, 209-218, 220, 223-227, 230, 240, 247, 250-251, 253, 255, 258-259, 263, 271-275, 278, 281-290
Also see "Satan"
devil's power, 8, 167, 240
devil's retaliation, 187
in the grip of the devil, 1, 130
read a person's thoughts, 177
yell out your sins, 176
discernment, xxxiii, 59, 80, 84, 86-87, 89, 95, 97-100, 108, 112-113, 116-118, 121, 135, 146-147, 151, 164, 169, 174, 183, 203-204, 206-207, 209, 216, 221-222, 265, 284, 286-287
charismatic gift of discernment, 99, 183
discernment of spirits, 98-99, 108, 221, 284, 286-287
discernment process, 98, 151, 164, 207
discernment team, 98, 112, 135, 147
disguised as "angel of the light," 30
medical and psychological sci-

ences, 99
occult spirits, 142
role of common sense, 18, 98, 100, 148, 166, 205
Rules for Discernment of Spirits, 99
trauma, 101-102, 120, 123, 133, 149, 172
various forms of discernment, 98
The Divine Comedy, 26
Divine Providence, 37, 48, 104, 215
Eastern Catholic Church, xxxiv, 57, 61, 138, 184
envy, xxii, 21, 38-39, 141, 239, 252, 274
Eucharist, 15, 91, 146, 150, 164, 185, 225-226
evil, xxi-xxiii, xxv-xxix, xxxi-xxxiv, 3, 5-6, 8-14, 17-19, 21-24, 28, 30-31, 33, 37, 40-44, 46, 48-49, 51-52, 58, 60, 63, 65, 68, 71-72, 78, 82-83, 89, 95, 97, 99, 101, 104-105, 107-111, 113, 118-122, 126-129, 133-136, 140-146, 148, 150, 154, 163, 166-167, 172, 180-181, 183, 186, 188, 196, 199, 203-205, 207-215, 217, 219-220, 223-228, 238, 240, 247, 249, 255-256, 259, 261, 265-266, 271-272, 274-276, 279-280, 284, 287-290
spiritual remedy against evil, 13, 95
excommunicated persons, 70, 90
exorcee, 81, 156, 158, 164-168, 171, 179, 185
exorcee persecuted, 185
exorcism, xxi, xxiii, xxv-xxvi, xxviii, xxx-xxxiv, xxxvii, 1-14, 20-23, 31, 37-38, 42-43, 45-47, 51, 56-72, 74-90, 92-98, 101, 106-107, 109-110, 112-116, 123, 128-129, 132, 134-139, 145-146, 148, 154-176, 178-188, 190-199, 202-203, 207, 211-212, 214-215, 217-218, 222-228, 238, 250-251, 255-265, 269, 277, 279-280, 283-290
Also see "Exorcism Against Satan and the Fallen Angels," "ministry of exorcism," and *"Rite of Exorcism"*
canonical restriction of solemn exorcism to ordained priests, 138
"casting out" demons, 4, 113, 129, 199
charismatic gift, 99, 138, 183
does not work automatically, 57
electronically recording exorcisms, 76
feeling pain during exorcism, 171
holy visions during course of exorcism, 180
judicial process, 60, 155
keeping records of exorcisms, 76
length of exorcism sessions, 165, 191, 207
"line of demarcation" between deliverance and exorcism, 114
major vs. minor exorcisms, 68
number of exorcisms needed to liberate a person, 161
person unconscious, 120, 170
practical advice for petitioning an exorcism, 92
preparation for an exorcism, 156, 158-159
reasons why a demon would not leave, 182
resistance to going to an exorcism, 161
restrictions on the laity, 138

role of angels in an exorcism, 180
role of prayer support for an exorcism, 157
scrutinies, 63, 68
signs of departure, 87, 182
solemn exorcism, xxxiv, 62-63, 68, 75-76, 78, 83, 94, 96, 128, 138, 148, 182, 190, 264
spiritual abuse, 197
spiritual work of mercy, 57
use of relics, 15, 111, 163, 225-226
use of the Eucharist in an exorcism, 164, 226
violence, 169
what is exorcism not, 59
what victims feel after exorcism, 184
where demons go when cast out, 183

exorcism, images of, xxx
as spiritual warfare, 57
eschatological sign, 58
means of evangelization and conversion, 58

Exorcism Against Satan and the Fallen Angels (Exorcism of Pope Leo XIII - Part III of the 1614 *Rite of Exorcism*), 22, 43, 71, 79-80, 250, 262-263

exorcist, xxx-xxxii, xxxv, 1, 3, 5, 10-12, 14, 21-23, 30-31, 34, 37, 44, 47-48, 51, 58-60, 62-64, 66-69, 72-77, 79-80, 82-90, 93-94, 96-100, 105, 107, 112, 115-116, 122-125, 128-129, 138, 147-148, 155-170, 172-187, 190, 201, 204, 211-212, 214-215, 221, 224-227, 256-258, 265, 278, 284, 286, 288-290

appointed in the diocese, 64, 75
charge for his services, 67, 207
identity to be kept secret, 67
International Association of Exorcists, 66
mentoring, 65
order of exorcist, 73-74, 138
"priesthood of the faithful", 63, 129
subdeacon, 73
training, xxxiv, 55, 64-66, 76, 148, 157, 201, 203, 216
various reasons why there are not more exorcists, 64

Fathers of the Church, 25-27, 63, 221, 285
Also see "Tertullian"
Foot of the Cross, 142, 145, 183-184, 257
Also see "*axis mundi*"
Fortea, Fr. José Antonio, 11-12, 44, 82, 148, 156, 162, 177, 186, 286-287, 290
Fourth Council of Carthage, 62
Freemasonry, 91-92
Gaudium et Spes, xxi
ghosts, 7, 103-105, 289
Gibson, Mel, 23, 30
Also see "*The Passion of the Christ*"
Good Shepherd, 95, 161, 209
Goodman, Felicitas, 38, 277, 286
grace, state of, 27, 36-37, 46, 88, 158, 177, 209, 213, 217
Grob, Rev. Jeffrey S., 63-64, 136, 138, 184
guttural voice, 170
Hampsch, Fr. John, 103, 220, 287, 290
healing, xxxiii, 1, 11, 50, 57-58, 63-66, 72-73, 75, 82, 85, 97-98, 100-

Index

103, 106-107, 111, 115, 119-124, 126-134, 138-139, 148-149, 151, 153, 156-157, 162, 165, 172, 180, 185, 190, 199-202, 206-209, 214, 219-222, 260, 267-269, 283-284, 287-289
   Also see "Anointing of the Sick," "prayer - prayers for healing/inner healing/physical healing," and "Project Rachel"
   Charismatic Renewal, 131
   Church's concept of healing, 127
   faith healing, 132
   healing services, 133-134, 267-269
   Lazarus, 105
   level of repentance, 122
   post-abortion healing, 133
   regulations regarding healing services, 134
   Sacraments of Healing, 131
   spiritual healing, 57-58, 65, 75, 82, 85, 97-98, 107, 120, 131-132, 156, 200-201, 208, 222
Hollywood, xxi, 159, 170
Holy Spirit, 1, 10, 19, 22, 36, 39, 43, 53, 56, 58, 66, 108, 125, 138, 140, 231, 239, 241, 247, 249, 252
Holy Trinity, 59, 140
Hostage to the Devil, xxviii, 42, 80, 84, 167, 288
humility, 44, 67, 81, 89-90, 99, 106, 135, 140, 146-148, 160, 162, 178, 223, 225-226, 278, 289
   overcoming the pride of the devil, 106
image and likeness of God, 59
The Imitation of Christ, 128
in persona Christi, 10, 58
Incarnation, 39, 53, 231

Inde Ab Aliquot Annis (*On the Current Norms Governing Exorcism*), 43, 71, 134, 139, 260, 270, 283
infestation, 33, 44, 53, 100-101, 105, 117, 119, 132, 152, 215
Instruction on Prayers for Healing, 72, 73, 126, 131, 134, 139, 260, 267, 283
Jericho, 6
Jesus, xxiii, xxvi, xxxv, 1-6, 8-14, 22-24, 38, 48-54, 56-57, 59-60, 62, 73, 77-78, 82, 97, 102, 108, 126-127, 129-130, 133-134, 136, 139-145, 147, 150, 154-157, 162, 171, 183-184, 186-187, 198, 206, 230-231, 233, 235-239, 243-247, 249, 251-253, 265, 271, 274-276, 279, 281, 283
   Also see "Cross," "Eucharist," "*in persona Christi*," and "Incarnation"
   ambassadors of Christ, 11
   Blood of Jesus, 8, 142-143, 184, 186-187, 194, 247, 251, 281
   Body of Christ, xxix, 5, 66
   Good Shepherd, 95, 161, 209
   Jesus as Judge, 155, 184, 237, 241, 244, 248
   Kingdom of Jesus, 3-4, 8-9, 24, 32, 40, 48-49, 85-86, 89, 127, 129, 141, 145, 154, 236, 271-272, 276
   Name of Jesus, 3, 10-13, 52, 77, 108, 130, 134, 136, 141-145, 150, 171, 233, 244-245, 251-253
   New Moses, 8
   Paschal Lamb, 8, 239
   Sacred Heart, 13
Jews, 7, 12
Judas, 23, 246
judgment, xxxiii, 5-6, 59, 70, 91, 93, 96, 106-107, 109, 142, 155, 165-

166, 183, 207, 231, 272-273, 275
  end of the world, 252
  final judgment, xxxiii
  Last Judgment, 59
  nether world, 14, 17
  pool of fire, 14
Kingdom of Jesus, 3-4, 8-9, 24, 32, 40, 48-49, 85-86, 89, 127, 129, 141, 145, 154, 236, 271-272, 276
Kreeft, Peter, 26, 28, 35, 104, 221, 287
The Ladder of Divine Ascent, 128
LaVey, Anton, 49
Lazarus, 105
liberation, 7-8, 57, 94, 102, 117-122, 127, 135, 140-141, 158, 162, 183, 185, 260, 263-264, 266
  degrees of difficulty in expelling demons, 117
Litany of Saints, 80, 180, 194, 257, 258
liturgy, 8, 58, 73-74, 257, 268-269, 274
Lord of the Flies, 23
The Lord of the Rings, 212
Lozano, Neal, 57, 220, 263-264, 287
Lucifer, 2, 10, 19-20, 24, 31-32, 47
MacNutt, Francis, 101, 127, 138, 220, 288
Magisterium, xxii-xxiii, xxxiii, 70, 92
Magnificat, 80, 248
malice, 6, 24, 38, 178, 202, 214, 246
manifestations, demonic, 11, 29, 65, 106, 113-114, 150, 167-168, 190, 264, 275
Martin, Malachi, xxvii-xxviii, 40, 42, 80, 84, 124, 167, 288, 290
McManus, Fr. Dennis, 39, 50
Medina Estévez, Jorge A., 75
Michel, Anneliese, 37-38, 82, 179, 215, 277, 286-287
Milingo, Emmanuel, 89
Ministeria Quaedam, 73-74
ministry of exorcism, xxxi, 6, 9, 10, 47, 57, 64, 70, 112, 135, 138, 159, 178, 198-199, 203, 269
Moonies, 89
Moses, 5, 7-8, 246
movies, demonic, xxviii, xxx, xxxii, 29, 42, 49, 167, 170
  The Alien, 29
  The Exorcism of Emily Rose, xxx, 42, 167-169, 215, 277, 290
  The Exorcist, xxx, 47-48, 88, 159, 167, 180, 290
  The Matrix, 52
  Rosemary's Baby, 49
Muslims, 12-13
Name of Jesus, 3, 10-13, 52, 77, 108, 130, 134, 136, 141-145, 150, 171, 233, 244-245, 251-253
Nazi concentration camps, 109
Neumann, Theresa, 179
New Age, xxviii, xxxii, 72-73, 122, 149, 167, 214, 221, 283, 285, 288
New Moses, 8
non-Catholics, 70, 77, 204
objects, religious, 163
obsession, 33-34, 44, 108, 112-114, 148, 152, 202, 211, 215
occult, xxxi-xxxii, 3, 17, 37, 43, 53, 67, 72, 101-103, 111, 119-120, 122, 142-143, 149, 152, 157, 166-167, 172-173, 182, 187-188, 192, 202, 204, 206, 210-214, 217, 283, 288
  Also see "witches," and "witchcraft"
  occult practices, 142, 173
On the Current Norms Governing

Exorcism (*Inde Ab Aliquot Annis*), 43, 71, 139, 260-261, 283
oppression, 7-8, 33-34, 152, 159, 182, 186, 195, 266, 278
Orthodox Christians, 11
Padre Pio, 14-15, 140, 179
pagans, 48, 68, 74, 82, 103-104
Paschal Lamb, 8, 239
The Passion of the Christ, 23, 30, 179
Passover, 8
patience, 121-122, 161
   God's patience, 13
Peck, M. Scott, 162, 288
   Also see "*People of the Lie*"
Penance (Confession), 9, 131, 138, 157-158, 176, 186, 210-211, 213, 225
People of the Lie, 162, 288
Pharaoh, 7, 231, 246
pope, xxvii, 14-15, 17, 20, 22, 43, 62, 71-73, 79-80, 90, 92, 154, 199-200, 250, 259, 262-263, 271
   papal audience, 72, 90
   power of the keys, 56
   power to "bind and loose", 4, 9, 12, 62, 138
   Vicar of Christ, 62
Pope Benedict XVI, 72, 199-200, 259, 263
   Also see "Ratzinger, Joseph"
Pope John Paul II, xxvii, 14-15, 72, 90, 154, 199, 271
   catechesis on the fallen angels, 271
   Pastores Dabo Vobis, 199
   performed three exorcisms, 90
Pope Leo XIII, 22, 43, 71, 79-80, 250, 262-263
Pope Paul VI, 17, 72-73, 199
   Sacerdotalis Caelibatus, 199

possession, xxviii, xxxi, xxxiv, 7, 11-12, 31, 34, 37-40, 42-43, 45, 49-50, 53-55, 57-58, 68, 70, 80, 82, 84, 94-97, 99, 106, 109-114, 116, 119, 122-124, 128-129, 134, 136, 148-149, 155-156, 159, 161-162, 170, 175, 177, 179-180, 182, 185, 187-189, 211, 215, 223, 236, 249, 263-265, 275, 278, 280, 286-289
   Also see "gutteral voice," "infestation," and "obsession"
   bondage, 7-8, 113, 135, 140, 142, 239, 253
   a Christian can have a demon, 108
   co-existence of spiritual, moral and psychological factors, 113
   different from mental/psychological disorders, 4, 99-100, 110, 115, 121, 132, 223
   family as antidote to demonic possession, 54
   full possession, 34, 42, 49, 68, 112-113, 119, 129, 134, 148, 264
   how to know when a person needs an exorcism, 106
   no inadvertent possession, 42
   partial possession, 34
   perfect possession, 40, 43, 124
   re-possessed, 186-187
   self-destructive behavior, 50
   signs of possession, 94, 97, 109-111, 189, 223
   state of perfect possession, 40
   "symptoms" of possession, 110
   temple of the Holy Spirit, 39, 53, 108
prayer, 9, 13, 15, 20-22, 43, 57, 60, 63, 68-69, 71-77, 79-83, 85, 87-89, 93, 98-104, 107, 110-113,

115-120, 123-124, 126-128, 131-135, 137, 139-152, 155, 157-159, 161, 163, 173-174, 177, 180, 182, 185-187, 190-196, 202-203, 206-208, 211, 218-219, 221, 225, 229-230, 236-237, 239, 242, 244, 250, 253, 255-269, 275-276, 283-284, 286

Also see "Athanasian Creed," "Litany of Saints," "Magnificat," and "Prayer to St. Michael"

deprecative (i.e., petitioning) prayers, 140, 266

exorcism prayers, 79-80, 83, 110, 191, 194, 260, 263, 269

imperative (i.e., commanding) prayers, 145

prayers for healing, 72, 103, 126, 131-132, 134, 139, 151, 260, 267-268

prayers for inner healing, 132

prayers for physical healing, 132

prayers of deliverance, 101, 139

prayers of forgiveness, 141

prayers of intercession, 140, 257, 268-269

prayers of renunciation, 142

prayers of repentance, 141

prayer team, 85, 87, 98, 112, 120, 147-149, 157-158, 165-166, 172, 180, 182, 193

Prayer to St. Michael (by Pope Leo XIII), 79-80, 250, 259

pride, xxii, 15, 21, 31, 39, 67, 106, 178, 252

Project Rachel, 133

Protestants, xxxiv, 12, 78, 190

prudence, 62, 67, 70, 86, 148, 223, 261, 269

Public Ministry of Jesus, 4, 8, 73, 129-130, 141

purgatory, xxi, xxix, 31, 103-104, 290

Ratzinger, Joseph Cardinal, 71, 91, 263-264, 266, 280

Also see "Pope Benedict XVI"

repentance, 6, 13, 33, 54, 101-102, 119, 122, 132, 141, 210

Also see "prayer - prayers of repentance," and "Penance"

impossibility of for demons, 33, 54

Rite of Christian Initiation of Adults, 68

Rite of Exorcism, 1, 20, 31, 56, 60-63, 70, 72, 75, 79-80, 83, 94, 97, 109, 128, 137, 163, 185, 188, 223, 228, 250, 255, 260, 262-263, 286

Also see "Alcuin," "Athanasian Creed," "Exorcism Against Satan and the Fallen Angels," "Litany of Saints," "Magnificat," and "Weller"

1614 *Rite of Exorcism*, 20-21, 60, 63, 79-80, 94, 109-110, 136-137, 155, 181, 188, 223, 228, 250, 255, 257, 259, 262-263, 286

1999 *Rite of Exorcism* (*De Exorcismis et Supplicationibus Quibusdam*), 61, 72, 75, 255, 260, 270, 283

Exorcism Against Satan and the Fallen Angels (Exorcism of Pope Leo XIII - Part III of the 1614 *Rite of Exorcism*), 43, 80, 250, 262

exorcism in secret, 68-69, 83

exorcism of place, 80, 161

General Rules Concerning Exorcism (Part I of the 1614 *Rite of Exorcism*), 94, 97, 223

power of the Church's prayer, 81

Praenotanda (preliminay notes of the 1999 *Rite of Exorcism*), 72, 267, 270
Ritus Exorcizandi Obsessos A Daemonio (Part II of the 1614 *Rite of Exorcism*), 228
use of Latin, 60, 82, 256, 258
The Roman Ritual, xxv, 1, 56, 79, 97, 223, 284
Rules for Discernment of Spirits (from *The Spiritual Exercises of St. Ignatius*), 99, 108
Sacraments, 1, 9, 46, 57, 70, 72, 75, 79, 131, 138, 176, 185, 208, 210-211, 213, 217-218, 268-269, 284, 289-290
　Anointing of the Sick, 9, 131, 133, 138, 151
　anti-sacrament, 52
　attempted "spiritual marriage" (demonic), 28
　Eucharist, 15, 91, 146, 150, 164, 185, 225-226
　Holy Orders, 73, 128
　Penance (Confession), 9, 131, 138, 157-158, 176, 186, 210-211, 213, 225
Sacred Heart, 13
saints, 9, 34, 37, 48, 56, 63, 80, 128, 140, 163, 177, 180, 194, 200, 210, 215, 217, 219, 225-226, 242, 251, 257, 266, 290
salvation, xxvi-xxvii, 6, 11, 13, 20, 25-26, 45, 48, 58, 71, 89, 91, 124-125, 129, 131, 147, 154, 199-200, 233, 252, 271-272, 275, 280-281
Satan, xxii-xxiii, xxv-xxvii, xxix, xxxi, 2, 5-6, 19-24, 26-28, 31-32, 43, 47-50, 71-72, 80, 127, 143, 145, 154, 178, 184, 188, 234-236, 238, 250-252, 259, 262, 271-276, 282, 285-286, 289
　Also see "Beelzebub," "devil," and "Lucifer"
　ancient serpent, 20-22, 241, 251, 282
　beast, 14, 21, 231, 282
　falls from the sky like lightning, 154
　father of lies, 20, 83, 273
　huge dragon, 20
　Kingdom of Satan, 32, 71
　morning star, son of the dawn, 17
　a murderer from the beginning, 20, 38, 51, 273
　Prince of Evil, 31
　prince of this world, 3, 6, 23, 59
　Satan's expulsion from heaven, 2
　seraphim angel, 32
　set up his throne above the heavens, 17
　spiritual criminal, 60
Satanic Ritual Abuse, 118, 120, 123
　mind control, 123
Satanism, xxviii, xxxii, 6, 122-123, 289-290
Satanists, 67, 108, 123, 197
Scripture, Sacred, xxii, xxvi, xxxv, 5, 21-22, 24, 28, 51, 103, 105, 113, 133, 159, 163, 210, 219, 272, 274-275, 281, 285
seminaries, xxiii-xxiv, 11, 65, 200, 216, 263
　Mundelein Seminary, 11, 263
Sign of the Cross, 8, 181, 226, 258
signs, 8, 85, 87, 94, 97, 99, 109-112, 114, 127, 129, 175, 177, 181-182, 185, 189, 223-224, 227, 239, 281
sin, xxi-xxiii, xxvi-xxvii, xxx, 8-10, 13, 30, 33, 41, 46-47, 51, 58, 68-

69, 71, 83, 86, 91, 101-103, 108, 116, 119-120, 127-128, 130-132, 135, 141, 143, 155, 157-158, 173, 176-178, 186, 198, 209-210, 213-215, 227-228, 230, 237, 272-274, 280
    Also see "blasphemy," and "vice"
    mortal sin, 33, 46, 68, 158, 213-215
    Original Sin, 102-103, 274
    sin against the Holy Spirit, 10
    venial sin, 46, 213
slavery, xxvi, 7-8, 122-123
Sodom and Gomorrah, 6
The Spiritual Exercises of St. Ignatius, 99, 108, 128, 157
    Rules for Discernment of Spirits, 99, 108
spiritual warfare, xxiii, xxvi, xxix-xxx, xxxiii, 12, 57, 67, 71, 78, 148, 192, 205, 210, 217-220, 222, 289-290
    battlefield, xxi, xxiv, xxvii, 193
    combat, xxi, xxiii, xxvi, 10, 12, 48, 63, 137, 180, 199, 215, 219, 289
    spiritual weapons, 11-12
St. Alphonsus Liguori, 69, 83
St. Anthony of the Desert, 140
St. Gabriel the Archangel, 180
St. Gemma Galgani, 37, 215
St. Ignatius of Loyola, 34, 108
    Also see "*The Spiritual Exercises of St. Ignatius*"
St. John, the Evangelist, 39, 205, 273
St. John Bosco, 37, 215
St. John of the Cross, 128
St. John Vianney, 140, 200
St. Joseph, 140-141, 179, 290
St. Luke, the Evangelist, 4, 113, 126, 137, 154, 234-235, 271
St. Matthew, the Evangelist, 4, 126, 133, 137
St. Michael the Archangel, xxxv, 2, 5, 47, 60, 79-80, 163, 178-180, 219, 250-251, 259, 288
St. Paul, the Apostle, xxix, 30, 56, 86, 88, 100, 108, 130, 142, 208, 213, 242, 251-252
St. Peter, the Apostle, 11, 88, 272
St. Raphael the Archangel, 180
St. Theresa of Avila, 128
St. Thomas Aquinas, 2, 18-20, 25, 33-36, 104, 175, 284
    Also see "*Summa Theologica*"
    De Malo (*On Evil*), 18, 33
Stallings, George, 90
suffering, xxix, 43, 85, 97, 107, 110, 115-116, 131, 149, 171, 188-189, 203, 215, 223, 272, 277, 280
    redemptive suffering, 277
suicide, 15, 23, 37-38, 107, 111
    Church exerts a restraining force, 38
    demons tempt, 177
Summa Theologica, 2, 19-20, 33-36, 104, 175, 284
temptation, 33-34, 48, 67, 69, 111-112, 122, 173, 217, 227-228, 276
Tertullian, 49
Tradition, Sacred, xxii, xxix, xxxi, xxxiv-xxxv, 11, 20, 24-25, 31, 41, 68-69, 103-105, 128, 156, 184, 191, 265, 272
Vatican, 20, 72, 79, 89, 260, 270, 283, 288-289
    Also see "Congregation for the Doctrine of the Faith," and "*Inde Ab Aliquot Annis*"
    Congregation for Divine Worship and the Sacraments, 72, 75
    Pontifical Council for Culture,

Index

73, 283
Pontifical Council for Interreligious Dialogue, 73, 283
Pontifical Councils, 73
Vatican II (Second Vatican Council), xxi, xxix, 70-73, 79, 198-199, 255-256, 270, 283
Vatican II documents (conciliar and post-conciliar), 70, 199
  Also see "*Christian Faith and Demonology,*" "*Gaudium et Spes,*" and "*Ministeria Quaedam*"
Presbyterorum Ordinis, 199
vice, 21, 146, 238
  Also see "envy," "pride," and "sin"
victim, xxx, 30-31, 35, 37, 39-40, 42-43, 45, 47-48, 83-85, 87, 99, 118, 123, 129, 135, 155-157, 167-172, 176-177, 179-181, 183-186, 191-192, 196, 214, 216, 224, 278-279
Virgin Mary, 15, 30, 84, 140, 170-171, 179, 181, 251-252, 266
virtue, 21, 48-49, 85, 89, 106, 135, 146-148, 160-161, 177, 217, 242
  Also see "courage," "humility," "patience," and "prudence"
  faith, hope and charity, 85, 140
Weller, xxv, 1, 20, 56, 83, 97, 109, 146, 156, 163, 168, 181, 223, 250, 284
  Also see "*The Roman Ritual*"
witchcraft, 37, 122-123, 149, 152, 186
witches, 28-29, 100, 149, 214, 277

About the Author

Rev. Thomas J. Euteneuer was born in Detroit, Michigan, in 1962, the fourth of seven children. He was ordained a priest in 1988 for the Diocese of Palm Beach, Florida and served in parishes in that diocese for twelve years before being given permission by his bishop to work full-time in pro-life ministry with Human Life International, where he has served as President since December of the year 2000.

Fr. Euteneuer has been performing exorcisms for seven years with approval from numerous dioceses in the United States. His interest in the ministry was a natural outgrowth of his work in the pro-life field, which deals with the organized power of evil on a global scale. Exorcism has allowed him to combine both his years of pastoral experience with his expertise in the pro-life movement; and in the last several years, he has performed dozens of full exorcisms and many dozen deliverances on afflicted persons. Fr. Euteneuer's book, *Exorcism and the Church Militant*, is accompanied by two companion editions: *Demonic Abortion*, which explains the demonic nature of abortion and the culture of death from an exorcist's point of view; and *Discernment Manual for Exorcists and Pastoral Ministers*, which is intended to equip persons engaging in spiritual warfare with all the proper tools of discernment.